This Life I've Bled

A MEMOIR

Jacquelyn Johnston

DEMETER

This Life I've Bled
A Memoir
Jacquelyn Johnston

Copyright © 2021 Demeter Press

Demeter Press
140 Holland Street West
P. O. Box 13022
Bradford, ON L3Z 2Y5
Tel: (905) 775-9089
Email: info@demeterpress.org
Website: www.demeterpress.org

Demeter Press logo based on the sculpture "Demeter" by Maria-Luise Bodirsky
www.keramik-atelier.bodirsky.de

Printed and Bound in Canada

Front cover artwork: Michelle Pirovich
Typesetting: Michelle Pirovich

Library and Archives Canada Cataloguing in Publication
Title: This life I've bled : a memoir / by Jacquelyn Johnston.
Names: Johnston, Jacquelyn, 1961- author.
Identifiers: Canadiana 20200375237 | ISBN 9781772582475 (softcover)
Subjects: LCSH: Johnston, Jacquelyn, 1961- | LCSH: Johnston, Jacquelyn,
1961-—Health. | LCSH: Johnston, Jacquelyn, 1961-—Mental health.
| LCSH: Mothers—Canada—Biography. | LCSH: Motherhood. | LCSH: Parental
grief. | LCSH: Loss (Psychology) | LCGFT: Autobiographies.
Classification: LCC HQ759 .J64 2021 | DDC 305.42092—dc23

This book contains scenes of violence, sexuality, and coarse language. Reader discretion is advised. Also, this is the story of my life. In it, I have tried to adhere as closely as possible to the truth as I recall it. However, in the process of writing it, I've learned that memory creates its own truth sometimes. I have changed the names of most of the characters to protect the identity of the innocent and the guilty. It is my sincere hope and wish that no one is offended by their portrayal within, but that is unlikely. Please forgive me and don't sue me—the lawyer will get more than you will. I suggest you write your own book and say what you will about me. That is the best revenge and my safest bet that what I haven't already damaged of my reputation will remain intact because it's hard to write a book, bitches.

For all my children

Contents

1

Writing on the Wall

Unlike most people, I am consciously aware that my bloody life could end today. Everyone's could. We're all just one breath away from death, our last one. I wake up one day in 2005, around noon, to the sound of my doorbell ringing in a subsidized housing unit in Port Coquitlam, a suburb of Vancouver, British Columbia, fondly known among us as the white ghetto. I live there with my two daughters, Shiloh and Keziah, ages fourteen and twelve. I am forty-four years old. At the door is their Uncle Gary, my forty-year-old brother.

"Come on, Sissy, get up. Whatcha doin'?" He gives me a hug as he comes in and sets a six-pack of beer on the table covered with undone homework, dirty dishes, papers, clutter, and Keziah's hair extensions borrowed from a friend, which creates an eerie sense that someone has been scalped. "I brought breakfast," he says with a smile as he pops open a can and hands it to me and then cracks himself one. "Cheers," I say, trying to swallow the trepidation that always accompanies a visit from Gary.

Even though I'm not typically a day drinker at all—I just have my afterwork six-pack at most unless I have company and it turns into a party—I find myself quickly downing a few beers. I'm a guzzler, not a sipper, no matter what I'm drinking, as though the goal is to finish the job and move on, which doesn't bode well with alcohol. We go out to the patio to smoke, and Gary entertains me with the story of his most recent fight with his wife that morning, hence his appearance at my place: He is avoiding the ogre. After we finish the six-pack and some cigarettes, I send Gary to the nearby pub while I have a shower. No matter how crazy things get, I always feel better if I have time to get ready.

Guys have it so easy: shit, shower, shave. Lesbians have it even easier: shit, shower, ha. There is a whole regimen of personal grooming some women go through, and despite its laboriousness, I can't go without and feel right. So, after showering and blow-drying my bobbed hair and applying makeup, I put on a pair of jeans and a red top and matching boots, and walk over to The Hook and Handle Pub.

Gary is sitting outside at the smoking tables. "What took you so long, Sissy? I almost gave up on you."

"Well, it takes time to look this good. I'm here now. Who's our waitress?"

After a few drinks there, we stop at the beer and wine store next door and buy more beer, cigarettes, and rum and coke, Gary's everyday drink. We go home and continue the party. Soon the girls come home from school. They run over to give Uncle Gary a hug. Once he came over from the pub with about ten pull-tabs and let my younger daughter Keziah open them. She couldn't believe her good fortune. She said of Gary, "Almost like a real dad."

Of course, she has a dad, my ex-husband Boris, but he isn't carefree and generous like Gary, especially toward her. He used to call her "the little wedge" because he felt she tried to come between him and me. I just felt guilty and sad for her when he sent her away to go play or watch TV in the other room. He wanted me all for himself.

The girls don't like it when I drink, although everyone expects it of Gary by now. They nuke some chicken nuggets from the freezer and disappear upstairs, just as Screwy Louie, my current live-in boyfriend arrives. I go by the nickname Wacky Jacquie, so when he introduces himself at a bar one night as Screwy Louie it seems obvious that he is "the one," for now.

He borrows my van to do some transmission business that I don't understand. Louie is always ready for a beer. He's probably already had a few while he was out driving around.

"Hey, Gary, how's it goin,' buddy?" Louie's frenetic energy amps up the room. The voices get louder as we all try to talk over each other. Half-smoked cigarettes are everywhere and taking over the house instead of staying outside where they're supposed to be. By now, moderate chaos is the prevailing mood. I am starting to feel the uncomfortable prick of my conscience about the girls and the neighbours.

Louie tells the girls to order a pizza while he and Gary go on another beer run. When they get back, I am pissed off that they bought bottles.

"Why, Jacquie, what's the difference? The beer tastes better out of the bottle."

"Yeah, and when it gets knocked over as it always does, there's broken glass everywhere that I have to clean up."

"Nothing's gonna get broken. Everything's fine."

But not inside of me, it isn't. My nerves are on edge. I hate the environment of drunks. I have old triggers from my childhood. Now, as an adult, I am conflicted, playing my mother's sober role while being drunk and allowing this craziness in my own home. I know how my kids feel, only it is worse because there is no one sober here except them. I hate myself for putting them through it.

Suddenly, I hate Gary, and I hate Louie too.

"I have to get out of here," I yell and head back to the pub. That night, strangely, the waitress brings me a free drink, a shooter.

I say, "Thanks," wondering who it is from. The place isn't all that full, but I can't guess who it is. Another shot arrives.

Thankfully, by this time, a woman I know and her brother come in and sit with me. When the third shot comes, I ask the waitress who sent it. She points to a guy sitting at the bar. He smiles and waves, and I motion him over. "Why are you buying me drinks?"

"Well, I saw a beautiful woman sitting alone so I thought..."

By this time, I am hammered, and I allow my friend and her brother to protect me, since he is obviously trying to get me drunk so he can fuck me. They walk me out, and I stumble the two blocks home. When I get back to the house, I reach that point that some alcoholics do, when something snaps in their brain and they go straight to blind rage. I start yelling at Louie and Gary and go upstairs to my room, where Louie follows me.

Suddenly I despise him, him and his skinny chicken legs, his removable dental plate, and the way he uses my money, home, vehicle, and kids. I want to kill him, to rip that plate out of his mouth. I hit him. He tries to stop my flailing arms. We crash around my room, banging into things, and I am fighting with a fierce intensity that flows like a lava stream from within. I want him dead. He is trying to call the cops on his cell phone while resisting my blows. My brother Gary remains conspicuously absent from the scene.

Louie speaks up. "Stop it, Jacquie. Fuckin' settle down. Stop it or I'll have to hurt you."

"You can't hurt me."

But I'm wrong. He throws me to the floor, and my ribs crack as they hit the corner of the bookshelf. Ouch. The next thing I know, the cops are there, trying to get the story.

"Who lives here?"

"I do."

"Who are these gentlemen?"

"That's my brother. That's the asshole that used to be my boyfriend."

"Does he live here?"

"No! He's homeless again just like when I met him."

There are two officers. One takes Gary and Louie outside. The other stays inside to talk to me. Now, I'm in a smart-aleck mood. I don't like cops. For good reason. I've seen one beat an innocent man in my driveway, years before, while his peers watched. Another time I'm drinking with Gary, and a cop wrestles with me, then puts handcuffs on me, pushes me in the back seat of his cruiser on my back, and calls me a whore. He stands around with some guys from the bar who have come out for the show while I pound his car's roof with my bare feet. When he gets in the driver's seat, I call him an immigrant because he looks Chinese. Tit for tat. I spend that night in jail, singing "Burning Ring of Fire" for four hours as loud as I can. I have no voice the next day. But I'm not going to let them silence me.

So, as I was saying, I am being lippy, rude, and obnoxious. But I feel pretty safe now. I am back in my own home, and Gary and Louie are gone. We finish our business, and the cops walk out into the breezeway, where I notice the boys have left some things, one of which is a red beer backpack that triggers my anger because Louie got two of them free by buying ninety-six cans of beer. Which we drank one weekend. He said he got them for the kids. For fuck's sake. I don't want my kids to have stuff like that. Nothing says white trash hypocrites like beer backpacks at Christian school. He also gave them free *Maxim* men's magazines. Louie has some kind of criminal record and is on probation. I don't know what for. It's always an awkward question in a new relationship. This is the lowest I've ever stooped to be with a man.

I see the backpack, and I kick it with my foot. It slides across the cement and comes to rest touching the toe of one of the officer's boots. "That's it. That's assaulting a police officer." He comes over to me, wrenches my arms behind my back, whips my wrists into tight cuffs, and shoves me hard up against the rough, stippled building wall. I see a drop of blood from my nose fall and splat on the ground.

"I'm taking you in."

"That's bullshit. I didn't assault you, you fucking liar." But he has me where he wants me. I can feel his smug satisfaction. I mouthed off to him, and now I am the mouse in his big cat mouth.

"You'll have to take off those high-heeled boots. Find some other shoes."

The other cop reaches into my closet, grabs a pair of flipflops, and says "Let's go."

"What about my kids?"

"You should have thought about that sooner. Let's go."

I start screaming as loud as I can. "Police brutality, help! Someone help me."

No one comes, not so much as a curtain flutters. This is the white ghetto. Nobody cares. The girls tell me later they heard me screaming. I guess it was embarrassing for them. Here they were, fourteen and twelve, trying to go to sleep. Years later, Keziah is diagnosed with post-traumatic stress disorder from this incident, and it reappears in her journal writing.

I am quiet for the ride to the station. What is left to say? It is over. I lost. I know what I have to look forward to in the drunk tank from my previous visit, after drinking with Gary one Father's Day a couple of years ago when the girls were with their dad. I couldn't believe I ended up there, never imagined it was possible. What had happened to my life for me to end up at rock bottom so quickly? Lots of people lose their marriage, home, job, and bank credit. Losing them all together was a blow I didn't know how to absorb. I sank to the bottom of the bottle like a rock. And here I am back in the drunk tank looking forward to nothing. No pillow, no blanket, no heat, no toilet paper. Just the punishment of the minutes threatening to suffocate me under their weight. I'm not going to scream. I'm not going to sing. I am going to succumb.

We arrive at the station. As I approach the desk, a butchish female officer is checking me in. "May I have a phone call, please?" I ask politely. "I get one call, right? I'd like to call my kids and tell them I won't be home tonight." She looks at me with a combination of disbelief and contempt and spits, "You're a mother?"

When she says that, all the shame and sadness and regret I feel about what my children have gone through rises in me, and I keep thinking about it as I sit locked in my hollow cell with no phone call. The accusing question about my role as a mother burrows into my soul like a steadily chomping maggot. My side hurts, and, trying to stay warm, I wrap the loose fabric of my short-sleeved red top hanging below the tighter V-neck fabric stretched across my breasts over my arms. I want to try to explain or defend myself. I have to respond.

What is a mother? Is it someone who gives birth to one or more children and cares for them? Or just someone who gives birth? Or just someone who gets pregnant? I have been pregnant six times in my life. Three times I terminated the pregnancies because I didn't think I would make a good mother. Once, I gave birth to a little boy, and before he was two years old, he died. That makes me a grieving mother. Now, I have two girls who are at home in bed while their crazy drunk screaming mother is in jail. I have always been a grieving mother, whether I have my children or not. Mothering is the hardest thing I've ever done. I can't imagine how much harder mothering well could be or how to go about it.

I want to explain to that dyke bitch that I married a man I met in church in good faith, who betrayed me and left with me with nothing but two children to raise on my own. Had I known this would be the case, I wouldn't have had them. They don't deserve what happened. I don't know how to deal with my losses. Rage and bitterness threaten to engulf me daily. I drink to escape. I hate my ex-husband. I hate my life. I am depressed and feel utterly trapped in my misery.

I am sure she doesn't care about that. Yet her comment demands a response. What can I say? What can I do?

Suddenly, I remember I am wearing an internal form of feminine hygiene called a menstrual cup, which is just like it sounds. It's a little soft plastic cup that you insert into the vagina that collects the menstrual flow. To empty it, you stick your finger in and pull it out. Can be a bit messy, but I've been using them for years as an alternative to tampons. I'm surprised they're not more popular, but I learned about them on late night infomercials. You can wear them safely up to twelve hours.

I realize I have one in, and I should remove it. Thankfully, this time my cell has toilet paper. So I pull out my little cup half full of warm blood, and I am inspired. I dip my finger in it and write on the cold white tile wall with bold red letters:

YES, I AM A MOTHER.

2

Daddy and Me

I hold my breath as I run through the cloud of dust created from the school bus's tires grazing the dusty gravel as it stops at the side of Highway 3A in Creston, British Columbia, where I live. I am ten years old. I wave to Mr. Davis, the school bus driver, to show him I've safely crossed the highway and because he's nice. I like him.

I walk the rest of the way to our house, cutting through the yard full of apple trees. I can only run short distances because of my asthma. Once, at the drive-in theatre, Dad complains about the static on the speaker. My mom says reproachfully, "Len, that's Jacquie wheezing." In the backseat, I try to control my breathing to minimize the irritation, but it's hard to breathe quietly when you can hardly breathe at all.

I step into the house and smell a strange, fleshy, metallic odour. I follow my nose and the light downstairs to find my dad skinning by the furnace. His hands are slippery with blood. He throws the vulnerable naked body of a small animal into a garbage bag and pulls another furry creature from the pile of unfortunates caught in his traps. What was that, a marten, a weasel, an otter?

"Hiya, Sue-Sue." That's my dad's nickname for me. My sister April is Missus, my brother Gary, Bowser. Our nickname for him is Len Morton.

"Wanna learn how to skin a marten? Watch. First you cut around the ankles with a sharp knife like this." He deftly rotates the blade around the small legs.

"Then a straight cut from ankle to tail, following the dividing line between the soft belly fur and the guard hair. Then, once you have the bottom opened up like that, you just grab the fur and peel it off like a sweater, gently tearing it over the front paws and nose. You have to be careful though to watch the scent glands, especially with weasels. If you nick 'em, they'll really stink up the house. Most women don't like the smell. It's kinda like crude oil. I kinda like it."

He throws another skinny body into the garbage bag. It looks so small without its coat but athletic, with its muscles and sinews showing; the meat is a purplish red. I go upstairs.

My dad seems to be in a perpetually bad mood when he's at home, although peeling the skins off small animals is a placating activity, as is hunting and killing large animals and fishing. His other favourite thing is drinking. Although I have to say, looking back, I don't know what he drank, particularly, and I don't recall seeing it in the house a lot, no doubt an influence of my teetotalling mother.

Dad has a business selling fish and seafood in a refrigerated one ton truck around the interior of British Columbia, driving from town to town, spending about twenty days a month on the road. I begin to recognize a certain look on his face—barely perceptible to others but obvious when you know him—that indicates he'd been drinking before he arrived home.

One particular night, he is in the mood to dance. Mom has already had enough of him and disappeared, gone to read in bed or maybe sleep.

"Sue-Sue, come and dance with me."

Dear god no, please don't make me do this. "No thanks," I say.

"Come on, whatsa matter with you? Dance with your daddy."

I shake my head. "I don't want to."

"Whattaya mean? Come on." And he pulls me by the hand to the middle of the living room floor. I can feel the rhythm of the music, but he's moving in another way I can't follow. I feel so awkward. I hate this. I want to run and hide, not for the first time. The next thing I know, his leg is between my legs. Oh god, please let this be over. Please make the music stop.

When I am in my early twenties, living away from home, and he is living between my mom and his girlfriend, I write him a mean hateful letter saying I wish he'd die, but that's too good for him. I wish he'd suffer first and then die. I say this in the letter. He phones me and says, "That was sure a crock of shit letter you wrote me."

All right, let's do this, voice to voice. Let's have it out. "No. It wasn't. It was the truth. You're an asshole, and you ruined my life, our whole family's. I hate you."

"Well, I can't understand why I was such a bad father to you. I never molested you or anything."

I scream in frustration. "Really? That's the only thing you have to your credit? Don't you realize it's all the other things you didn't do that you should have and did that you shouldn't have? I can't talk to you." Slam.

I'm shaking. How can he think that not molesting his kids makes him a good father? No father should do that. It's only right and decent and expected that fathers don't molest their children. You don't get credit for it, any more than you get credit for not killing and skinning them. Was making me dance with him when I didn't want to molestation? I don't think so. More likely, a moment of drunken indiscretion. Anyway, he only did it that one time.

Many years later someone said to me, "Well, maybe he deserves credit if he thought about it but didn't do it."

And that put a whole different spin on it.

*

On neighbouring farms near a grain elevator labelled Griffin, Saskatchewan, there once lived a boy and a girl. Her name was Myra, the youngest of four sisters. His name was Len, the oldest of four siblings. They attended the same one-room school. Len was good at drawing maps and helped Myra with hers. Len was a handsome lad by his late teens, wearing a greasy ducktail and black, geek glasses, as was the fashion in the late 1950s. Myra was a petite five feet, with a nineteen-inch waist, which matched her age when they married in October 1960.

Those were my parents before they were parents. My mom, Myra, claims the first time she saw my father, Len, drink and get drunk, was on their wedding day. It wouldn't be the last. As it was October and the opening of hunting season, her honeymoon was spent at a motel in Williston, North Dakota, a small town a few hours' drive from Griffin, while he shot birds out of the sky.

By July, Myra was due to give birth to their first child, who managed to arrive barely nine months after the wedding night. A honeymoon baby. Len experienced a second big change in his life—first a wife and now a child in less than a year. An interesting fact is that he dropped my mom off at the hospital in one car and picked her up in another, having traded the first one in for another model. Apparently, this sudden changing of vehicles was common behaviour for him.

The baby was a little girl, which was probably secretly disappointing to her father. They named her Jacquelyn, after the oh-so-popular Jackie Kennedy, wife of the American president. Her middle name was Susan, for the nurse who delivered her, as her impatient rush to get this journey started meant the doctor missed her arrival. That's how I came into the world.

I guess if I have to choose one time from my childhood that defines my dad's drinking when I was growing up, it would be Christmas, 1970, when I was nine. Probably every child of an alcoholic has a Christmas story. Mine goes like this. Christmas Eve. My family is at home, waiting for Dad to arrive in the fish truck as usual so we can enjoy our late dinner. On Christmas Eve, our tradition has become to have lobster tail for dinner. We have to wait for Dad to get home with the truck that holds the lobster.

Now that I'm a grown alcoholic in my own right, well, recovering alcoholic, I can imagine that Dad might have popped into a pub on his way home to have a celebratory drink or three for the drive home. Or perhaps someone gifted him with a bottle, or he gifted himself with one. Almost assuredly, he's been drinking before he arrives home.

Mom has the rest of the meal prepped and ready to go once the lobsters are boiled. My younger sister, April, aged seven, and baby brother, Gary, aged five, and I are squatting near the Christmas tree, giving our gifts a final, satisfying going over, in anticipation of finally opening them tomorrow morning. We shake the packages, listening for telltale clues of their contents. We organize them according to size. We discuss our best guesses.

Finally, we hear the familiar rumble of the fish truck coming up our driveway, which we call our lane.

"Girls, is the table set?" Mom calls from the kitchen.

"Yes," we say in unison.

A moment later, the door opens, and Dad enters with a cold gust. His hands are full—a newspaper, a lard can that he hides the money in, dirty coveralls, a paper bag holding booze, and the lobsters.

"Finally. That bloody summit." The summit between Creston and Salmo is always a source of some driving trouble—snow, ice, avalanche, gravel, traffic.

"It was rough, was it, Len?" my Uncle Ron, Dad's younger brother, says with the same cynical curl of his lips he always has. He is having dinner with us tonight, either because he's living with us then, as he did for awhile, or because he lives by himself next door, which he did until he died at fifty-two, although he shared that house with three wives consecutively when he wasn't living alone.

"Bloody awful," my dad says. "I need a drink. Here, Myra, take these lobsters and get 'em going. I'm hungry."

The adult chatter in the other room fades as we resume our concentration on our gifts.

"Okay, let's count and see who has the most."

Soon Mom says, "Okay, everybody, let's eat."

We sit down, and my mom prays. "Father, we thank you for all your gifts and that we can be together." Her voice always catches with emotion when she prays. I sneak a peek at Uncle Ron. His head is not bowed nor are his eyes closed. "Please bless this food to our bodies' use. In Jesus's name, amen."

We set about the task of devouring our delicious dinner, although between the lobster and the melted garlic butter, it's rich, and I can only eat so much before I get a headache. My dad is talking. I don't know about what because it doesn't interest me. My head is full of visions of sugarplums. For some reason, something in his voice changes, and I look at him sitting at the head of our dining room table, and what to my wondering eyes should appear but a tear. And then another one appears around my dad's eyes and rolls down his cheek. I am seized by a paralytic anxiety attack at this strange happening. What is going on? What on earth?

I look at my sister, and we telepathically communicate *Let's go*. We make a hasty exit to our bedroom, where we close the door and lean against it, clinging to each other. I notice that Uncle Ron is laughing as we depart. Why is Dad crying and Uncle Ron laughing? And why is Mom not saying anything to us? Why do we eat lobster on Christmas Eve? We're probably the only family in town that does. What just happened at our dinner? No explanation is offered.

But a very strange thing happens the next day. It is Christmas morning. We kids get up, and see our presents from Santa, and since Mom and Dad aren't up yet, we very carefully unwrap some of our other gifts a bit to get an idea of what they are. We then retape them because we're supposed to wait for them to open the other presents. At our house, we each got one big unwrapped gift from Santa, as well as a wrapped gift from Mom and Dad to maintain the illusion that they weren't him, I guess, and a few presents from various aunts and family friends. Finally, they come out, Mom in pink, baby-doll pyjamas that reveal the valley between her tiny breasts. Dad looks normal. We open our gifts, and Mom goes for a shower before putting the turkey in the oven.

The weird thing is that Dad stays home all day. I am extremely nervous, wondering if there's going to be another crying episode. At some point, before or after dinner, our whole family sits and watches TV in the same room, the only time in my life. Sammy Davis, Jr. is singing and tap dancing. Sammy Davis, Jr. is a very lucky Black man, I think, to be on TV with a glass eye. He is inspiring, making me think maybe I can be on TV someday. I can't tap dance, but I have two good eyes, well, with my glasses, and maybe I can develop another talent I could perform.

The fact that my dad cried at Christmas Eve dinner, that he spends the whole next day with us, and that neither event is ever explained is typical of the perpetual elephant in the living room feeling of our family when I was a kid. And somehow Santa Claus and the reindeer and baby Jesus in the manger are in the midst of it all. They are never clearly explained either.

A couple of days later, after some unusual tension and fighting between Mom and Dad, I say, "Mom, where's Dad?"

Her face tweaks as she says, "I don't know where he is."

That's it. That's all I'm going to get. End of story. Yet I sense there's more going on. He hasn't been here for two days after storming out of the house, and he's not at work, or she would have said so. I guess she really doesn't know. Ah, that's it. That's what's making me uncomfortable. She should know. He's her husband. Is she worried? Probably. Should I be worried? I don't know the implications at this point of not having a father or of being raised by a single mother. I only know of two divorced mothers among my friends' parents. Dysfunctional families like mine (only they weren't called that then) are the norm. Personally, I think I would be just as happy without my dad, happier, in fact. He takes Mom away from me, upsets her, and makes me tense. It's peaceful when he's away on the fish truck. He's usually grumpy when he's at home.

Dad is away for three days before he comes back. It's many years before I hear where he was. He storms out of the house after an argument with my mother about his drinking. He jumps in his truck, which has the boat conveniently loaded and ready to go. He drives to Kootenay Lake, grabs his rifle from behind the front seat of the truck, puts the boat in the water, and drinks and drives his way to the other side, with the express intention of offing himself. He takes the rifle, gets out of the boat, and stumbles through the trees to find a good spot. Instead, he finds a cabin out of which an old man comes.

"What are you up to there, son?"

"Aw, I don't know. I came here to kill myself."

"That sounds pretty serious. Why don't you come inside and have a coffee with me, and I'll hear some more about it?"

I don't know whether the old man talked my dad out of it or whether he talked himself out of it. But he came home and lived with us for quite a few more years before he went to live with his girlfriend, Bunnie. He lived to enjoy killing many other creatures than himself, though. Maybe he was trying to kill his pain.

*

"Mom, why doesn't Dad go to church with us?"

I'm standing in the bathroom looking in the mirror, watching Mom brush my long hair that rises magically with every lift of the static-y hairbrush. I'm seven years old. I'm wearing a blue dress she made me, and white leotards covered with knitballs that only come up to within three inches of my crotch.

Her face pinches into an awkward expression. "Your dad used to go to church all the time."

"But why doesn't he go now?"

"Well, he works a lot, and he's tired."

"So am I." I yawn then, part real and part pretend, to show her.

Somewhat exasperated, she blurts, "Well, I heard that he was taking a faith healing course from a man called Bennie Screwum. One week, Bennie Screwum wasn't there to teach the class. He had disappeared with the offering and the church secretary. Your father never went to church after that."

"Oh." Finally, a real answer. Kind of makes sense. My dad felt disappointed. Someone he thought was good was bad. Do I have to go to church until that happens to me? I wonder. I've been going to church already for at least three years since I was four. Before we move to Creston when I am six, we live in Calgary, Alberta, in Grandma and Grandpa Morton's basement suite. They are my dad's mom and dad. They take me to church with them. Every Sunday, Grandpa walks me down the stairs in the church to a small, cool, dark room and leaves me there. The teacher tells us stories; we sing and draw pictures.

One day after the story, the teacher asks a question. The answer to most of her questions is God, so I put my hand up for this question: "Who forgives you?"

"God," I say. Is that your final answer? Bzzzt.

"No, it is Jesus."

I feel sad, ashamed, and stupid. I don't like church anymore. Maybe this is how Dad feels. But I still have to go.

In Creston, Mom takes us to the United Church for several years. Then Mom and Dad rent out our basement suite to a family from Australia with three children. Mom and the woman become friends. "Y'know, Myrna," the woman from Australia suggests, "the Baptist Church has great programs for the kids. Good Sunday School and a group every Friday night. Our kids love it. You should try it."

So then we go to the Baptist Church for several more years. I go to youth group every Friday night up until high school when it just becomes too uncool. My favourite thing about that church is the year we get a sticker book and stickers for memorizing Bible verses. I stash God's word in my heart against the day when Christians might be persecuted and not have Bibles to read, like my Sunday School teacher says. I like memorizing things. It feels like exercising my brain. In hindsight, it probably gave my obsessive compulsive nature a good workout. I take pride in reciting things back perfectly.

Our church shows a movie called *A Thief in the Night* that I see when I am about ten years old. It is terrifying. It's about the Rapture—that impending event that in a moment sucks all the Christians off the earth and leaves the rest of humanity one last chance to decide if they are going to accept Jesus or suffer the consequences. However, if they do, they are subject to persecution by the leaders of the world system who are Satanically inspired. I cannot forget the images of a man waking up in the morning alone in bed, going to the kitchen to look for his wife, and finding only the Mixmaster in a lonely spin. Or the wife who finds her husband's electric razor buzzing in the sink. It is the one and only horror film I ever see. I can't handle it. Morbid thoughts overtake my mind before bed. My fear is that I won't be good enough to go in the first wave, and I'll have to hide from predators, not knowing who to trust. This movie is considered family entertainment in the church. Dear god.

Then, as a result of my Mom receiving the Holy Spirit at camp when I was about fourteen, we start sneaking in some services at the Pentecostal church, where they believe in speaking in tongues, prophesying, laying on of hands for healing, and such. The Baptist church is okay but kind of dry, straight, and limited in viewpoint. Baptists don't clap or dance when they sing like Pentecostals do.

By the time I'm in my teens, I'm beginning to wonder about religion. How is it that all these churches are worshipping the same God but in so many different ways? Why so many denominations? Why can't we agree? I have doubts about the whole system.

My dad's parents, Grandma and Grandpa Morton, were devout Christians, who believed in the operation of the gifts of the Holy Spirit mentioned in the Bible. They'd experienced what they believed was an outpouring of God's spirit in modern times, which was known as the Latter Rain Movement in the 1950s. Google it. My Grandma spoke in tongues when she prayed. She and my Grandpa had four kids. My dad was the oldest. They'd grown up in Saskatchewan and were not allowed to smoke, drink, swear, dance, or even play cards, all tools in the devil's workshop. They were forced to attend meetings and came under Grandma's wild hand, back in the days when disciplining children usually involved corporal punishment. I guess I can understand why my dad likes killing things. I would too if I couldn't swear or dance and was hit a lot as a kid. All four of their children became alcoholics by my labelling system.

I have to say that over the years, especially after he quit drinking in 1985, my dad seemed to draw a lot of peace from being in the outdoors. Maybe his passion for hunting was more about being in nature, in the quiet, where he could think and feel unencumbered by the weight of his responsibilities at home. We ate a variety of game, including venison, elk, moose, and even bear as well as duck, geese, and partridge.

In the 1950s, the premier of Alberta, Ernest Manning, gave a group of families, including the Mortons, a land grant outside Canmore, Alberta. Not only did he serve as the premier of Alberta for twenty-five years, from 1943 to 1968, but he was also a Christian and hosted a radio program called *Canada's National Bible Hour* for nearly half a century. As long as the families used the property in the service of God, they could keep it free of charge. Later his son, Preston Manning, became the founder and leader of the Reform party, from 1987 to 2000.

Reggie and Daffy Morton, my grandparents, along with four or five other couples, began the construction of Bow Valley Conference Grounds—consisting of a girls' dorm, a boys' dorm, a family dorm, a kitchen and dining area, washrooms with showers, and the Tabernacle, where religious services were held on a sawdust floor several times daily during camps. Bill Roycroft, the youth pastor, told the story of his childhood prank of tipping the offering plate into the sawdust floor so that the contents could be surreptitiously removed later.

The families would drive out on weekends, from Calgary or wherever they lived, to Canmore, a small town near Banff and nestled in the majestic Rocky Mountains, to work on the project. It was a labour of love by like-minded people, who wanted to build a place of worship for the glory of God.

I was about ten or eleven years old the first time my sister and I travelled by Greyhound bus (back before the beheading days, although mind you it felt pretty risky even then!) to Calgary, where my grandparents drove us to the outskirts of Canmore and the conference grounds of Bow Valley Camp.

Grandma and Grandpa had a silver trailer that they'd placed on the property years before while the camp was being built. It had a very distinctive odour, one which I never smelled again until almost forty years later when I was in the psychiatric ward of the Royal Columbian Hospital in New Westminster, British Columbia. I think the smell came from the wooden cupboards. You can imagine my surprise, and the irony, of discovering in my semipsychotic state that Grandma and Grandpa's trailer and the psych ward smelled the same, which is yet more evidence for my theory that religion and insanity are linked.

We would go to Grandma's trailer to say hi, knowing we'd be offered homemade oatmeal cookies or other treats. Grandma worked in the big kitchen and put us to work serving tea and coffee to the camp goers who sat at long dining tables on wooden benches. After meals, we had to help with the cleanup, usually scraping plates.

On our first visit, April and I were assigned a room in the girls' dorm, a bunker full of bunk beds covered with thin, dusty mattresses. I was allergic to dust, so my chronic asthma began pretty much on our arrival and progressed in intensity throughout the week.

That was how I was introduced to the concept of faith healing. People laid hands on me and prayed feverishly as I wheezed and gasped away, feeling like I might draw my last breath in this strange, beautiful but dangerous-for-me place. When Tom Roycroft, the main speaker and author of a book on the spiritual gifts prayed for me, I knew they were calling in the big guns, and I felt an extreme pressure to get well, lest I be the faithless one to prove his prayers to be of no effect. Believe me, I wanted to breathe.

I still wonder how I made it through that week. Somehow, I survived with a minimal amount of oxygen. Hey, maybe that explains some of the stupid things I did later in my life. Oxygen deprivation might have caused some brain damage.

Besides asthma, what I remember about that week was making a burnt match cross in Mrs. Baker's morning class and learning the memory verse "God commendeth His love toward us in that while we were yet sinners, Christ died for us." I also remember the song "Come Now and Let Us Reason Together" and, again, feeling extreme pressure and some uncertainty as Mrs. Baker went around the room, speaking in tongues and praying for us to be filled with the Holy Spirit and do likewise.

Nobody in the class spoke in tongues. I sat there feeling like I could do it, as if something would come out of my mouth if I opened it. But did I dare be the only one? What were the implications of that? I actually felt a pressure on my tongue, as if words were sitting there, waiting to be released, but somehow I was too terrified by the whole bizarre situation to do anything. I sat mute.

It was later, when I was telling some of the girls in the dorm about speaking in tongues, making fun of it actually, that as I started to imitate the sounds I'd heard coming from my teacher. I felt them flowing from me, and I experienced an internal sensation like a peace filling my soul. I spoke in tongues frequently after that. It gave me a sense of relief to know I was praying perfect prayers that the Holy Spirit in me and God Himself could understand between them. It was especially helpful in times of stress, at least as effective at warding off nervous energy as anything else I knew.

Of course, I kept the experience to myself back home, as I sensed there could be some stigma attached to speaking in tongues back in the Baptist Church we were from. Nobody there did it. It was a private thing, kind of like spiritual masturbation.

Canmore is near the Rocky Mountains, and afternoon trips into nearby Banff for hiking, swimming, or shopping also included the drive through some awesome scenery, often with wildlife. And that was just the other campers! We often spotted bighorn sheep, bears, and whitetail deer along the roadways and fields.

At the Tabernacle, morning and evening services were held. We'd sing about how the redeemed of the Lord would come singing unto Zion, the mountain to the North, the city of the great King. It was easy to imagine Almighty God inhabiting a place of such majesty. The Rocky Mountains are truly spectacular, giving one a proportionate sense of human smallness against the sheer magnitude of the mountains' towering faces. I didn't doubt that God was near the camp.

And there was an eclectic assortment of His people—big, small, fat, tall, and downright odd. People would come and go during the week, pulling up in their broken-down cars, hauling trailers, or driving school buses full of kids, all their own. There were plenty of opportunities to make new friends, with the comforting knowledge that if they turned out to be too odd, I wouldn't likely see them again until next year, if ever.

Meals were served in the dining hall, where a bell was rung at five o'clock. People lined up, grace was said, and the food was doled out by volunteers, who ate last if there was anything left. I remember mashed potatoes and roast beef. Attending Alberta farmers donated meat and vegetables. Everything was free back then, with a little wooden donation box on the wall that nobody seemed to use. Of course, there were always faithful families quietly giving in the background, but as a kid, I didn't realize that and was just impressed with what a good deal it was.

Grandpa was always in the dish pit or the sewer pit, keeping things going and flowing. A dish pit is what the dishwashing area was called; it had deep stainless steel commercial sinks for washing and sanitizing dishes. A sewer pit was a huge hole dug deep enough in the ground for Grandpa to climb in to access blocked sewer pipes. At the camp, the girls' washroom had two or three toilets and one small shower with a wooden slat or cold cement floor. I can't remember which. I hated using public facilities, afraid that one of the bad girls would come in and pull back the curtain to reveal my scrawny nakedness. Actually, now that I think about it, that did happen. They threw a bucket of cold water on me. And they called themselves Christians.

There was a pond on the property where you could go if you wanted solitude or to contemplate the teaching from one of the services. There was a fire pit for rare smokers and evening singsongs. Kumbaya, my Lord. There was a tetherball pole and a couple of wooden teetertotters right outside the girls' dorm, where I saw a poor guy's tooth get knocked out by an errant jumper off the end.

A favourite activity of ours was walking the dusty road into Canmore to the candy store, which we kids did as often as possible, to feed our childhood addiction. I remember buying orange Beechnut cough drops, inspired by another camp founder's grandchild, even though I didn't have a cold. I guess a cough drop would be considered "hard stuff" when it came to candy. I felt a bit guilty. I've always had an exaggerated sense of guilt, an overly sensitive conscience as it were, that made me very susceptible to the Christian idea of Christ's unconditional forgiveness on the cross.

How I needed that warm cleansing blood to wash my dirty soul, to make and keep me whole.

Another thing I remember is Mrs. Graham playing her harpsichord and singing, "Oh the blood of Jesus, Oh the blood of Jesus, Oh the blood of Jesus, it washes white as snow," which made no sense to me and still doesn't. Speaking of washing, I don't know if the pond was used for baptisms in the early days. I think there was a lake nearby that was used but thankfully, when I was thirteen and getting baptized, the first time, they had a baptismal tank in the Tabernacle, which seemed to me more sanitary.

At the end of the week, Grandpa Morton emceed the "Program," a little show where we kids performed songs and verses and displayed our crafts onstage in the Tabernacle. I'm not sure why he got that job other than he was on the board of directors for many years and could be kind of entertaining with a microphone in his hand. I have few memories of him speaking to me directly, but I recall him smiling at me during his jokes at camp. One year, I gave an object lesson that I'd heard somewhere, with a string, about a naughty, knotty boy, in which I made slipknots to represent his sins and then pulled them out with a quick tug on either end of the string to represent Jesus's forgiveness. It went over well, and years later when attending camp as an adult, I had people mention it. Well, I guess it was just Bill Roycroft. He never forgot and teased me kindly.

Actually, another person who never forgot was my Uncle Harry. When Grandma Morton passed away just before her ninety-sixth birthday in 2010, we were in Calgary for her funeral. At the reception at Uncle Harry and Aunt Marilyn's, he insisted on gathering up all the kids and making me perform it in front of everyone. I'd only done it once before, thirty years ago, so it was a little rough. And it sounded kind of lame, talking about little Johnny's sins of not listening to his mother when she called him to get up in the morning. Et cetera.

When I was done, the kids bolted back downstairs, and one voice was heard, "Thanks a lot, Grandpa." It was then that I realized that I really should have updated the sins, like Johnny stole his friend's iPod or something. We laughed.

I would be remiss if I didn't mention what an impact Bill Roycroft and his lovely wife Barb had on my life and the lives of so many others. Bill was unlike other preachers I had heard. He used original material, kept me interested, and made me laugh. And he played the guitar. He was in charge of the teens at camp, and I was thrilled when I got to attend his evening sessions. I loved the music and listening to his stories that imparted insightful spiritual truths. He literally shared his life, giving personal examples and revelations.

He was unorthodox, wearing jeans, t-shirts, cowboy boots, and sometimes a cowboy hat over his red hair and freckled face. He was quirky, fond of Willie Nelson, Dr. Pepper, and baseball caps. He had distinctive handwriting and found a way to find something to say whenever he passed by. He made us feel like we belonged, no matter how nerdy or insecure we were on the inside. A chronic asthmatic, I could relate to his struggles as a diabetic.

Many years later, after my daughters had attended camp and gotten to know Bill and Barb, they greeted me at the door when I arrived home one day with tearstained faces.

"Mom, Mom, someone died." My heart stopped.

"Who? Is it Grandma Myra or Grandpa Len? Auntie April or Uncle Gary?"

"No, Bill Roycroft!"

I was surprised at how his death from complications after a fall in his sixties affected them. Either I'd raised extremely compassionate children, or he'd influenced their lives as much as he had mine.

*

In July 2000, I took my daughters Shiloh and Keziah, then aged eight and six years, to visit at my mom's in Creston, where she was living with her second husband, Grandpa Hans. I was thirty-eight. My dad, Grandpa Len, lived down by the river on the flats in Creston; he spent most of the time trapping beavers and such, while his wife, Grandma Bunnie, lived in a shack in Yahk, British Columbia, about thirty miles away. He went there once in a while for food and laundry.

Late one afternoon, we have a small supper at Grandma Myra's before we go to have supper with Grandpa Len, just in case the girls don't like his food. I drive Mom's still new Chrysler Intrepid off the highway and along the dirt road, as two-to-three foot high weeds scrape the undercarriage and my conscience.

It's hard to describe Dad's camp. Mini dump. Junkyard. Salvaged scrap pile. Desecration Desert. Used goods and bads. Trashy Treasures. Crap City. None of these names really capture the full essence. Forgotten Field. Recycled Wreckage. Hell's Heap. No, there are no easy words. The man uses a shower curtain reclaimed from the town dump for a tablecloth. He tells us the dogs do the dishes. A pink vinyl toilet seat cover with embroidered flowers balances on the edge of the boat. Bits of discarded carpet are strewn around on the ground—tarps, wires, pails, rubber boots, 8-track tapes, pickup trucks, campers, blankets, propane tanks, duct tape, radios, dangling speakers, the top of an ironing board, an antler. These items are all kind of connected in some inexplicable way, creating a delicately linked mayhem.

Everything is camouflaged in the same colour, undertone, because for as long as it was wherever it came from before here and until now, it had been exposed to sun and wind and weather and dirt and dog hair and mould and rust and dust and such. Any original colour is mostly a memory now. In the midst of this mess, Grandpa Len produces a truly delicious meal of mashed potatoes and elk meat cabbage rolls and cans of cold pop and iced tea. The food was cooked back in Yahk by his demoted, I mean devoted, wife, Bunnie. He feeds what we can't eat to the dogs, and we go down the bank to the boats.

A homemade, half-sunk dock becomes our gateway to the river. We manage to clamber into the biggest of the three boats. Shreds of red paint cling bravely to this unseaworthy-looking vessel. The small hull contains flotation devices of various description. A thick, stiff, mouldy orange life jacket goes over Keziah's head. The date on it is 1970. I probably wore it when I was a kid.

There is something eerie about all this old stuff. It was meant to die and rest permanently in waste disposal heaven, but my dad is a grave robber surrounded by skeletons of material veterans who've lost the war with time.

Anyway, the river is calm as far as I can see through the thick haze of blue smoke coming from the chugging motor. The dogs follow us along the shore. Keziah is gleeful as Grandpa pulls the first fish into the net. She sampled fresh Kokanee salmon from her step-grandpa Hans's weekend fishing trip and is now hooked. Grandpa Len has found a friend. When he asks if we should go back or keep fishing, Keyz yells, "Keep fishing!"

Eventually, we go back to the dock. Grandpa goes to shore to dig worms, and we fish from the boat in shallow water to catch chubs. These will be stored whole in glass jars in the summer sun to be used as bait for winter trapping. Mm, mm. When the last worm disappears with the fading sun, we climb the ladder back to camp for our dessert. I ask, "Dad, do you have a sink somewhere so the girls can wash their hands?"

"Sure, I got sinks everywhere," he says, and a big silver mixing bowl is plunked down on a lawn chair, and water appears from a jug. Dad retrieves a huge watermelon from a cooler somewhere and hacks into it lengthwise with a long knife—surely not the one he cleaned the one edible fish with, I'm thinking hopefully—and invites us to sit on an outdoor couch sheltered by the overhang of a camper. We hold enormous pieces of the sweet fruit, and the juice drips freely.

"You can even spit the seeds on Grandpa's living room floor," he tells the girls. "Just throw the rinds past the road into the grass."

As long as I can keep my mind from thinking about what my body is making contact with in this place, I can enjoy the simple peace of it. But soon, the mosquitoes are making a meal of us, and it's time to go. We take the gifts kindly chosen by Bunnie, which are wrapped in a black garbage bag, and climb back into the green Intrepid, aptly named for this trip. I stop to put the chain up after I drive over it and think it's mighty thoughtful of Dad to warn people with a sign that says KEEP OUT.

This is one time I really enjoyed being with Dad. He's inherited the Morton hospitality and served us graciously, never apologetically or self-belittlingly as Mom and I do. He seems peaceful and content, having freed himself from the constricting bonds of matrimony while availing himself of the benefits of marriage, which are at his disposal when needed.

The girls instinctively give him a hug goodbye, and I sense he is a bit awkward with this display of affection, but he receives it, nonetheless. It's really amazing to see him now so differently than I did for so many years. I didn't speak to him for a couple of years after our last conversation about my hateful letter. But one day I was at my brother Gary's place when he called, and I answered the phone and we just started talking as usual. I wonder who has changed more, he or I.

3

First Loves and Losses

It's summertime in Creston, 1976. My sister April, age thirteen, and I, just turned fifteen, walk into town to see a movie at the Tivoli Theatre. It's getting dark as we walk home talking. As we approach our yard from the highway, we notice some movement by the gas tank. For the sake of convenience with all the vehicles we've acquired—fish truck, Dad's pickup truck, Mom's car, snowmobiles, boat—we have a gas tank in our yard. A dark figure appears to be stealing gas. We break into a run toward the intruder yelling, "Hey, what are you doing? Get out of here."

It is a male. It looks like Brett Turcott, one of our neighbours, but it's hard to tell for sure in the dark. He starts running away from us. We keep running into the house, which is dark except for the hall light.

"Dad, Dad," I yell, "Someone's stealing our gas."

A minute later, my dad comes running down the hall to the doorway where we are standing, totally naked, pointing a handgun upwards to the ceiling. I don't know where to look. I am totally freaked out that I am seeing my dad naked with a handgun but also curious. There is a gun rack with rifles hanging on the wall, but he must keep the pistol in the bedroom.

"Where is he? What's going on?"

"Well, someone was stealing our gas, but they're gone. It might have been Brett Turcott."

"Well, if they're gone, there's not much I can do about it." I'm not sure what he was planning to do anyway, go outside naked and shoot at someone? Maybe just scare them off.

"Yeah, sorry."

He turns around and goes back to bed. April and I cling together, trying to stifle our relieved laughter on this night of double trauma.

"Did you see it?" I ask April.

"Of course. I wish I hadn't. How am I going to get that out of my head?"

"I know, me too. I had no idea he had a handgun."

*

Now I realize this is telescoping, but it's the perfect time to tell it. It's many years later, and I'm the mother of two daughters. My friend has given me a book from the seventies about sensual massage, when I express a passing interest in learning massage. The book contains instructions and full-nude pictures of hippies rubbing each other. My ten-year-old daughter comes across it one day and starts looking at it. She finds the page with a long-haired, bearded guy lying on the floor face up. She says out loud, "Weird."

I say, "What?" and look over to see what she is looking at.

"Is that really what it looks like?"

"Yeah, that's pretty much it."

"Huh. I always pictured it with the balls on top."

I laughed. "Depends how you're looking at it."

*

In grade five when I was ten years old, I became obsessed with all things sexual. The girl who sat behind me, Cindy, was the first in the class to have developing breasts. Each day, my fascination grew with her emerging cones. Her thin t-shirts created a tantalizing view, enabling me to see the distinction between the flesh and the skin of the nipple. I had to be discreet. I stole glances whenever possible, making up excuses to swivel around in my seat. Once she got annoyed and said, "Stop staring at me." But I couldn't help it. The attraction was a driving force that controlled me.

I began to pray for my own breast development. I would lie in bed with my hands cupped over my little maple buds and beg God: "Please give me big breasts, please. Help my breasts grow larger, Lord. Please supply them with nutrients and energy to grow faster. Please Lord. For your glory. In Jesus's name, amen."

Night upon night, I petitioned with little change in sight.

Slowly and imperceptibly, they began to grow, and three breastfed kids and forty years later, they're massive. When I lie on my back, they're like huge sugar cookies with gumdrops on top. When I get a mammogram, they spread into a ten-inch pizza dough, 38 DD. What can I say? Hallelujah, thank you Jesus, and be careful what you wish for. Truly, despite all that has happened to shake my faith, I cannot deny that He answered my prayer, glory to God. Although apparently according to some Christians, "No" is an answer, too.

However, there are downsides to having large breasts. First, that's the first thing everybody sees. Guys see big boobs and equate it with a measure of your sex factor. They respond instantly by making comments, trying to cop a feel, and assuming you're loose. Which of course I was. Am. Three kids later and too lazy to do Kegel exercises, what do you expect? Also, they don't give you credit for having any brains. Second, large breasts limit the clothing styles you can wear. Spaghetti straps, halters, and backless dresses just don't work. There's no such thing as a strapless bra that really works. My breasts are heavy. They need straps to hold them up. The straps dig into your shoulders over time, creating permanent ridges. Big breasts also sag more as you age. The bigger they are, the harder they fall.

Some of the happiest times in my life were nestled in a papasan chair with a baby at my breast, enjoying mutual bliss. That would have been my ideal job, providing babies with suckle services. I had plenty of rich creamy milk. My kids were like little Michelin men, their thighs a series of stacked sausage rings. I didn't like men and boys in general. They seemed coarse and stupid, base and mammalian. They were uninteresting to look at, with boring clothes and plain bodies. They needed a nice car to get me to pay attention. I was actually scared of guys in high school. The only ones I liked were the ones who turned out to be gay at the ten-year high school reunion.

When I was thirteen, my best friend Peggy—who ditched me the following year to join the popular crowd because she hated the way I bragged, which was a painful but effective correction to my behaviour—got a job babysitting during the Blossom Festival. This was the Town of Creston's annual fair held during the long weekend in May. She told me to come over and hang out with her, but I had to leave before the people got home because she hadn't asked if she could have company.

So I rode my bike over, and we hung out. The house belonged to an older couple whose children and their kids were home visiting, so she was babysitting the grandchildren of the homeowners. The kids were asleep in bed. Peggy and I daringly shared a beer from the fridge. Next thing we knew we heard noises outside.

"They're home. Get going. I'll see you at my place," Peggy said. I was sleeping over at her house. So I went out the back door with my heart pounding as the people were coming in the front. I rounded the house to the side where my bike was parked, put my hands on the handlebars, looked up, and froze. In the corner of the bushy hedge was a squatting white figure. What was it? A lawn ornament, an elf? In the darkness and with my bad eyes, I couldn't tell what I was looking at. Until it spoke.

A woman's voice said, "Who are you? What are you doing? Where do you think you're going? Let go of that bike and come inside. I want to talk to you."

If there's one feeling I abhor, it's the feeling of being caught. Cornered, condemned. Guilt is an unpleasant emotion. I swear my veins were full of it. The pissing grandma successfully avoided having to explain why she was peeing in the bushes in her own front yard and used her full authority to interrogate Peggy and me as we sat on the couch. Peggy was reproved, and I was released. What a night.

When we got back to Peggy's, we set up a bed of blankets on the living room floor. We were watching TV and rehashing the events of the evening.

Then Peggy said, "I want to kiss you." Could things possibly get any weirder? I didn't know what to do, so I said, "Okay."

She leaned over and put her lips on my lips. My stomach flipped. We began touching each other's bodies, starting at the top and working our way down. The way it's supposed to be done, boys.

Her fingers stroked the backs of the butterflies dancing in my belly, and by the time her hand was at my panty line, I shuddered with the ecstasy of it all but pushed her hand away. Enough already. It was too much. I was wet, quivering. She was my best friend, and this was a crazy night.

"Let's try and go to sleep now," I said. "I'm tired."

We never spoke of the incident again, ever. She married one of her brother's friends shortly after high school and had three kids. Of course, I eventually got married and had three kids, too, but that might never have happened if I'd met the right woman. In fact, I've met many women I lusted for and longed to be with, but as far as I know, they were all straight. I had no idea who or where the lesbians were or how on earth to show interest in a woman without freaking her out. No other women ever expressed any interest in me.

Well, there was this one hairdresser I had when I lived in Lethbridge. She'd always press her body against me when she was cutting my hair. She was cute, too, short blonde hair, but I was so clueless back then. I didn't realize. She invited me to the pub where her baseball team was going after a practice, and I went but didn't see her. The next time I booked an appointment, they told me she'd joined the army. I was shocked, but by then, I'd finally put the pieces together and realized I was too late.

And once, many years later when I was in Montréal on an adventure, I'm getting ahead of myself here, a nice waitress gave me an invitation, but I foolishly chose a guy again and lost that chance, too. As much as I wanted to be with a woman, I always went with men because it was easier, more familiar, socially speaking, if less satisfying.

It takes courage to be different, to be true to your self. You risk judgment and rejection, being labelled and shunned. Some people also feel betrayed, as though you've been lying to them or hiding from them all along.

My first real love is a guy named Harry Hall I meet when I am in my grad year, 1979, in Creston, my hometown. I am seventeen, and he is twenty-three. We are acting in the Creston Drama Club's play, *The Mousetrap* by Agatha Christie. I am Mollie Ralston; he is Sergeant Trotter. Somehow our romance develops as it often does in theatre while we are having fun together a few times a week. Harry is tall, with long hair, long legs, long everything. I'm not sure I ever actually see *it*, as our lusty liaisons take place on the couch in his mother's trailer after she's gone to bed. It's dark except for the muted blue glow of the TV and quiet except for Meatloaf's low crooning of "Paradise by the Dashboard Light."

Harry seems responsible. Not so much that he uses a condom but enough that he doesn't come inside me, which is almost the same thing. We only consummate our love a few times before I find a poem written about another girl on his dresser when he's not home. Heartbroken, I resign myself to graduation festivities without a date. However, the consolation is not having to be seen with him in public again in the suit he wore to prom, a salmon polyester number. The only one he owns.

There's always a silver lining.

After graduation that June, I enjoy some summer at Kootenay Lake, then head to Calgary in my yellow land yacht, a used Chevrolet Impala and gift from my parents, to room and board with my recently bereaved Aunt Lorna, my mom's older sister, and my cousin Tim, a year older than I. Aunt Lorna's husband had a sudden, unexpected fatal aneurysm while curling, at the age of forty-eight. She was forty-nine, and the shock put her into instant menopause.

I get a job at AGT, Alberta Government Telephones, as a directory assistance operator. AGT has just begun using computers, so I am trained for three weeks and begin taking calls for just over five dollars an hour, a good wage, almost two dollars above minimum. Calgary is in a big oil boom, and money is everywhere. While technically my job is to look up local phone numbers for customers, people consider telephone operators sources of information, so they call requesting the time frequently or wanting taxis, which is difficult because we are not supposed to choose one company over another and some drunk people have trouble remembering the name of a taxi company. Once, someone even calls and asks me how to cook a chicken. As if I know. "I'm not actually sure, but my mom cooks everything at 350 degrees for an hour."

The worst call I ever take is from a gentleman with a thick accent, Italian or European anyway. "Good afternoon, directory assistance," I say.

"Yah, I vud like da number for Mr. Somebody."

"Uh, okay, what is the person's name, please?"

"Mr. Somebody."

"I'm sorry, sir, that's not a real name. What is the last name of the person you want?"

"Not a person. I vant Mr. Somebody."

"Sir, I'm sorry, but I can't help you if you won't cooperate."

Slowly, "Mr. Somebody."

"Okay, I checked, and there is no listing under Somebody." By this time, my voice is raised to a low yell, and my supervisor gets my attention.

"Sir, I'm going have my supervisor come on the line. One moment, please." I listen.

My supervisor says, "Sir, what is the listing you want, please?" By this time, he's as annoyed as I am with our communication.

"I tell her already so many time. I vant Mr. Somebody."

"Is that a business or residential listing?"

"It's a business. Dey make da sandwich. Mr. Somebody."

"Okay, I think the listing you want is Mr. Submarine. Is that correct?"

"Dat's da one. Mr. Somebody."

I quickly look up the number, give it to him, release the call, and shriek, "Oh my god!" It is evident that my ability to handle people is not the best. The way I deal with it is to go drinking with one of the other operators, Sharon. The legal drinking age in Alberta is eighteen, a year younger than in British Columbia, although that is not the reason I move to Calgary. I just wanted to get out of Creston, and Calgary is the closest big city where I have relatives.

One particular night, I am out with another friend from Creston who is going to postsecondary school in Calgary and celebrating her birthday. We are at a bar where there is a tall guy playing a guitar and singing on a small stage. On his break, I approach him.

"Hi, I was wondering if you'd mind singing happy birthday to my friend Debbie."

"Sure, no problem. What's your name?"

"Oh, it's Jacquie."

"I'm Rick."

"I really like your music, Rick."

"Oh thanks, yeah, that's good."

Somewhere between the happy birthday song and last call, I give Rick my number. He's tall, dark, and handsome. We start dating. I go to his gigs with him, then we go to his place and have sex. His apartment is sparsely furnished—couch, coffee table, TV. He reads *Omni* magazine. He dabbles in photography, plays his guitar every day, and smokes pot but doesn't offer me any, which I inwardly think is kind of rude. He drives an old station wagon to haul his gear and rides his bike. He likes doing outdoor things, like camping and cross-country skiing.

He calls my boobs orbs. One night we start making out on the couch. He pulls his erect cock out of his pants. "Would you like to suck it?" he asks. My inner voice says, 'No, I don't think so.' My outer, pleaser voice says, "Yeah, I guess. I've never done it before."

Everything is okay until he starts pushing my head down so his penis blocks my windpipe. How am I supposed to breathe? I don't like this.

One month, my period is late. Uh-oh. This isn't good. I don't have a doctor in Calgary, so I go to one whose phone number I get a lot of requests for as an operator. He is an older man, gruff. When he confirms my pregnancy and I tell him I want to terminate, he seems angry, scolding, "You're the eighth one this week." I go to Planned Parenthood. A worker named Mandy tells me the drill: "The easiest thing is to go to Spokane, Washington. I'll give you the address and phone number of a clinic there. Call and make an appointment. I think it's about 350 dollars American." She explains birth control options, but it kind of goes over my head.

The thing is I am a Christian. I should not be having premarital sex. It's called fornication. I know this, and I am ashamed of myself, yet to my body, it seems a very natural thing to do and expected, except the cock sucking sometimes seems unnatural. Plus, now that I've lost my virginity, what's the diff? When I tell Rick I am pregnant, he says, "Do you want to get married?"

"No thanks," I reply. I don't really love Rick forever. He's just my boyfriend for now. Getting married because of a pregnancy has proven to be a mistake for the previous generation. Rick is in his early thirties, and I am eighteen. Ever since I was a kid, I've never seen myself getting married or having children. It seems to me like a boring trap. I'd rather do anything than that.

Rick says, "I wouldn't mind having a kid."

I would. I can't imagine having a baby. I certainly couldn't take care of it myself, wouldn't know how. I tell Aunt Lorna, who is not a professing Christian, and therefore safe.

"Honey, you know you can have this baby if you want to. I'll help you, and I'm sure your mom will help you. I want you to know you're not alone. We can make it work. Don't worry about that. I just want you to do want you want. It's your decision."

I don't even have to think about it. To me, pregnancy equals abortion. It's the only option for me.

I feel guilty. I know my mom considers it murder. I can't deny the reality that if I don't interfere, a child will appear. Women have been dangerously and clandestinely procuring abortions for centuries, but now abortion is available and safe, I hope. What I really want is for this child to abort itself, so I won't be responsible for its death. I run around the park. I do jumping jacks. I pray for a miscarriage. And I make an appointment at the abortion clinic in Spokane.

Rick is on board: "I have to play until midnight. Then we can pack up my gear and get on the road. We'll get there in time for your appointment in the morning." I am so thankful that I have a job and can pay for this. I like being financially independent. I can't ask Mom. I don't mind paying for it. Rick seems okay with my decision, and I appreciate his support in driving me down there.

So back to what I was saying about birth control. I never use anything other than withdrawal because by using birth control, I condone my own sin. Stupid, I know. Reckless. Proven fail. I just want to get this procedure over with and get on with my life and never have sex again.

We carry out the plan, driving through the night to Spokane. I leave Rick in the car to sleep while I go into the clinic. I am nervous, guilty, and ashamed.

"Hello, I'm Jacquelyn Morton. I have an 8:00 a.m. appointment."

"Okay, Jacquelyn, I'll take your payment and then you can have a seat. Someone will be with you in a moment."

Soon a woman in scrubs approaches me. "Jacquelyn, come with me please." She leads me into a small room with two single beds in it and hands me a gown. "Just get totally undressed and put the gown on. It won't be long."

Moments later another girl, apparently a patient, enters the room and goes to the other bed. "Hi," she says.

"Hi, do you mind if I ask how old you are?" I ask.

"Twenty-two," she says.

I knew it. At least she waited to make this mistake. I feel stupid, scared, and embarrassed but not alone. I'm not the only one. The woman in scrubs returns.

"Jacquelyn, it's time. Come with me, please."

We go into the operating room where a masked and gowned male doctor is waiting. At 350 dollars a pop, I bet he lives in a really nice house, I think to myself. I am seated in a reclining chair. My cold, white, shaky legs are spread so that a series of slim-to-increasingly-thicker metal rods can be inserted into my cervix and the contents of my womb removed. I am given a sedative. I begin to feel woozy, choosy, prochoice, I hear a voice screaming, yelling, it's very telling. I'm in pain, straining, draining, hurting, squirting, blurting, "Someone stop the screaming."

The nurse says, "Shh, we're almost done now, okay."

I realize it's me screaming from far away, from deep down. Finally, the sounds abate. It's over. I'm sent back to the little bedroom to recover. I am given a surfboard-sized pad that will surely shout my shame and a prescription to prevent haemorrhaging. I sit reclining for half an hour or so, and then I go, stepping still somewhat shakily from the screaming place into the bright sunshine of a summer day. It is July 24, 1980, two days after my nineteenth birthday. I've just received the best gift ever.

I am happy, relieved of my sinful burden. It's my little secret, not my public shame. Thank you, God. Thank you that I live in a time when this is available to me. I go to the car and wake Rick.

"I have to get a prescription filled. Apparently, there's a pharmacy around the corner." I go in and hand the pharmacist my Rx. I see the same look on his face as the doctor's in Calgary—judgment, disgust. I try not to cry as I wait.

On the drive home, I lie down in the back seat of Rick's car. The guy at the border crossing looks at us, as only a border guard can. He waves us through. We get back just in time for Rick to drop me off at home, unload his equipment, and work again. I'm thankful for his help. Maybe he wishes we'd kept the baby and stayed together. I just wanted to move on, maybe even move away to avoid the temptation of having sex with Rick. I realize I got pregnant at almost the same age my mom had with me. Had she ever wished she'd had a choice?

This never would have happened if I'd had a girlfriend.

4

Covenant Players

Shortly after my first abortion at the young age of just barely nineteen, which I know I'll never tell my mother about, she and I are visiting on the phone. "Jacquie, did you know that Betsy Harris, your school and church friend, is going to California to join an acting group? They performed at the church, and she was so impressed she wanted to join."

"Really? I didn't know Betsy likes acting. But that sounds interesting. I'd like to hear more about it. Do you have her phone number?"

"Oh sure, it's in the church directory. Just a minute while I find it." Mom gives me the number and when we're finished our conversation, I call Betsy.

Betsy says, "The group is called Covenant Players. They came to our church and I talked to them and decided to join. It's a good way to get out of Creston and travel. It starts in August. The training is in California for three weeks and then we go on tour."

"I might be interested. Is there anything else I need to know?"

"Well, it's a year commitment. You do two tours in that time with a break in between."

"Do you get paid?"

"A little bit. You pay for your own food during training, but once you're on the road, they cover meals and shelter, so you don't need much money."

"Well, I've got a bit saved, so I should be okay. This sounds interesting. I think I'd like to come."

"Okay, so we need to book our flight and let them know when we arrive so they can pick us up at the airport."

Arrangements are made. I give notice at the telephone company and quit my job, a job that could become a career with many lucrative benefits and opportunities to climb the corporate ladder. I know this, and I also know that a nine-to-five job in a cubicle or office talking to strangers on the phone for a second only to connect them to others for the rest of my life is not my destiny. I want to write a book. There's nothing interesting about a rut job, marriage, and children. I need adventures to keep those pages turning.

Off I go, away from Rick and back toward God, hopefully, putting on my metaphorical boots to march in God's army and avoid the devil's territory. God is right: I strayed, and I paid. I'll stay safe by doing Christian theatre for awhile. Plus, it sounds like a good chapter for a book, my adventures as a touring actor.

As the plane descends over Los Angeles, I can't count the backyard swimming pools of every imaginable shape that dot the landscape. We land, get our luggage, and step out into the heat of a woodfire pizza oven, which is California in August. There is no breeze rustling the tall palm trees. Within minutes, sweat is gathering in the small of my back. We wait on the sidewalk with our small bags.

"Are you sure they're coming, Betsy? It's so hot. Let's go back inside where there's air conditioning."

"No, they won't be able to see us. They should be here soon."

Sure enough, a white van rolls up and a tanned, blonde woman gets out and helps us put our baggage inside. "Hi, I'm Charity from CP. How are you doing?"

"We're hot. I hope the van has air conditioning."

"No, sorry, but I can open the windows." Which is the equivalent of being hit in the face with warm pillows. Charity begins narrating the trip like a tour guide, allowing for our questions.

"How far is it to where we're going?" I ask.

"Oh, it'll take us about forty minutes or so, depending on traffic, to get to Reseda."

"Where do we stay?"

"New recruits are sharing rooms in a motel. It's right next to St. James Church where we do training."

"Where do we get food?"

"Oh, there are places around. A few blocks away there is a small grocery store, and there's a Jack-in-the-Box right across the street."

We pass the famous white HOLLYWOOD letters on the hillside.

I imagine a series of fortunate event scenarios in which I am discovered and become a famous actor. I may be on the brink of something bigger than I think.

When we arrive at the motel, we are assigned separate rooms. "Go ahead, Bets," I say. "I'll be there in a minute."

"Charity, may I talk to you for a sec? Um, I have a little issue. You see, I recently had an abortion, and I have to go for a six-week checkup." This is difficult to say out loud.

"That's no problem. I've had three abortions. Just tell your unit leader when it's time, and they'll make arrangements." Three! I think to myself. That's a lot. Is that even possible? And how do you call yourself a Christian with a track record like that?

"What's a unit leader?"

"Oh, well when you get assigned to a tour area, you'll have a unit leader who's in charge of the group. Don't worry. It'll be fine."

"Okay, thanks."

I go to check out my room, which is next door to Betsy's. There are four girls per room. One of my roommates is a naturally beautiful young woman who doesn't know it. Seeing her in a white bra and panties makes my mouth water. I hope she's in my group.

We start training the next morning at 8:00 a.m. What was I thinking? I am not a morning person. The principal of my high school threatened to not let me graduate unless I started showing up for home room. I have always had a hard time waking up in the morning. That's when I'm most tired. I don't think you can change your natural sleep rhythm easily. Every morning my mom would call to wake me, sometimes coming in to shake me, and I'd momentarily rise from the murky depths of unconsciousness to acknowledge that I knew my presence was requested, only to sink back into sleep. These moments of hanging in the balance between wakefulness and asleep were as sweet as stolen kisses, akin to hovering on the edge of an orgasm, as irresistible as the siren's song. Inevitably, I'd sleep on as the rest of the family trotted off into their days, and I'd finally rouse myself after the school bus had departed, forcing me to walk the mile or so to school, arriving late.

At night, I loved the stillness of the sleeping world, the feeling of solitary wakefulness. I have a theory that one's sleep-awake schedule is related to their time of birth. I was born at 1:00 a.m.; therefore, that's when I feel awake.

Standing in a large circle on a cement pad under a warm sun that gets hotter as the day progresses soon makes me question the sanity of this decision. But I can't turn back now. I just got here. Onward into hell I go. We do acting exercises and drama games, learning to project our voices from the diaphragm, moving farther apart. We walk in a circle as instructions are called out: "Louder, I can't hear you. Now you are an old man. Feel his joints. How does your body move? What is your posture?" And in one of those rare magical moments where my effort meets internal creative force, I am an old man. I can feel it.

The founder of Covenant Players is Charles M. Tanner, known as Chuck, a middle-aged man who induces a hush when he graces the cement pad with his presence. Older CP'ers are in awe of him. Apparently, he was a film director in Hollywood who changed directions and decided to start a nondenominational touring company using drama to communicate the gospel. He has written some seven hundred skits, sketches, and plays. Unfortunately, some innate jealousy or insecurity in me reacts poorly to people in authority who, I'm told, deserve my respect. He looks like an ordinary guy to me—tall, middle aged, thinning hair, and glasses.

The best thing about those three weeks is a long walk I take one day to a strip mall where I find the coolest, cutest outfit of white cotton harem pants and an embroidered peasant top with a gathered waist. It becomes my uniform and is the best thing I have to deal with the unbearable heat.

After the training and learning some simple sketches, it is time to be assigned our touring areas for the first six months of our year-long commitment. I am nervous with anticipation. As the announcements are made, I hear, "Jacquelyn Morton, your area is West Virginia and Virginia. Your unit leader is Susan Colton." People are milling and scrambling to form smaller groups, teams of four, usually. My friend Betsy is being sent to Alabama and Georgia. I look for a name tag that says Susan Colton and find it attached to a tall, blonde woman from Minnesota, who looks to me well suited to digging potatoes. The other members of our unit are twenty-three-year-old Jane from California and nineteen-year-old Derek from New York. I am also nineteen.

The next morning, we load our CP van with luggage and necessities. Susan consults the map to determine her route. Essentially, we'll be crossing the United States from the west coast almost to the east. She says, "I had this same tour last time and I love it. The people are great. Is everybody ready? Let's pray. Lord, we ask for You to bless this trip, keep us safe, provide our needs and use us to do Your will. In Jesus's name, amen."

She puts the van into gear and our journey from California to West Virginia begins. The way the structure of CP works is that on each tour of each area, the leaders try to set up performance dates for the upcoming season as well as to book shows while the team is in the area.

Most performances are in churches, as part of the Sunday services, but we also perform in schools and prisons, basically anywhere someone will pay us. From the seven hundred or so skits, there are several themes—such as stewardship, forgiveness, sacrifice, friendship, et cetera—that the ministers and pastors can choose from. Then we get busy building a show to their specifications. We learn and rehearse and perform within days sometimes. The skits and sketches are relatively short, requiring only simple props, costumes, and sets. Susan assigns roles and offers direction.

With so many, I obviously don't remember them all, but they're all generally just promoting the tenets of Christianity in some form or another. I recall the first skit we learn in California being one person sitting on a park bench by themselves and being joined by another person, and they have a conversation. I don't remember what it was about, but I recall it contained the word "precedent," and I didn't know what it meant. In another one, I played an angelic narrator. I was wearing a white dress I owned that seemed fitting. We didn't have costumes per se, as most of the skits were about ordinary people. Sometimes we'd stay after the service/performance briefly to talk to people. Mostly, it was just thought-provoking entertainment for churchgoers who didn't usually get the Word of God presented theatrically or in such a down-to-earth fashion. For schools and prisons, the shows were intended to give the audience a positive message of hope and encouragement.

We are on a shoestring budget, with a staple diet of peanut butter and jam sandwiches while on the road. The other aspect of the CP ministry is to make connections and find supporters all across the United States and Canada, so we can stop in a city and find someone who will put us up for the night.

Susan, a Mennonite CP'er of five years, is in charge of everything.

She is the driver, navigator, and show booker, and bears full responsibility for the trip. My role is to whine and complain about everything—the food, the hours, the conditions. When I learn she is a virgin at twenty-eight, there is a deep, internal clash. The perfectionist in me is jealous. The postabortion, lazy, irresponsible part of me is ashamed of me for my sin and of her for not getting laid by her age, even though it could be a personal choice. The result is that I decide I don't like her and do little to make her job easy. Often, she and Jane, who is a quiet, pleasant, cooperative person, naturally pair up, as do Derek and I, as we discover things we have in common, starting with a sex life.

Derek has curly, frizzy hair and small silver fillings in many of his teeth, even in the front, which gives the impression of braces. I like his vibe right away. There's something different about him that I don't identify until one boring, hot, humid day when Susan is piloting the van past the cornfields of Iowa and Derek and I are riding in the back. I have a thought buzzing in my head like a big ol' bee, and it's making me nervous. I want to talk to somebody about it before I talk to Susan. I wonder if I should trust Derek. He is about my age, from a suburb of New York, and I feel more comfortable with him than with the girls. Maybe that's because he has a sordid past like me.

"You might as well know I'm gay," he says conspiratorially.

"Oh, really?" I reply nonchalantly. Maybe that's why I like him. He doesn't give off that typical male hunger that I usually feel. I don't go around saying I am gay because I've had so little sexual experience with women, even though I secretly long for them. I've liked girls since I was in grade four or five. I don't understand boys, and most of them seem stupid or mean. I used to have little crushes on my female teachers. I fixate on the body parts of women I find attractive. It might be their breasts or teeth or hair or fingernails. I rarely find men attractive, David Cassidy being the big exception. He's beautiful. Bodies without boobs seem kind of boring. But it isn't just that. Usually men's clothes and shoes are dull coloured and unimaginative. Some men do have nice muscular legs but almost always gross feet.

Of course, I'd slept with a few men but not because I wanted to, with the exception of my first love, Harry, who wrote poetry, but either because I was drunk, they wanted me to, or I thought that's what they wanted. After Harry, I moved to Calgary just after my eighteenth birthday and met a few guys at bars I slept with before I met Rick. It was more about acceptance than passion. The world expects women to sleep with men.

So that doesn't bother me in the least about Derek. In fact, I envy him. However, it sounds like being a gay man in New York is a bit different than me having a girlfriend. Derek tells me he's had sex with strangers in alleys. I picture him squatting between a dark figure's legs, or would the dark figure be squatting between his legs? How do gay people have sex exactly? When someone's confessing, one has to be delicate when pressing for details or risk collapsing the exposé. I'm not quite that desperate.

When ugly or older men in bars bother me or want to dance, I tell them I'm a lesbian to get rid of them and secretly hope another woman hears me. Sometimes they look at me like a freak as they back away. It isn't exactly true, but I wish it were.

I decide to risk it. "Hey Derek, I need to talk to Susan about something, but I'm nervous."

"What is it?"

"Well, just before I came here, I had an abortion, and I'm supposed to have a follow-up checkup. Do you think she'll take me to a clinic? I don't really want to tell her because I feel bad about it, you know how straight she is, but I pretty much have to."

"Of course she'll take you. She has to. Don't worry about her. God forgives our sins. She has no right to judge."

"Yeah, I guess you're right. I just feel so ashamed. I know it was wrong, but I just couldn't go through with the pregnancy. I was too proud. I didn't want my mom or my grandparents to know I'd had sex."

"I know how you feel. I did something too. On my last tour, I was staying overnight at a priest's house. He said he was going to take a shower before bed. I thought nothing of it until I heard him calling me. When I went to the bathroom door, it was open. I hesitated, but I went in. I knew what I was doing, but I'm so weak. I gave up sex when I found God, but it was so strange. Here am I trying to serve God, and temptation is right in front of me. I gave in. It still bothers me. I don't know what to do."

"You should tell someone at the head office, so he doesn't do it to someone else."

"It's my fault. I had a choice."

"Not really. He set you up. We're weak. It's like you said to me, 'God forgives our sins.' In fact, that's the whole reason Jesus died."

"Yeah, I guess I believe that in my head and for you, but I don't always feel it."

"Me neither."

Eventually, I manage to tell Susan my problem. She looks a little shocked but makes arrangements. I have a minor infection, so I have to get something to clear it up. We carry on. One of our gigs is at a prison in West Virginia. We are not allowed to wear skirts for this performance so as not to entice the inmates, which doesn't make sense to me because I look damn good in pants. I am astounded to see that all the inmates are Black men.

I don't remember much about our show other than we had a very appreciative audience. At the time, I thought it was odd that most of the inmates were Black. In fact, it took about another thirty-plus years before I read an article that explained the high percentage of Black people in American prisons, as part of the legacy of slavery. After enslavement became illegal, imprisonment for even small crimes became a way to perpetuate racism and oppress Black people in the United States. I was stunned, but it fit with my experience and observation with the Covenant Players at that time and made so much sense, as horribly distasteful as it was.

They seem happy to see us, and we mingle briefly after the show, guards watching intently. One inmate in particular asks for my address so he can write to me. I give him the CP address and tell him to send it in care of. He writes, and I write back. Then I don't hear from him for a couple of years, when he writes me at an address that I haven't given him, to say he's being released and wants to visit me. Scary. I don't reply.

We do some shows, meet some nice people, survive some van problems, and enjoy the beauty of the Virginias, which are lush, treed, and mountainous, slightly reminiscent of British Columbia. I feel comfortable here and hope to return.

One day, we have no plans for a show and therefore no place to sleep. Susan says, "I'm going to call AJ and Fiona Morton." This is my own last name, coincidentally. "They're a lovely couple who may let us stay with them tonight."

She goes to use a pay phone and comes back to the van where we're waiting, smiling. "They said yes. Let's go. It's a bit of a drive from here. They live in the country."

We arrive at dinnertime, conveniently for us, and they feed us. AJ is a good-sized man, and by that, I mean tall and solid but not overweight. He wears jean overalls and has shoulder length-hair, looking like a farmer-hippie-Jesus-freak combo. His wife, Fiona, is pretty, petite, and quiet. They have two small children, a boy and a girl. Fiona is always tired and in bed first. After dinner, AJ starts talking about the things of the Lord, not preaching, exactly, but sharing his faith, reminiscent of Bill Roycroft from my camp days. One by one, the others drift off to bed, with Derek and me the only listeners left.

"Y'all have to come to the meeting tomorrow night. I'll be speaking. It's a group of us locals who fellowship once a week. I usually speak."

By now, my eyelids are bobbing at half-mast. I like AJ. He is charismatic and impresses me as a sincere Christian. "I've enjoyed our talk," I say. "But I'm falling asleep now, AJ. See you tomorrow. Goodnight."

The next day, I work on my lines a bit. We have a show booked for the following day. That evening we go to the meeting and listen to AJ speak again. I don't think Fiona and the kids come. She is probably tired of listening to him. I sense some vague annoyance or tension coming from her direction. AJ seems like the kind of guy to extend hospitality freely, well, not just seems like, he is. He probably enjoys the audience, as I sense Fiona may be tired of listening to his voice. But she is the one looking after two small children and having four extra people to feed for several days. AJ never leaves for work. I get it.

When we get home from the meeting, Fiona is already in bed, and Jane and Susan are making their way, when Susan calls to check in with the home office, and she gets off the phone looking stunned. "Everyone, I need to talk to you. I've just been told that we've had an issue with some parents of CP'ers thinking Covenant Players is a cult and sending deprogrammers after their children. Please be aware of anyone suspicious coming around us and let me know right away. Goodnight."

Then, only AJ, Derek, and I are left sitting at the kitchen table. Derek is agitated. "AJ, do you think we could be in a cult? I came here to follow God. Now I'm concerned."

"Well, Derek, Jesus says, 'My sheep know my voice.' You have to search your heart. Pray and ask the Lord to show you."

I say, "Well, I have noticed everyone treats Charles M. Tanner almost like God. I've heard that cults use sleep deprivation on their members.

I'm always tired. And they pretty much control us, don't you think, Derek?"

"I have to know if I'm doing the right thing. I came here to serve God. What if I'm unknowingly serving Satan? I need to know." Derek is quite a purist when he isn't sucking strange dick in the alleys of New York or in creepy priests' bathrooms.

"Well, maybe we shouldn't take a chance. I mean, there must be some reason those parents hired deprogrammers."

"I'm ready to quit. We have a show tomorrow night, and I don't know my lines for our performance yet. I'll leave if you will, Derek. What do you say?"

"I don't want to let Susan down, but I can't take a chance on being wrong about this. Okay, let's tell her in the morning. I'm going to pray some more about it now. Goodnight." Poor Derek is practically gnashing his little silver teeth.

That leaves AJ and me. We talk about the situation a bit more. He says he can help us arrange some flights home tomorrow. Then he says, "Is there something you want to talk to me about, Jacquie?"

"Why do you say that?"

"Just sensing there might be something." This makes me think maybe God is speaking to him, so I might as well confess.

"Well, just before I came on this trip, I had a boyfriend and I um... well, I got pregnant, and... I ended up... you know..."

"Having an abortion?" AJ says in his soft, caring voice.

My eyes fill with tears, and I nod, looking down.

"Jacquie, I forgive you. God forgives you. You just have to forgive yourself."

I cry quietly and then look at him. With his long hair, he reminds me of pictures of Jesus. His eyes are kind. He takes my hand. I feel as though a heavy weight has been lifted off me. I feel forgiven. It's okay now. I feel light. I can go home. This is what I came for, without even knowing it.

"Thank you, AJ. Thanks for everything. See you tomorrow." We hug, and I go to bed. The next morning at breakfast, Derek tells Susan that he and I have decided to leave. It is a mutiny of sorts. She's the whitest white woman I've ever seen, potato white. She's visibly upset and says, "But we have a show tonight!"

"Sorry, Susan, but we have to do what we feel is right."

51

"Excuse me. I have to call the head office." When she returns, she says, "Okay, you're done. You are officially persona non grata, which means no one in Covenant Players is to speak to you and vice versa. You can never come back."

If we were Amish or Jehovah's Witnesses, this would be called a shunning. The lack of forgiveness is in stark contrast to my conversation with AJ some hours before. Now AJ is in the background, quietly helping Fiona with preparing breakfast. I am happy with my decision, although it made things a little awkward for my friend Betsy and me. We still talk, although when I emailed her for some memories for this book she said, "All I remember is you were a good actor and I was terrible, and you left and I stayed. Go figure." Which wasn't helpful at all. I don't really believe Covenant Players is a cult, but I've had my experience and that's enough of that.

That afternoon, a shuttle bus comes to take me to the airport. AJ is standing outside with me. "You better go," he says.

Or what? Or he'll kiss me on the mouth instead of the forehead? I can feel it. I'm not sure how I feel about that, knowing he's married. Part of me would like that but it's time to go home.

I feel light, weightless, as if I can float or fly my way home. Speaking of which, where is home? I don't want to go back to Calgary and Rick. I don't want to go back to Creston, although that's where I'll stay until I make a new plan. The weightless feeling lasts three days, the same amount of time Jesus was in the tomb.

5

Dark Days

After regrouping me, myself, and I at home in Creston, my mom and I have our little talk about CP. "I'm so sorry, Jac," she says. "It never occurred to me that Covenant Players could be a cult. I didn't really look into it as I should have. I guess I just assumed a Christian organization would be legit."

"It's okay, Mom. It's not your fault. No harm done."

But her response is typical of the arm's length way she deals with things pertaining to her children. My sister doesn't understand why she didn't insist on open doors when boys were in our bedrooms, or why we never had a curfew. I guess she expected us to know what the standard was and behave. Her parenting is of the liberal variety, and I guess she's distracted by other things.

I decide to move to Lethbridge, in southern Alberta, as a friend from Bible camp named Cherie has a two-bedroom apartment and invites me to stay with her. I plan to apply at AGT and get my telephone operator job back. But AGT doesn't hire me, and shortly after I agree to share the basement suite with Cherie, she moves back to Calgary, leaving me scrambling for a roommate.

When my unemployment insurance runs out, my mom steps in with her chequebook and suggests I go to university. She is a firm believer in a good education, lest we get stuck with a less than good man. So, I move to Lethbridge and enroll at the university there as a mature student. I am nineteen. I find myself quickly gravitating to the drama department. I love acting. There is a magical quality to becoming someone else. I like losing myself completely in a character. I find the black space of a theatre womblike and inspiring.

But university is stressful because I'm a procrastinator and have a hard time getting to early classes and staying awake through lectures. I've always been poor at time management. I begin drinking at university pubs on weekends and smoking pot occasionally. Rick comes down for a visit. I'm not sure when my Christian resolve dissolved, but we have sex. Soon after, I miss a period again. Oh God, no. Please don't let me be pregnant again, please. But God is not please'd. A test reveals that I am indeed pregnant. I speak to my female doctor about getting an abortion. She is serious. "Well, the law is such that in order to procure a therapeutic abortion, the mother must be in danger for her life."

"I'll kill myself if I have to have it, I really will. I feel suicidal."

"I will have to take your case before a board of fourteen doctors for a review." This is 1981. I'm hoping the doctors aren't all male. She says: "You mentioned you've already had an abortion. I'll warn you—the board does not take that lightly. I can't guarantee anything. Also, there is a window. A therapeutic abortion cannot be performed after twelve-weeks gestation. Unfortunately, there is a break for Christmas. It will be very close if they approve it."

"Please try. I don't have any money to do it any other way."

"I'll call you when I get an answer."

My nerves are shot over Christmas, waiting to hear. I call Rick and tell him. He agrees to split the 150 dollar surcharge with me if I am accepted. I am on Mom's dime and have to do this without her knowledge.

Finally, in January, I am given the green light. I am so happy, thankful, relieved. And guilty. One night, I have a dream. In the dream, I go to the bathroom, and the baby falls into the toilet. I'm so glad, but as I stand up and look into the toilet bowl with one hand on the flusher, its large, alien-looking eyes open in its large head. It looks directly into my eyes, and I feel it's telling me it knows what I'm planning to do. Its gaze doesn't waver, locked into mine. I feel convicted of murder by my planned victim. I flush and awake with a shudder of horror.

My roommate, Janet, drops me off at the hospital for day surgery. I am given a general anaesthetic and awaken in the recovery room with a sore throat from a tube and feeling nauseated. It's over, just a dark escape from consciousness while the deed was done. But nothing erases the memory of that knowing, connective stare from the baby in my dream.

I continue with my studies. There's a cast party in a small theatre in the drama department. After a few drinks, I decide to check out the view from the lighting booth. When I get up there, I find Charlie, another mature student, although he is older than me and is married with small children. He is the go-to guy (long before people said "go-to") for lighting.

"I don't know anything about sound or lighting," I announce.

"Well, you could learn. The sound board is here in the booth, obviously. To hang lights, you go out onto the catwalk and put them in position, then control them from here. These coloured plastic films are called gels. You can put them over the bulbs to create different colours."

Shortly after that, the alcohol sends me into a turn that leaves me spluttering to Charlie about how guilty I feel about my second abortion a few months ago. He comforts me with a hug. He is a heavy guy, with shoulder-length hair and glasses, a nice guy. The next thing I know, Charlie is saying hi to me at school, inviting me up to the booth, wondering if I'd like to go on a picnic. I know this may seem hard to believe, but what I thought then was it was okay to hang around with him because I was not interested in him or attracted to him; plus, he was a family man. Surely that makes him safe.

So, I go on the picnic, where he exposes me to deli foods, like Kuhne's pickled gherkins, a sweet, tangy, crunchy pickle that has been my favourite ever since, Swiss cheese, smoked gouda, sliced meats, baguette, strawberries, and wine. The guy knows how to do it right. And for all that, I only indulge him with a little kiss, a peck, really. Soon he separates from his wife, to my chagrin, but thankfully they reunite as I continue to express disinterest.

While not fucking Charlie, I am fucking other guys. For me, alcohol leads to kissing, which leads to sex. I did go on the pill after the second abortion at my doctor's insistence and after my sad conclusion that my love for Jesus didn't protect me from pregnancy.

I feel guilty a lot and tired. I feel guilty spending money Mom sends me on booze, knowing she wouldn't like it. She is anti-alcohol. I feel guilty that I've had two abortions before my twenty-first birthday. My behaviour is decidedly not Christian, yet the standards of Christian behaviour that I've been taught are always with me. Like the voices in my head that point out my errors, showing me my life as a bad report card or as a mirror that reflects the worst possible image of me—the figurative white robes Jesus clothed me in when He saved me are filthy, bloody, and tattered.

I drink to forget how far I've fallen from God's will for my life, but each drink is a further fall. I can't control my drinking. Once I start, it doesn't end until I throw up, get laid, or pass out. I drive drunk all the time. It doesn't really occur to me that I am an alcoholic like my father. I've never heard him describe himself that way. Most young people drink like I do, I think. I occasionally encounter a normal drinker, around whom I feel embarrassed and ashamed, normal being a social drinker who has a drink or two and then stops.

There are a couple of new guys who start attending classes at the University of Lethbridge. Word travels that they are prisoners from the local jail. One of them, a guy named Doug, takes a lot of drama courses. He is older, balding but handsome. Over time, we become casual friends and I ask about the jail thing. "What are you in for, if you don't mind me asking?"

"Well, I've actually served my time and been released recently. I was charged with buggery. What happened was, I was in Deer Ridge Park one night and there was this guy, he was drunk. I had a mickey on me, and we walked and talked and drank a bit, and then I had sex with him and left him there. I guess he choked on his vomit because apparently they found him dead."

"Oh."

"Yeah, it wasn't my fault that he died or anything."

"No."

This is in about 1982 or 1983. I'm not sure if the charges meant that homosexuality was illegal then or doing it in a public place was. You'd think doing it with someone who died after would be a different charge, like homicide or accidental death or something. He didn't give me all the details, and I didn't press.

One night, Doug calls me. He is staying at the motel where I worked the summer between my first and second years of university, for some forgotten reason. "Come on over. Let's catch up."

"Okay, see you soon."

When I arrive, Doug asks, "Do you like gin?" He has a large bottle of Tanqueray.

"Yeah, I love gin. It reminds me of my Aunt Liz, my dad's sister. It's her drink."

"Well, let me make you a drink." He puts ice, gin, and tonic in a glass and hands it to me.

After a couple of drinks, Doug says, "Let's go for a drive."

"Really? Okay, where are we going?"

"Wherever."

It quickly gets dark after we start out. I feel a bit unsure of this venture. We see a young man walking on the side of the road. Doug slows down and says, "Open your window," and then louder to the guy, "Hi, how are you doing? Would you like a ride?"

"Uh, I'm okay, thanks." I can see uncertainty in his eyes.

Doug says, "Where are you going?"

"I'm just headed home."

"Well, get in here next to my wife, and we'll give you a lift."

I look at Doug who is motioning me to move over toward him, which I do. I see. We're doing some improv acting tonight. The guy looks obligated to get in and does.

"How's your night been?" Doug purrs.

"Okay." The guy is looking uncomfortable.

"I'm Doug, and this is my wife, Jacquie. What's your name?"

"Uh, Dennis."

"Well, it's nice to meet you, Dennis. Would you like to have a drink with us before we take you home? Where do you live, by the way?"

"Uh, no thanks. Actually, this is good. You can just let me out here please. It's right up there."

"Are you sure? Okay then, have a good night." The guy gets out, and we drive on. I am very sensitive to vibe and I can still feel his discomfort as well as my own.

What was that about? Does Doug make a habit of picking up strangers? I find it odd. Therefore, I should be prepared when he shows up at a party my boyfriend and his roommates are having and tries to lure me away for some real fun.

I tell Doug, "I don't feel right leaving the party now. I just got here."

"Oh, come on. Your boyfriend will never notice."

"I have an idea. I'll see if he'll fuck me, and if he won't, I'll have an excuse to leave."

This is my reasoning capacity under the influence of alcohol and a stronger personality—a painful example of having no boundaries, of a person who can't say no to Dougs and of a crazy, manipulative bitch who doesn't deserve a boyfriend. I am not proud of this. He rightly dumps my sorry white ass after the episode.

I enact my plan. I draw my boyfriend Duane away from the party into his bedroom and push him onto the bed with fake sexual intensity. He's like, "What are you doing, Jac? This isn't a good time. We've got company. Come on."

Soon, I slip out the door with Doug, and I follow him in my car. We go over to another mature student's house where he is staying. She isn't home. We go upstairs, and there is a man watching TV. This man is a complete stranger to me. I assume Doug knows him somewhat, as they are both staying in the same house. Doug pulls me into a bedroom and says, "Let's get comfortable. Take your clothes off and put this on." He hands me a belted robe. I follow his instructions like a kindergartener listening to her teacher, yet I am thinking, "What the hell? This is fucked up."

He does the same. He then takes my hand and guides me back out to the room where the stranger is watching TV. The man briefly shifts his eyes to register our presence. Doug seats me beside the guy. Nary is a word spoken as we settle into position on the loveseat—stranger, me, Doug. Soon, with all our eyes glued to the TV, Doug puts his hand on my knee, and the robe falls away, exposing my bare skin. All action stops momentarily. Doug then begins to slowly caress my leg, drawing his fingers up to my inner thigh. I can see no evidence from the stranger that he is aware of Doug's doings. Ever so slowly, Doug undoes my robe and begins stroking my breast. I'm confused because Doug is gay, isn't he? What's going on?

I soon begin to detect furtive glances from the stranger. He can no longer ignore the show being staged for his benefit. I'm sure he's wondering what's going on too until Doug says, "My wife and I are going to bed. Care to join us?"

The man nods. He's a slightly less attractive version of Danny DeVito with dirty fingernails. We get into bed in the same formation, Jacquie sandwich. Doug is pushing me toward the guy. Doug stops giving me any attention, encourages the man to go down on me, fuck me. I am sick at what's happening. I am being used as a toy for Doug's enjoyment. I am completely weirded out by the events of the evening. The thought of this stranger touching me is disgusting. I try to play along, but finally I can't do it anymore and say so. I jump out of bed, apologetically dressing and fleeing.

Once at home, I sob. I feel so filthy, so stupid, so ashamed, so gullible. Not just because of the physicality of it but because I let it happen. I couldn't say no until the damage was done. My instincts were screaming, and I ignored them. I put Doug's desires before my own. I let him use me. I can't think of anyone else I know who would have gone along with that. Doug somehow knows that. Having no boundaries makes me a mark to be used. Christianity has taught me to be a nice person and has taught others they can use me, and I won't say anything—that I'll turn the other cheek. At least that's the version of Christianity I grew up with.

Somewhere around this time, I get my hair permed. The stylist puts the rollers in, adds the solution, wraps a piece of stretchy cotton around my head, and goes to another client while my hair processes. As I sit there, I feel something like a hot wire wiener stick pulled from a campfire run from my scalp down to my neck and hold its position. My instinct is to scream and to dunk my head in a pot of water, like a cartoon, where I am sure it will hiss and steam. Or to grab a towel and wipe the dripping, scalding perm solution off my neck.

I do nothing. I don't want to bother the stylist. I sit while my flesh burns. When the stylist finally comes back and removes the cotton, I hear her gasp involuntarily. I know she is seeing what I was feeling. She doesn't say anything, just wipes my neck gingerly with a wet towel. I have scabs for weeks.

Why do I let myself be hurt? What is wrong with me? I know this is not normal behaviour. Is it low self-esteem? Do I not consider myself worthy of good things? Do I think I deserve bad things because of my shame? Am I self-punishing? I think part of my doormat behaviour was learned growing up as a child of an alcoholic. And from his enabling wife, my mother. When my dad finally decided he should go live with his girlfriend, he told my mom to rent out the basement suite of our house so he could pay the mortgage on the house he bought thirty miles away for him and his girlfriend. She did.

But I also think part of it is what I came here to earth to learn. There is a theory called reincarnation that says we never die. We experience recurring lifetimes on earth to give us experiences to foster our spiritual growth. It even goes so far as to say we have spiritual guides that when we are in spirit form away from earth help us to review what we've learned in the past and what the best circumstances for further growth will be, right down to choosing our family of origin. So, we are here in bodily form or there in a spiritual body, with families and relationships in both places, and we leave there to come here and vice versa, trying to work things out with them, correcting the mistakes of the last round and the times before that.

All my life, I've questioned the meaning of life. Possibly, I chose a family who would expose me to Christianity, a religion that doesn't believe in reincarnation. Maybe I've been procrastinating on learning some of my lessons (I'll just do it next lifetime), and my spiritual guides thought it might help if I was told that I wasn't getting any more chances. The Bible says people are destined to die once and after that to face judgment. That's heavy. But it creates a sense of urgency and an understanding of the importance of living your best life.

It has taken me a long time to learn to set boundaries and overcome the shame of being used. I still struggle sometimes. Many years later, I married a man named Boris, who was a Christian. He expected us to follow a Biblical hierarchy, with God as the Head of the church. He would be the head of the household, and I would submit to him and obey him, as he did to God. I might have confused obedience and submissiveness with boundaries, but being married to a man who expected me to do everything he wanted was a good lesson. I rarely opposed him for the first ten years. But when I finally said no, I meant it.

During my marriage to Boris, a friend named Robyn loaned me a book called *Boundaries*, by Dr. Henry Cloud and Dr. John Townsend, published by Zondervan. It blew my mind. In the first chapter were examples of nice Christian women like me who were overworked, stressed, and resentful because they didn't know how to say no to people. They were women like me who feared the disapproval of others, especially when Christianity tells us to give freely. To me, setting boundaries means taking my feelings into account as much as the feelings of somebody who wants something from me and being able to say no without feeling guilty. Why couldn't women be taught these things when they're young instead of having to suffer for so many years first? There are many of us in the same boat.

But this is 1982, and I'm twenty-one, still young and eager for the adventures ahead of me. I have taken drama courses by now in beginning, intermediate and advanced acting, movement for the stage, theatre history, workshop production, as well as performing in plays produced by other students studying directing and the drama department itself. Near the end of my second year of university, the drama department receives a grant to hire nine students for the summer to do workshop format theatre production. Three shows will be produced, and all students will learn all processes of producing theatre, including sets, lights, and sound. I audition and am chosen, but I am not keen on the conditions or wage. When I get an offer to work part-time at the four-star hotel in Lethbridge, the Lethbridge Lodge Hotel, for more money, I take it. I love acting. I'm not interested in the rest of the business of running a theatre.

When it is time to start my third year, I am quite comfortable at my front desk job at the hotel. It doesn't make sense to me to spend Mom's money for two more years to end up with a BA in drama. What kind of a job can I get with that? Plus, school is stressful. I prefer the independence of making my own money. I know I can go back and finish my degree within ten years if I want to.

I meet a guy named Hank, twenty-three years my senior, who serves in the dining room of the hotel while I'm working there. He has a curly perm and prominent, almost scary dark eyebrows over brown eyes. He's tall and thin with nice teeth. He's been married and divorced twice and is engaged when we meet and start chatting. You'd think I'd remember how we start hanging out, but I don't. Hank is a recovered alcoholic who has replaced booze with pot. I drink less with him and smoke more. Hank has been involved with EST. "Est" is the Latin word for "is" and an acronym for Erhard Seminars Training, an enlightenment training program started by Werner Erhard in San Francisco in 1971 and which has since spread all over, including Lethbridge. The training has been described as equal parts Zen Buddhism and Dale Carnegie. According to Erhard, it was designed "to transform your ability to experience living so that the situations you have been trying to change or have been putting up with clear up just in the process of life itself." The program is rife with catch phrases, like "How's that working for you?" To me, it seems like the members are always verbally poking each other.

Hank wants me to go to a meeting, believing I'll benefit from the teachings. I know I want no part of it. I dislike groups and having group mentality being imposed on me, perhaps somewhat because of what happened in CP. If I want that, I'll go to church. But church doesn't fit my current lifestyle. And neither will EST, I'm sure. However, I agree to go to one meeting for Hank's sake, but I warn him that I'm not into it.

EST was a net for people with weak boundaries. I went in certain it wasn't for me. I must have said no half-a-dozen times that first night as they tried to recruit me. I refused all suggestions to give it another try. I never went back. Years later, a friend mentioned EST, and I said it's an exercise in learning to say "no." She laughed and nodded.

I like Hank, and I feel we have something special. He loves me. He is the first guy to give me an orgasm. When I look into his eyes when we are making love, I feel like I am hallucinating and seeing him transform into someone I've known before, as if we knew each other in another lifetime or something. Spooky. I guess that could be the pot we always smoke before sex.

He also comes from a strong religious, guilt-producing background— in his case, Mormonism. He went into the army in his youth to escape it. I call him Major Impact because of the deep feelings he arouses in me and his positive influence in my life. Happily, Hank has had a vasectomy. Bonus.

We both want to write books. He has a great idea we are going to title *The Boys in the Back Room*, about how the earth is a board game played by the "boys," super humans or gods or something, and the colours of the races—red, brown, yellow, black, white—are used by them to control and influence the politics on earth. We somehow come up with a plan to move from Lethbridge to Vancouver to write and dance. We love dancing. We go to a lot of bars and dance happily across from each other, freestyle, for hours at a time. We sometimes fantasize that bands should hire us to be the party starters, who'd get the dancing started, since there seems to be a general reluctance to be the first ones on the dancefloor. We don't drink much, he not at all, and me only a little, for budget reasons, mostly. But we never hesitate to shake our booties.

In 1985, after four years in Lethbridge, two in university and two working at the hotel, we rent a U-Haul and drive to Vancouver, staying in a motel on the North Shore while we search for an apartment in the West End. It is tough. No one wants to rent to two unemployed people. Finally, we find a couple of sympathetic building managers who take a chance on us.

We move in and start job searching. I soon get a job at a boutique hotel called the Wedgewood, a ten minute walk up Robson Street. Hank, in his early forties, doesn't have as much luck. He can't find a server position, despite the number of restaurants surrounding us. In desperation, he decides to try stock brokering, which he has some experience in but doesn't like.

I am disillusioned with our dream. Hank is a very positive, dreamy sort of guy. I become increasingly irritable and am downright miserable when I am taken off the front desk at work and sent upstairs with another girl to take reservations by hand in a huge awkward book. This is six months before Vancouver is hosting Expo '86. Travel agents are as overwhelmed as we are. They have long wait times to get through on the phone from the States or wherever, and then we don't have availability.

My mood is definitely dim. I want to have a threesome with a woman, with which Hank is happy to comply. One night, I am cranky and leave the apartment under the pretence of going for a walk. I go into a gay bar. It is dark and empty except for a few guys and a couple of big women who look like guys, definitely not what I am looking for.

Hank is getting on my nerves. Things in Vancouver are expensive, and pretty soon bumping up against reality scratches the veneer of our dreams. We don't have enough money. Here we are in the city of promise, with a hundred shows and things happening every night, and we can't afford any of it. One night I come home from work and he's made macaroni and cheese for dinner and offers it like he's hoping I'll be pleased. I'm not.

I hate to do it, but I break up with him. He goes back to Lethbridge with his tail between his legs. He cries tears. I feel like a raging bitch, but I don't want him around. I hate my job, so I come up with a better idea. I'll become an exotic dancer. I love dancing and performing, and I'm comfortable in bars. I especially like the idea of the "Look but don't touch" dynamic.

I start to diet, eating mostly grapefruit and drinking black coffee. I go to an aerobics class and buy a mini trampoline to bounce on after my exercise. I have energy to burn and run uphill to work. I see an ad in the West Ender for auditions for stripping at the American Hotel on Main Street. I call to make an appointment. When I get there, I realize it's a neglected part of town. It's grimy; the vibe is aching loneliness. It is

Good Friday morning at 11:00 a.m. There are a couple of grizzled old regulars drinking beer. I have been practicing to Cyndi Lauper's "Girls Just Wanna Have Fun." I've never seen a stripper, so I have to work from my imagination about what is sexy. I am nervous, as always, before stepping on a stage. I go out and do my thing, seemingly ignored by the few old men having their breakfast beers.

Afterwards, the woman I've danced for reviews my performance. "Have you ever seen an exotic dancer?" she asks. "Go to some of the clubs and check them out. Also, you need to lose this." She pinches the skin at the top of my butt. "Then come back and see me."

"Okay, thank you very much."

Within a few months, I'll be with a guy who tells me the perfect ass is an upside down heart. I had an upside down ass. But I'm getting ahead of myself.

I am having difficulty leaving my apartment except to run over to the nearby community centre to exercise. I dread going to work. I feel utterly alone in a city of 1.5 million people, knowing no one except people at work. I wonder who lives in all the apartments surrounding mine, aware that only walls separate us from one another. I get paranoid when I smoke pot. One day when I come home to my apartment building, there is a sign posted near the elevators in the lobby that says Please Stop Removing Posted Signs. I go to my suite, smoke a joint, and think it would be funny to remove that sign, so I do. But I'm terrified of getting caught. I get back to my apartment and start freaking out, trying to figure out where to hide it or how to destroy it. I call Hank even though we broke up and he's back in Lethbridge. I am panicking about what I've done, but I'm too scared to put the sign back. He tells me not to worry. I end up stashing it in a book but keep expecting someone to come and knock on the door and find it and kick me out of the building.

Finally, one day at work, I crack and start walking out. The owner of the hotel, Eleni Skalbania, sits me down to talk.

"What is the problem?" she wants to know.

"Everything. It's so stressful. The phones never stop ringing. Zoe downstairs just takes the one in the reservation office off the hook."

"What do you mean?"

"What do you mean what do I mean? It's so busy that she doesn't have time to answer the 1-800 phone, so it dangles by the cord on the floor. Twila and I are writing and erasing in pencil so many times we're wearing holes in the paper in the big reservation books. I'm sure we're making mistakes."

"I see. Well, just take some deep breaths. Do you want some coffee or water?"

"No thanks, I just want to quit."

"Okay, well go home now and rest. We'll talk again."

I give the front desk manager, Nowan—who has been sexually harrassing me by grabbing my ass and making suggestive comments before I moved upstairs out of his reach—my two weeks' notice. I sublet my apartment and buy a VIA Rail open ticket that's good for a year. I'm going to get the hell out of Dodge, travel across Canada by train from the West coast to the East, I hope, and see my country, having adventures along the way. I also buy a red knockoff Walkman and pack my bag. I feel free. I feel better than free. I feel wonderful, euphoric, happy, confident, amusing, and sexy. It wasn't until about twenty-five years later that I realized this was the beginning of my first bipolar manic episode. These episodes were characterized by a feeling of euphoria, heightened sexuality, impulsive decision making, grandiose schemes, loss of sleep and appetite, excessive spending, breaking off relationships, and increased interest in music, preceded by depression, anxiety, and irritability.

6

Trains, Planes, and Acid Trips

I am jumping on the train in a pink mini dress and no underwear to begin an adventure I think of as my sixties experience. A retro adventure in the mid-80s. I've decided to travel across Canada, hoping for interesting stories to tell when I get home. I have sublet my apartment for one and a half times my rent, I have some savings. And I've managed to get on unemployment insurance. I'm twenty-five and in great shape. It feels good. I'm vibrating with sexual energy. I put my Walkman earphones in and dance down the aisles of the train. I get a lot of dirty looks from women and surreptitious ones from men.

The engineer approaches me. "Are you traveling coach?"

"Yes, I am."

In a lowered voice, "Well, please feel free to use my cabin. Why don't you come by for a drink later and see it. I'm sure you'll be comfortable."

"Thank you. Maybe I will."

Foolishly, I do. He seems fairly drunk even before we have a drink together. Then he lies on his bed and invites me to join him. I pull my dress off over my head and remove my bra, admiring my svelte figure in the mirror.

"Oh my god," he says. "Come here."

After checking out my front and turning to see my rear, I look at him, bleary eyed and middle aged, and say, "Sorry, I just can't." I get dressed, thank him for the drink, and leave, thinking it's not a good thing to have a drunk engineer. Next thing I know, the porters are inviting me to have a toke, as they crowd into a tiny bathroom.

I like the bar car, which has an upper deck, the better to see the view through. There is an older woman up there, knitting. As I pass her, she hisses, "You should be ashamed of yourself." I have no idea what brought that on. It seems not everyone is enjoying the throbbing sexuality pulsating from my pores.

I get off the train in Calgary to visit relatives. I write in my Grandma's guest book, "On track!" After a few days, I get back on the train; the next stop is Winnipeg. I'm travelling light. One of my clothing items is a leotard, a tight-fitting black body suit with foot straps. I'm stopping in Winnipeg to visit a friend. While waiting at the station for the train to carry me to my next destination, I stride around in my suit, exuding sexual energy. I feel like Jesus as the crowd parts for me. I look up to the second level to see all the men have come out of their offices to watch. I smile suggestively. I feel so strong, so sure that I'm the best-looking woman in the place, that all eyes are on me, directly or indirectly. I feel high.

I call up my Winnipeg connection from the train station. He's the friend of a friend—a nice guy from a good family I'd met in Vancouver when he was out visiting a coworker of mine at the hotel. They'd met travelling in Europe. His name was Bobby. He was a cyclist, not professionally, but he biked downtown from Burnaby, which is quite a trot. We drive up to Grand Beach on Lake Winnipeg to spend the day. It's a busy place, lots of people, ice cream stands, nice sand. Bobby invites me to stay at his mom and dad's house overnight. We are supposed to be in separate bedrooms, but he changes the plan after his mom and dad go to bed. I have sex with him as a thank you for the accommodation, since he seems to expect it. The next morning, he drives me to the station, and I get back on the train, after a short, unsentimental goodbye hug with this one-night lover.

By this time, Rick, my old boyfriend from Calgary, had moved back to his native Ontario and was living in Hamilton so I went to visit him next. He was impressed with my svelte new figure and took me out dancing at a bar. I was being fun and flirty. At one point, he went to the washroom, so I danced by myself. I could feel the eyes of the mostly male, working-class crowd on me and could feel their hungry energy in the air. I felt a bit like a rabbit in the forest at night with yellow wolf eyes peering at me through the darkness. I was glad I was with Rick. On my own, I would have been devoured. Gang bang on the pool table, likely. That's how it felt. However, my feelings were out of whack. I mean in the literal sense of chemically imbalanced, although I didn't know those words for it at the time, and I was smoking pot on my trip, which heightened my sense of awareness.

To Rick's disappointment, I don't fuck him. I'm not in the mood for having sex, just feeling sexy. It's not really about him.

Someone has told me I'll like Montréal, so I head there next. In my heart, I am hoping to meet a woman. I do when I go for breakfast after staying at the YWCA hostel the first night. The waitress is young, cute, and friendly, inviting me out the next night. This could be it, I think to myself. At last.

I wander the streets for awhile, shopping a bit. I feel like I'm in a different country. Most people speak French. I don't. The architecture is old, European looking. I'm forced into the purchase of an outfit when I go into a clothing store. "Very beautiful on you," the old woman says, with a Jewish French accent. Her wizened husband sits by the cash register.

I stand looking in the mirror. The dress is a kind of muddy peach colour. It's a two piece, a long-sleeved top over a mid-calf-length skirt that's gathered at the waist. I tuck in the top to accentuate the waist. It's okay. Where would I wear it?

"Mm, maybe, I don't know," I say.

"Yes, I know. Perfect for young girl like you. Nice colour. Makes you look so beautiful. Good price, too. You not going to find so nice material and good price anywhere else."

I look through a rack. I hate being pressured like this. It's about boundaries. This woman is stronger than me. She is not going to let me out of the store until I buy it. Damn it. It's getting hot in here.

I just want to go. "Okay, I guess so."

"Very good. You going to be so happy."

No, I'm not. In fact, I never, ever wear that outfit even once. I give it away, brand new, tags on. The colour was weird; the skirt was too long. It just looked half-decent on me because anything looks good on a fit body.

After buying that stupid outfit that I have to carry around now, I realize I'm out of pot and wonder where to buy some. I ask someone on the street that looks like a likely smoker, who tells me to go to rue St-Denis. So, I wander down rue Ste-Catherine until I find it.

Walking up St-Denis, I see a small park with a fence upon which are perched various young biker-ish dealers calling, "Hash, coke, acid." With their French accents, it sounds like Ash, Coke, a-CID.

"Um, do you have any pot?"

"Ash, coke, a-CID. Pas d'pot."

"Really? That seems strange. Do you know where I can get some?"

Just at that moment, a small young guy comes toward us. He has a very nice mullet, a big hoop earring plus a stud in the same hole; he has a scarf wrapped around his wrist and hanging down as well as round John Lennon glasses perched on his biggish nose. His shirt is unbuttoned to the waist and tied there. His jeans are so skintight I can see a small bulge in his crotch. He has a petite but lithe, muscular frame.

"Qu'est-ce que tu fait?" he asks.

The dealers explain in French that I'm looking for pot. At least I assume that's what's going on. They don't speak much English.

"Where are you from?" he asks with an accent.

"Vancouver."

"Oh, I love Vancouver. I always wanted to go dere."

"Yeah, it's nice. So do you happen to know where I can buy some pot?"

"Oui, you're in luck. I can 'elp you. 'Ow much do you want?"

"Okay, great. I don't know. An eighth of an ounce?"

"'Ow about ten dollars worth?"

"Well, I guess that'll do for now."

"Hokay, de money please."

I dig a ten-dollar bill out of my wallet on a string. "Here."

"Now I 'ave to go get it. You come wit' me."

I look into his eyes. They are dark. Not just the colour, the feel. I feel uneasy. "I don't know."

I turn to the drug dealers and ask, "Is he safe?"

They burst out laughing and say, "Oui, oui, il est correct, la."

By this time, the little guy has begun to walk away, forcing my hand. "I'm leaving. Are you coming, esti?"

I follow him a few blocks. "Now you wait 'ere. I'll be right back."

Five or so minutes later, he returns with a small manila envelope and hands it to me. "I don't make any money on dis, so I ask dat you smoke a joint wit' me."

"Oh, okay, sure, no problem." We walk together until we find a good spot to roll a joint. We light it, smoke, and walk again. We pass a guy with a guitar, and he asks if he can do a song. He's good, really good. I have a soft spot for musicians; it's in my head.

"What are you doing in Montréal?" he asks.

"I'm just travelling across Canada to see it. I have an open train ticket. I want to go as far as Halifax. I'm also exploring the meaning of life and searching for the truth." By this time, we have walked in a big square and are back in the little park on St-Denis where we met.

"Let's sit," he says as we seat ourselves on a wooden bench.

"I'm going to tell you somet'ing. De way, and de trut', and de life is Jesus Christ."

I almost fall off the bench. This pronouncement from a drug dealer takes me by surprise. But my curiosity is piqued. Okay, he isn't exactly a drug dealer. He is more like a dirty rat, slinking through the underbelly of the city, smoking joints with tourists, bumming for spare change.

"Well, that's interesting," I say. "I've heard that before, but I'm wondering if perhaps there isn't more or greater truth to be found."

"Dere isn't. Everyt'ing begins and ends in Christ. He is de Alpha and de Omega. And I am my Fader's son, and all dat 'e 'as is mine."

"I'm staying at the YWCA hostel. I'd like to see the city. Would you like to be my guide? All the pot you can smoke."

"Oui, c'est bon. I believe de Lord as more t'ings to say to you. You should meet my friend Pierre. 'E is my brodder in de Lord."

For my part, I am happy with this serendipitous meeting. A good sixties experience should include hippies, and I have a feeling my new friend—who tells me his name is Jason, a strange name for a French guy, I think—and his friend Pierre will qualify as an eighties equivalent. He has no fixed address but is currently staying with a gay guy named Armand, even though he assures me he himself isn't gay. I can never really tell about anything he says. His stories are wild.

Jason is only nineteen, and I am twenty-five. He is homeless because he escaped from a juvenile detention centre. The story is that Jason's mother, a Québécois white woman, was being pimped out as a teenage girl by her father who worked in or ran or just forced her to work in a brothel in Montréal in the 1960s, before some political influence under Jean Drapeau had brothels shut down and she and her father had to go to court to face charges of prostitution. She then married a Québécois white man who worked as a doorman at topless bars and sold pencils and watches on the street. He was aware of her past as a prostitute and

70

allowed, even encouraged her to keep working for money so as to buy needed things, like furniture. As a result, about a year after they were married, she became pregnant from a liaison with an Asian man and bore a half-Asian son, Stephan, who is three years older than Jason. Apparently, mental health problems landed her in an asylum at some point, called Saint Jean de Dieu, run by the Sisters of Providence. There she was impregnated by a male psychiatric nurse who wore a turban. (I found an interesting bit in an online archive: "For the direct care of the male patients, the Sisters have provided a numerous staff of male attendants, who look after the sick, attend to the bathing, the changes of clothing, and assist in the domestic duties of the wards. A sister and a number of lay-nuns are daily present in every ward to oversee the conduct of the *attendants in their intercourse with* and treatment of *the patients.*" Italics mine. This lends credibility to the story. Also, interestingly, apparently Louis Riel stayed there briefly many years earlier.) She gave birth to a half-East Indian as it was called then, a son, Jason. She rejoined her husband for a period of time, in which he adopted both sons, but she eventually ended up back in the mental hospital.

Jason says he remembers her trying to feed him poop from the toilet on a spoon. So, since he was only three and his brother six, they had to be fostered out because their dad couldn't work and take care of them. He and his brother were separated and sent to live with relatives, then eventually strangers, foster families. Jason's behaviour was difficult to handle. He says the natural children would always be treated better, getting butter over margarine, et cetera. He was jealous. In one home, he claims the woman loved her dog more than she loved him. He tells me he secretly broke its leg. Move followed move, until he ended up in a facility, from which he ran away when he was sixteen.

My heart breaks hearing such a sad story. I am hooked. Poor, unloved, misunderstood little dear. So cunning and brave, living on the streets alone. So charming and talented, yet lost among the hordes, waiting to be discovered. The street is his playground as well as his field to be plowed. He lives off welfare and panhandling and the kindness of others. He has few possessions, just some clothes. Everything he owns can fit into a backpack.

He believes everything belongs to his Father and that as God's son, he is entitled to whatever he needs; therefore, picking fruit or flowers from somebody's yard is perfectly acceptable. To hear him talk sometimes, you'd think Jesus Christ was his brother. I am fascinated with his simple life, enchanted, almost. From that first day, we stay together, and he becomes my guide to Montréal. The city seems much more interesting when I am with him than it did on my own.

Whenever we come across a busker or someone with a guitar, he asks to play it. Homemade music in the streets, I love it. Jason knows how to work a crowd, too. His world is easy, full of possibility. We stop so he can join a hackey sack game or be the audience for a head shaving going on in the washroom of a Burger King. It's 1986. There are a lot of punks in those days in Montréal, with extreme spiked or shaved hairstyles, piercings and tattoos. Jason is a bit of an artist, too. He has a tattoo of a bird he drew.

I tell him I am having my sixties experience, and I want to meet some hippies. "You will," he promises. Later that day, we are cutting through a park, and from a distance, I notice a man with long, gray-white hair and beard and mesmerizing blue eyes that lock onto mine from a long distance away. "That must be Pierre," I think, and indeed it is. Pierre is tall, thin, and handsome, with leathery tanned skin. He and Jason speak French to each other of course, although Pierre can speak English as well. Very convenient, knowing two languages. It's like having a secret code against those who don't.

Once, much later, I heard Jason telling someone in French that my new glasses were ugly. I always hated choosing glasses, still do. I chose frames that I hoped wouldn't stand out, the plastic a pale flesh colour. They were the style then, large. My hair was medium brown. I was trying to grow it out from the super short cut I had when I met him. Of course, he liked long hair on women as well as his own. He didn't know I was beginning to understand French. I was hurt and wondered what else he said behind my back. I tried to learn French. I'd only taken it in grade eight in school. I got a B but didn't like it and didn't really remember anything except "Comment t'appelles tu?"

I made Jason help me learn the theme song from Da Giovanni, a restaurant that we frequented because you got a plate of spaghetti and sauce, coffee or tea, and dessert for 3.25. The dessert I always chose was pruneaux. I'd never eaten prunes as a dessert before in my life, but they were delicious. Jason was screaming mad by the time I learned that little jingle because I made him repeat it so many times. It was effective, though, because I still remember it, something like this:

> Da Giovanni, Da Giovanni, Da Giovanni, Da Giovanni
> La meilleure place à Montréal où les repas sont un régal,
> Da Giovanni
> Vous gouterez les meilleurs spaghetti,
> et la pizza et le ravioli; vous passerez une belle soirée,
> soyez en sûr quand vous irez chez,
> Da Giovanni, Da Giovanni

He used to tell me I was stupid, thick in the head, I think he put it, because I couldn't pick French up faster. What was funny to me later, as I did begin to understand some words and phrases, was that I realized people were usually speaking about mundane things, not the lofty ideas and concepts I assumed they were talking about, just because I didn't understand them.

Anyway, as a result of Pierre and Jason's conversation, I check out of the YWCA, but not before Jason and I have sex on the bed. He says he could tell right away when he met me that I was easy. And then we go to stay at Pierre's. Pierre and Jason like to expound on spiritual matters and seem to have a unique twist on Christianity. They are fascinating characters to me, the best of both worlds—pot smokers who talk about Jesus. My world seems more surreal and dreamlike every day. I'd wanted to have a sixties experience, travel, and meet some cool hippies, and the universe is obliging.

One night, Pierre, Jason and a bunch of their friends, or should I say acquaintances, fellow street people, and I go to a natural foods restaurant on rue St-Denis. Our group doesn't have much money, but we have tea and coffee and sit at a long table in the back, with Pierre at the head. I count eleven people.

"If we had one more person, we'd be like Jesus and the twelve disciples," I joke to Pierre.

"We are," he smiles. "Someone will come." Sure enough, within a little while, another body appears and joins us.

"I told you," Pierre says. Then, turning to the group he says in French, "Jacquelyn thinks we are like Jesus and the twelve disciples." Everybody laughs.

Pierre believes that we all have personal power that comes through the solar plexus, a spiritual centre near the diaphragm, and that exercising it increases that power. One night, someone decides we do a hit of acid. This is a first time experience for me, and I am a little nervous.

My Uncle Ron, Dad's brother, a drug aficionado, told me not to do acid until I was twenty-one. In fact, I am twenty-five, so I think I might as well embrace the experience. The drug is on a tiny little piece of paper, which is placed on the tongue, chewed, and swallowed. After the swallow is when the grip of fear takes hold. Kind of like after the positive pregnancy test. No turning back. I have agreed to be strapped into a roller coaster and have to ride it out.

The first time isn't so bad. Pierre and Jason and I leave Pierre's place to walk the streets. I feel strange. We go to Mont Royal and lie on the grass and take our shirts off to let the sun recharge our solar plexuses. I am a little worried about the cops, but the guys are unconcerned, no surprise, and encourage me to be free. I remember Jason expounding on his freedom as a son of God.

We are up walking all night. At some point in the wee hours of the morning, we go into an all-hours coffee shop, and Pierre demonstrates how he can affect people's behaviour by concentrating his energy on them. Maybe he overworks his solar plexus because he soon begins to complain of stomach pain. Around dawn, Pierre buys a round loaf of bread, which he eats a few bites of and then he and Jason kick it like a football around a park. I find this a disturbing waste. I don't understand why they find it funny.

A pale-faced guy approaches us, seeming nonplussed by the bread. "Hey, can I buy a joint off you guys? I've been doing coke all night, and I need help to come down." He looks haggard, and his hands are shaking as he smokes a cigarette. The guys agree to sell him one, and Jason rolls one that is mostly stems and seeds. This is back in the day when seeds come free with purchase and Marc Emery is just a kid dreaming of being rich someday and having his own room. They sell it to him for ten bucks.

I see the city streets in the grey predawn and think a similar scene must have inspired Kris Kristofferson's song, "Sunday Morning Coming Down." It is cold, lonely, quiet, and depressing.

Pierre's stomach pain increases in intensity until we decide we better go to an emergency ward. Apparently, he's had this problem before when he's done acid. While waiting for the doctor, and some treatment, I ask Pierre, "Do you want me to pray for you?" "Mais oui," is his reply, so I lay my hands on his stomach and ask God to touch and heal him. From that point on, the pain subsides, and we end up leaving the ward without medication and going home to bed, just as the world is waking up.

Since the first trip wasn't bad, I agree to do a second. This time, there is another girl named Amélie doing a hit with us. The effect seems to be stronger this time. Jason and I go for a walk, leaving Pierre and Amélie and her little girl back at Pierre's place. It is hot, humid, and the Montréal Jazz Festival is in full swing. Rue St-Denis has been closed to traffic and is a solidly moving mass of people. It seems they are all moving uphill, and we are moving down.

To me, it is a sea of eyes. As I look into each person's eyes, I feel as if I am getting a glimpse into their souls, as though I've momentarily stepped into their bodies and can feel what they are feeling. So my feelings are changing every few seconds as I make eye contact, and they just keep coming. Thousands of people fill the street, from one sidewalk to the other. By the time we get to the bottom of the hill, I've lost my ability to speak. I try to say something, but it is garbled. I want to explain how I feel but can't. I am overwhelmed with feelings of stupidity. I don't feel safe. I have to get out of the crowd. I somehow indicate to Jason that we have to go back. As we are walking back up the hill, I feel fantastic. The sun is shining; the sky is blue. My world is suddenly perfect, and I gasp with the impact of a revelation I am getting—that I am on earth for a purpose. I'd come from the light to tell others about the light and then to return to it. I can't contain my joy. I begin to weep with the wonder of being chosen for such an important mission. I am still crying when we get back to Pierre's, where I tell him my experience. He smiles knowingly, and we have a big group hug.

Amélie is the single mother of a two-year-old daughter. Still in a state of blissful euphoria, my eyes fall upon Amélie's little girl. "I must be hallucinating," I say. "I've never seen anything so beautiful." She has delicate, perfectly formed curls encircling her chubby face, with eyes like stars twinkling, tiny chiclet teeth that smile at me, and rosebud lips. All the clichés. She truly appears angelic, ephemeral, too good to be true.

Right then and there I decide, and say, "I want one of those."

Jason says, "D'accord, tout le monde, allez-y. Ma femme veut faire l'amour." Pierre and Amélie then leave the room so he can impregnate me. We make love, and as we are finishing, I become aware of a bright light in the background behind Jason's head. We are on Pierre's air bed mattress on the floor, but left a candle burning on a bedside table, which has somehow ignited Jason's shirt. Flames are visible. From my acid-laced afterglow haze, I say, "There's a fire. Quick, put it out!" He does, but we both take it as a sign from God that our union is blessed and a special child will be the result. It is fire from heaven.

In the New Testament, tongues of fire were seen as evidence of the Holy Spirit's presence. There was also the refiner's fire, which caused the dross to burn off and purify the vessel. There's also a verse that says, "Better to marry than burn." What does that mean? Unmarried people will burn in hell? Sexual burning, passion, lust, and desire are best expressed within marriage? And, of course, there are the fires of hell and the lake of fire as well as the burning bush. Lots of references to fire in the Bible, but we saw ours as being a good sign.

So much so, that when the boy child was born, we named him Emmanuel, which means "God with us." I asked my mom what she thought of the name before he was born. She said, "Rather pretentious." But it was actually a fairly common name in Québec.

My poor mom. I'm afraid I humiliated her by moving back to Creston for a while with my crazy Frenchman boyfriend, carrying an illegitimate child. That was in my hippie days, so I wore long dresses with thick grey work socks and running shoes. Yikes. I knew it looked awful, but I took pleasure in the comfort. That's why I'm secretly jealous of lesbians who don't give a damn how they look to men and always wear comfortable shoes. I'm not sure which aspect of my life and style was most offensive to my mother, perhaps all of it.

My sister April sent me what Jason called "preppie" maternity clothes. I wore them out of need but didn't feel comfortable in them. Actually, in my heart, I didn't feel right in either style. It's funny how clothes affect your feelings and how people know from the time they're very young what they do and do not want to wear. My Grandma Morton told me once that when I was little, I used to want to change my clothes several times a day. "And your mother let you!" she yelped in dismay. I didn't remember that, but sometimes just for fun, I'll stand in front of the mirror at home and try on clothes, experimenting with different looks and outfits.

At one point, my entire wardrobe consisted of two each of identical pants, tops, and cover ups, one black and one white. I owned one pair of black shoes. And that's all I wore, in different combinations. It was simple. I liked it. That's when I was morphing out of my hippie phase.

Later on the evening of the sacred fire, Jason and I have been out wandering around still high on acid and end up in a cavelike after-hours bar. As we enter, it looks to me like a pit of snakes, bodies draped over each other in the dark cavern of the room, sprawled across low couches, intertwined, serpentine. It is hot and humid in there, too, being a Montréal summer night. I hallucinate as I see Jason standing above me. I see him as I think Jesus must look, like the innocent Lamb of God, soft eyed. Perspiration dampness causes the shorter hair at the top of his head to curl and form a crown of thorns on his forehead. He appears glowing white to me, smiling in love.

Suddenly, his countenance darkens, and the crown of thorns is transformed into devil horns, and he is black and evil and deeply frightening. I am freaked out. Who is he really? I try not to let the terror overtake me. When Jason speaks to me, his voice is reassuring, know what I mean, Eve? That morning at about 4:00 a.m., high on acid, we marry ourselves, proclaiming our vows to stick together. From then on, Jason refers to me as "ma femme," his wife, his woman. When people ask if we are married, we say yes.

Later that morning, we go to Armand's, the gay guy's place Jason has most frequently been staying at, to get his few belongings. I remember being alone in the bathroom, looking in the mirror and wondering what I'd done. I feel a swirl of emotions and a sudden rush of tears. Is this just the drug wearing off or is it me? I feel so weird and scared. I'm married now. Can I go through with this in the light of day? Who is he, really? What if I just change my mind and go home back to Vancouver?

But the thought of going back by myself and not seeing Jason again makes me cry. I'll stick it out. The image in the mirror is mine, but it looks unfamiliar. My eyes don't look right. I don't feel right. But I wipe my tears, take a deep breath, and shakily go out to rejoin my new partner.

I feel a little like I've betrayed Pierre by coming back to his house as Jason's wife. I sense there was a little competition between them for me. I like Pierre. He'd been an architect or an engineer but couldn't handle the pressures of the game and playing house, so he dropped out. He rents an upstairs apartment on rue St-Hubert and sublets rooms out to students to pay the rent and supplement his welfare income. He rolls his own cigarettes and smokes pot when he can get it. I hear him call Jason "Sylvain" and ask why. Pierre says, "That's his name."

Jason says, "My name is Jason. Sometimes he calls me Sylvain." Odd, I think. Jason and I are together about a year before he finally admits to several lies he's told me, including the fact that his real name is Sylvain St-Onge and he just chose the name Jason because he liked it and wanted people to call him that.

He also told me he had a black belt in karate, when in fact he'd had a few lessons where he'd learned a couple of signature moves that he used to create the impression that he was a pro. He admitted he didn't break his foster mother's little dog's leg either. So from then on, and now on, I call him Sylvain, which is a much nicer name for a French guy.

One day, we are passing through the Metro, Montréal's subway system. Buskers can sign up to sing for periods throughout the day. Sylvain and I stop so he can talk to a musician, whose guitar case is open. I notice a small book lying inside it. Catching his eye as Sylvain is talking to him, I use my facial expressions to ask if I can look at it. He nods. It is a Catholic prayer book with devotional readings. I hold the book in my hands, and it opens to a page entitled "Blessed is the Mother of Children."

This is after our fiery impregnation and seems like a message from God to me. Signs and messages are prolific. If you believe God speaks to His people, you expect to hear from Him, and I sometimes think you hear what you want to hear. Maybe we extract meaning from the chaos that surrounds us to reassure us that we are not alone.

I've always been aware of this, and it messes me up because I can't tell if it's me, God, or the devil I'm hearing. The Bible says the devil is a deceiver and appears as an angel of light. God's sheep are supposed to recognize His, the Shepherd's, voice. But I often have doubts about where the voices are coming from.

I'd often play Bible roulette when seeking guidance, flapping the pages of my Bible and letting it fall open of its own accord, believing the first verse my eye fell upon would be God's message to me. It's akin to reading a horoscope or a fortune cookie, having cards read, consulting a psychic or believing an animal in your path is an omen. People want to believe in something.

While staying with Pierre, I decide I am going to move to Montréal. I call to tell my mom, and she sounds very concerned. "Hey Mom, I've met some great people. They're Christians. I'm going to move here."

My mom informs me that the couple who were subletting my apartment in Vancouver are going to be leaving sooner than expected, and I have to be back in Vancouver by July 1 to pay the rent. So I modify my plan and decide to take Sylvain back to Vancouver with me. He is thrilled. Going to Vancouver and California is a dream of his. He has no reason to stay in Québec, except his welfare cheque, which he donates to Pierre for letting us stay there.

So we go back to the West Coast on the train. It is strange. I feel like a completely different person than I was a month earlier. Now I believe I am pregnant. I have a conversation on the train with a little girl who I am sure must be the reincarnation of one of my aborted children. Gone is the exhilarating energy I'd felt before. The trip seems long and slow. So much for my plan to become an exotic dancer when I get back. Now I am going to be a mother instead.

7

Keep on Trakkin'

As soon as we get back to my apartment in Vancouver, we decide I will dispose of my belongings, and we'll move back to Montréal. So I put up a moving sale sign in the building, and most days someone is there to buy a toaster or some cutlery or to look through my closet. I love trading my stuff for cash. I had loaned my car to a friend of a friend and suggested he buy it by making payments to my mom, who had loaned me the money to buy it. I'm not sure if she ever got fully paid.

I meet a guy in the neighbourhood from Iran, who says he is interested in buying some of my stuff. His name is Jim, another unlikely story, but most likely in the immigrant tradition of choosing an English moniker people here can understand. He comes to my apartment and says he is interested in all of it. I have a nice Kenwood stereo system, furniture my mom and dad and bought me new for my suite in Lethbridge, a waterbed, and my mom and dad's old orange vinyl and wood dining room set, very cool retro, plus a closet full of clothes and kitchen stuff. Nothing of any great value except the stereo, which I want to keep, but it no longer fits my new lifestyle. My music is in my man now.

Some people come by later and want to buy the couch and chairs. When Jim returns I tell him this, and he gets kind of mad and says he wants everything, and he'll give me five hundred dollars. So I call the people back and disappoint them. On the sale day, Jim's brother comes, too. They speak in Farsi and hand me half the promised amount. I don't say anything. No boundaries means no defense against marauding intruders. I tell Jim if I come back to Vancouver I might want to buy some of my stuff back, especially the eight-hundred-dollar stereo. Mom won't let him have Grandma Kaiser's thirty-year-old Electrolux vacuum. I have to ship that to Creston for her on the bus. Ironically, I borrowed it back several years later and used it for many more years. It saw its eventual demise many years later while in my possession.

So July 1986 is spent in Vancouver in my Alberni St. apartment, hosting Québecois acquaintances who are financing their West Coast Trail expedition with welfare monies acquired with my supplied rent receipts and hanging out at the beach at English Bay. I do my last hit of acid then, too. Bad trip. Sylvain is teasing me, saying, "Look at you," and it makes me feel horrible to be made fun of and laughed at, but I can't respond in any normal way, and now I feel completely insane and am afraid I'll never be normal again. I beg God to let me regain my sanity and promise I'll never do acid again. He does, and I don't.

One day while hanging out at English Bay, we run into Sylvain's half-brother Stephan and his girlfriend Sylvie. They haven't seen each other for years. What a random coincidence, or is that redundant? They also come to stay with us briefly. We talk about getting a place together back in Montréal. None of us have fixed addresses or phone numbers, so we use telepathy to stay in touch. We just start thinking about them, and within a few days, we bump into them somewhere on the street. One of my dreams is to perfect the technique and start teaching classes to put the cellphone companies out of business. Bandits that they are!

One day, the four of us are exploring Gastown. Those three have done acid, and now have gone outside to smoke a joint while I sit inside a rubby-dub pub. Soon, Sylvie and Stephan are back.

"There's a problem," Sylvie says. "The cops are chasing Sylvain. They saw us smoking the joint and came toward us. He took off running. One cop pulled his gun and told him to stop but he didn't. They're still chasing him."

He has all the cash we have, about five hundred dollars, in his bag. He spends the night in the Main Street lockup, screaming his head off. The cops won't even let him speak to me on the phone because he won't stop yelling. "There's something wrong with him," one cop tells me.

We'd all four spent the previous night at Jim the Iranian's place because my apartment was now empty and all my belongings were at Jim's, along with the contents of several other households. I suspected he was in some kind of buy and sell business of used goods. Sylvain and I had slept on a pile of mattresses stacked about seven high. And a strange thing happened. At some point in the middle of the night, I felt a tickling sensation, and when I woke up in the morning, I discovered my nightgown had been cut open right up the back. I was annoyed, as I'd paid over thirty dollars for it at a home party and really liked it. I found it odd and told Sylvain Jim must have done it, but nothing was said about it.

So now I am stuck with no apartment, no boyfriend, no money, and nowhere to go, except back to the weirdo's place. Sylvie and Stephan have left, so I am on my own until Sylvain gets out. We had planned to catch a Greyhound bus later in the day that he got caught and stop for a visit in Creston on our way to Montréal, but now all I can do is wait.

I eat cold boiled potatoes and feta cheese at Jim's. One night, he insists I eat some goat soup he's made. He also wants me to drink some hard liquor he's bought just for me. I am suspicious. He told me before how he and his friends had drugged girls in university so they could have sex with them. I feel like I am being set up. I go into the kitchen and try to quietly pour my drink down the drain. "What are you doing?" Jim asks. I am a little bit scared of him. He is a relative stranger to me who's already ripped me off. I don't trust him, but who knows how far he'll go.

Sure enough, sometime in the middle of the night as I sleep on Jim's couch, I feel a faraway stirring between my legs. I try to wake up but feel as though I am lying on the ocean floor and the weight of the water is paralyzing me. I groggily manage to open my eyes enough to see Jim crouched by the couch with his hand under the blanket. I know what is happening, and I feel powerless to stop it. I say, "Oh just go ahead and get it over with," and try not to think or feel anything as I fall back to sleep.

I wake up mad, though. I am extremely angry at being in that stupid position and angry at Jim for taking advantage of me. I ask God to "Get him." When I open my Bible, there is a passage in Ezekiel where Jonah was mad because God didn't do what he wanted, and God told him he had no right to be mad, so I take it as a message and try to let it go. Fortunately, Sylvain appears in court the next day and gets out of jail, so we can leave the city. I don't want to, but I tell him what Jim did.

We get on the bus and make the fourteen-hour trip to Creston, where we go to stay at my brother Gary's place. Actually, the house is our family home, which Mom kept when she and Dad finally got divorced after twenty-five years of marriage. But Mom has remarried and moved into a house a few miles out of town with her new husband, Hans. She "rents" the basement suite of the old house to my brother and has other tenants upstairs. I put rents in quotation marks because I don't think my bro Gary actually gets around to paying her rent very often, but he occupies the space when he is in town from doing the fish truck run. Gary quit school at sixteen and started working in the family business with my Uncle Ron and has been doing it ever since.

Seems like an ideal place for us to stay, since he isn't even around much. I am getting unemployment insurance, and Sylvain is getting welfare. We are double income no kids, DINKs, before the phrase was coined. Because Creston is a small town, we are easily identifiable. Sylvain is a social creature, walking into town to go for coffee or to the pub to play pool and chat. He is soon known in town, and people come by. I'm not exactly sure when we decide to stay the winter but that becomes the plan. Montréal winters are severe. Things are good where we are, until Gary tells Mom he doesn't want us staying with him. I'm not sure why. Maybe because Gary spent a thousand dollars on a garbage bag full of weed to sell and Sylvain just couldn't help helping himself. How could Gary possibly miss a joint or two when he had that much is Sylvain's attitude.

By now, I am several months pregnant and panicking about where we can move for a short-term stay. Fortunately, we see an ad in the paper for a furnished basement suite rented out by a kind-hearted Christian woman who lives upstairs. She is the single mother of a teenage son. The suite is decent and affordable. We move our few belongings, just clothes, mostly, and settle in. For years, I resent both Gary and Mom for making us move, especially since Sylvain and I paid rent. Yet when Gary and his wife finally split up, he slept on my couch rent free for a whole year, making more money on unemployment insurance than I was working part time, and left the place with drunken damage. Why didn't I ask him to leave sooner? I guess because I love him and he was company and he helped me with stuff sometimes, like cooking, driving the girls around, and becoming my younger daughter Keziah's best friend. But I'm getting ahead of myself.

At the time, I also had vivid childhood memories of what could happen when he got angry. Once when he was about eight years old he grabbed a rifle off my dad's hunting gun rack in the hallway and threatened to shoot my sister, April. Of course, there were no adults at home, but we told on him, and he got in big trouble. Discipline in our house was all done by my dad. Mom couldn't, and wouldn't, spank us. She hadn't been raised with it, whereas plenty of whacking went on in the religious Morton household. I only remember getting a couple of spankings. Gary got it the worst, but he was the worst.

Sylvain and I go out to Yahk, thirty miles from Creston, for my dad's birthday. Sylvain dresses up like a clown. My dad likes him, unlike the rest of the members of my family. We sleep overnight in the tiny spare room. I now realize my dad is a hoarder. Not an extreme one like the ones on TV, whose houses are full of garbage they have to climb over, but a moderate one. One time in his yard at Yahk, I counted fourteen boats, five campers, two snowmobiles, and several vehicles. He buys stuff with the intention of selling but rarely does. It sits and rots. I am overwhelmed with the amount of junk, but Sylvain thinks the little spare room we sleep in is magical.

Dad and Bunnie's house is interesting, to say the least. Trophies from Dad's kills adorn all four walls of the tiny living room, including the whole top half of a bear, whose outstretched claws threaten to scratch your head or snag your eyes as you walk by. Antlers and other appendages extend from the walls, leaving only a small safe area in the centre of the room. Bunnie puts family pictures on the mantelpiece, and when it is full, Dad says, "Don't send any more. We got no room." So he doesn't know what his grandkids looked like after about the age of three.

There isn't much floor space either due to an abundance of large dogs that are always underfoot. My dad loves his dogs more than his grandchildren. They are hunting dogs, of course, labs and spaniels. I am allergic to animals, so when he lived with my mom, the pets had to stay outside, but in his house, they cuddle up on the couch with him. Dog hair is everywhere, including on the pillowcases of the tiny guest room. And the scent of dog permeates every surface, and assaults you at the door. It is even worse in the confined spaces of his campers. I have to hold my breath and let it out slowly and breathe in again very slowly to acclimatize.

Once many years later, I took my two daughters to visit him at his camp on the river on the Ktunaxa First Nations reservation near Creston. The bloody carcass of a deer was lying in the snow in the yard. "That roadkill is the dogs' lunch," Dad said. "I couldn't believe it. They even chewed the nose off."

This time I'm thinking of the therapy costs associated with this kind of childhood trauma, trying to shield the girls' eyes and ears. Inside the camper, Merle Haggard croons on an 8-track player powered by a car battery. This is in the new millennium. Over the narrow bed, strung up like socks on a clothesline, is a line of pelts drying, from which, I imagine, fleas drop onto Dad's sleeping body beneath.

Dad happily proclaims the benefits of his location: "The river is right there. I just walk over and get my dish water, and I can drop the boat in anytime." How he can live this way is beyond me, but this self-sufficient solitary existence suits him fine. Should the world ever suffer some major disaster, the first thing I would try to do is find Dad. He knows how to survive.

April 16, 1987. Sylvain and I are living in my hometown of Creston for the winter, waiting for the arrival of our baby before we go back to Montréal. My dates are uncertain, so my doctor decides to induce labour. Sylvain and I go to the hospital and they start the drip.

"Can you believe it? Our child is coming today. I'm so excitable," Sylvain says.

"Excited. You're so excited, although they're both true." I'm having regular contractions.

"Breathe, my love. Are you okay?"

"Yes."

"Good. I'm going to get a coffee."

My mom comes in on her way to work at her job as a payroll clerk at one of Creston's three sawmills. "Hi, hon. How's it going?"

"Okay. The contractions hurt, but I guess that's normal. So far I've been able to breathe through them."

"Great. Well, I'm glad you're doing well. Can I get you anything?"

"No thanks, Mom. I'm fine."

It feels strange, emotionally awkward to have her here while I am in this condition, being vaginally examined periodically. The last time she visited me in the hospital was when I was there in grade five with a severe asthma attack. I remember she brought me an Archie comic and a slightly pink chicken leg and thigh pulled too soon from the family dinner. I know she is not in favour of us having this child. She suggested we give it up for adoption, as unemployment insurance and welfare aren't viable incomes on which to raise a child.

I blurted, "No, I want this baby. I've already had two abortions." Her face crumpled and she cried out as though I'd gut punched her hard. I felt bad about hurting her, but there was no room for argument in this decision. I'd set a boundary, and I was defending it. I hear people say they're either from a close family or they're not. I don't know what kind of family ours is. Both, I guess. It's hard to explain.

Mom leaves just as Sylvain returns. "I saw your mom was 'ere. 'Ow are you doing, my love?"

"Fine, but the contractions are getting stronger. Can you stay with me please?"

"Hof course. I just want to go talk to the nurse and find out when the baby will be born."

"She doesn't know. Ow, ow, ow, ow. Here comes another one."

"Breathe." We'd practiced the *th* sounds, and his accent was improving. "Remember the prenatal class."

I had, in fact, done the exercises, practicing while lying in bed at night at home, and I am managing to get through it. I want to do it as naturally as possible. Three hours after they start the drip, I feel a primal urge to push.

I yell, "I have to push!" and the nurse, Susan, coincidentally my Uncle Ron's second wife—small town—comes running to check between my legs and gasps, "You're crowning, Jac. It's time. Push."

Two more big pushes, and Emmanuel Morton St-Onge arrives in the world without waiting for the doctor. I did the same twenty-six years ago, coincidentally having the middle name Susan, after the nurse who delivered me at the time.

Sylvain is crying. I am overwhelmed with a feeling of wonder that a fully formed human being has just emerged from my body. The baby is okay but jaundiced. They keep him and me in the hospital for a week. Sylvain is beside himself with impatience for us to come home. I think our stay is excessive and being done to give us some time to adjust before I'm alone with Sylvain and the baby. He comes to visit every day.

My generously sized boobs now come into their own, fulfilling their true calling as baby feeders. Breastfeeding is a learning process for both of us. My dad and his wife, Bunnie, the girlfriend he left my mom for, come to visit just as I'm trying to get Emmanuel latched onto my breast. I'm in a hospital gown, with my chest half-exposed, sitting in a chair with a pillow on my lap. Dad watches with interest, as he might a hockey game.

I am uncomfortable and stressed, and think it's completely inappropriate, but I seem to be the only one. I tease my baby's lips with my nipple. Latch, please latch. I just wish they'd fucking leave already. Do I have to say this? Fuck. Blessed is the mother of children indeed.

Coping with Sylvain and Emmanuel induces mild postpartum depression. Anxiety and irritability are my prevailing moods. Sylvain constantly tells me what to do or not to do with the baby, usually in opposition to my own instincts. Like most fathers, he's somewhat jealous and resents the time the baby takes from me. My nerves are shot.

Now that our winter in Creston is over and our baby has been born, we resume our original plan to return to Montréal. Why I'm not sure. We fly back to Montréal when Emmanuel is six weeks old, arriving with no place to stay. I am floored by the realization that comes over me at times—this child depends on me, on us, for everything. He trusts us to feed, clothe, clean, protect, and nurture him until he can do it himself. He doesn't concern himself with the acquisition of necessities or their cost. That's our job. His is just to grow and to allow the life force that got him here to sustain him and turn him into himself while he gets to figure out who that is.

He lives from my breastmilk only for the first six months, meaning we are never far from each other. Wherever I go, he has to come. I sometimes want to give him a bottle so I can leave him with Sylvain, and I can have a break, but everyone says the breast is best, so I continue. It's very convenient when we are homeless in Montréal to be able to feed him anywhere, well, except a park bench, of course. I was covered with a blanket, but the police told me I wasn't allowed to breastfeed in public. This was 1987. Thanks to whoever fought to have the laws changed since then.

I sometimes can't believe that our free country is so overtaxed and overregulated. When I was in Mexico about thirty years later, I saw an entire family on a bicycle in a town with no stop signs, and they were all smoking and texting. No, they weren't smoking, but the rest is true. Okay, they weren't texting either. That would really be dangerous.

So, we spend our first night back in Montréal with our baby in a shit-hole hotel on rue Ste-Catherine. The room is small, with a double bed made with burn-hole sheets; the bathroom is down the hall. The walls whisper atrocities witnessed and base human urges filled.

"This is disgusting, Sylvain," I say. "I can't believe we paid for this.

They should pay us to stay here. Emmanuel doesn't belong here. Neither do we. It's so gross I can't stand it. I don't want to touch anything. Look at the carpet, what's left of it. It looks filthy. How do we know the sheets are clean? We have to find something else tomorrow. I'm not coming back here. Maybe Pierre has some room."

8

Montréal Deux

Pierre doesn't have room for us at this time. So, we hang out on the street, with Sylvain asking anyone he knows even remotely about a place to stay. A middle-aged guy named Guy takes pity on us and says we can stay with him temporarily while we look for something else.

Guy lives on the ground floor of a small row house. There is nothing in his living room except a geodesic dome made of straws. I think he was another engineer who'd had a meltdown. His kitchen wall is his guestbook, where visitors can draw and write their names. Sylvain draws a big ugly spider.

"Aren't you worried about your landlord?" I say.

"All it takes is a coat of paint. Easy."

I come from a home where there were few rules, but one of them was don't poke holes in the walls. The notion of writing on them also seems wicked to me.

The day after we arrive, Sylvain says, "I'm going to make some money. See you later." He takes the guitar and case I'd bought him.

Guy and I visit. I nurse the baby. We look through the newspaper at the weekly specials on groceries at the Boni Choix.

"I like to cut de coupons out," Guy says, producing scissors from a drawer in the kitchen.

"Me too," I say.

"We would make a good team," Guy says.

Uh-oh.

Late in the afternoon, there is a knock at the door. Guy goes to answer it, returning with a handful of change he puts on the table and pushes toward me.

"Dat was de cops. Dey picked up your man. 'E's in jail overnight."

"What?! Oh my god, again? Why does this keep happening?"

"Je ne sais pas. Maybe you need a real man to take care of you, not a boy."

I smile uneasily. "What I need is some dinner. I'm getting hungry. What about you? Why don't you take that change and get us something to eat, please?"

"I 'ave some bouillon. I will buy de pain and de fromage. I will be right back."

Guy returns shortly with the food and begins to heat the broth. He pours it steaming into bowls and then sets a cutting board and a knife on the table. He pierces the loaf of crusty, soft bread—a French baguette—and hacks off generous chunks of Swiss cheese. This simple meal is one of the best I've ever eaten.

He continues his sales pitch over dinner. "You har a nice woman. Why har you wit' a boy?"

"I don't know." Sylvain is twenty, and I am twenty-six.

"We could cut hout coupons togedder, take my scooter to de store to shop. Cook togedder, do de dishes."

I look at his curly graying hair, his fat stomach, his hovel. He's a nice guy but... nah. "Sorry, I'm already married," referring to our private ceremony, confessing our vows to each other on acid in a bar at 4:00 a.m.

"It probably won't work hout. Den you'll come back to me. Let me just put de tip inside has a hengagement, a promise dat you'll come back to me."

Holy shit. I am alone in a guy's house, and just like at Jim's, he wants to fuck me while my man is in jail. I've gotta stop meeting guys like this.

"I'm sorry. You're so kind. I like you, but I can't. I just can't. I have a baby."

Sylvain returns the next day.

"I can't believe the cops picked you up again. What for?" I say.

"Because they're assholes. They like to harass me. I wasn't doing anything."

"Come on. They don't put people in jail for nothing. Anyway, we need to move on. I don't want to stay here anymore. I'm having trouble with Guy. Don't say anything. Let's just go."

We beg Pierre, and he reluctantly agrees to let us stay temporarily.

Pierre's place is on rue St-Hubert, a row house typical of Montréal architecture. We will have to stay in his room. There is a sign on the clawfoot tub in the bathroom reminding everyone to clean it before they leave. Pierre isn't keen on the baby, understandably.

Fortunately, we don't stay with him long because Sylvain runs into his half-brother on the street, and we make plans to move in together, Stephan and his girlfriend Sylvie, and Sylvain and I. Sylvie finds us a house to rent in the country, a small town about seventy miles from Montréal, called Waterloo. The house is old and small but has two bedrooms, which is all we need. We acquire a mattress from somewhere, and Emmanuel sleeps near us on a pile of blankets.

The landlord lets us paint the bedrooms. It's fun. Everything is going well until everyone but me is complaining of red, itchy bumps. Emmanuel is covered in them. The former tenants had a dog that left its fleas behind when they moved.

We have to treat the house. That means removing everything to the front lawn and doing umpteen loads of laundry and bedding in hot water. Sylvie sprays the house, and we have to wait for it to defume, so we hang out in the front yard with all our belongings. It suddenly occurs to me that's where the term flea market comes from.

Living with Sylvie and Stephan is fun. I like having help with the baby. It is a hot, humid summer, though. One day Sylvie suggests we go to the lake to cool off. We get our gear together and off we go. On y va. It's a long, hot walk into the country. We see an unusual dwelling. It's a small dome house that looks like an igloo made out of cement blocks and covered with plasticine. We get closer to have a better look, and a woman comes outside. She is tall and slim, with long hair.

"Oh bonjour. We are just looking at your house, very cool."

"Would you like to see inside?"

"Yes, please, love to."

It is cool inside. She has an altar with rocks, sticks, and feathers set up. I've never seen anything like this. She also has a small daughter living with her. She tells us her name is Sappho. Interesting.

We trudge on through the long dry grass. Ahead there is a bunch of women playing volleyball, topless. What is this? Surprises around every corner. It turns out one of the women is Sylvie's sister. She calls out, "You want to play?"

"No thanks, we're going swimming," we answer. Even though I

wouldn't have minded watching, I'd be afraid I'd look like a perv. I was far from being comfortable enough to lob a ball around bare breasted, even if it was in the middle of nowhere. We had managed to get an inner tube from somewhere.

"Here we are," Sylvie says suddenly.

This is not a lake. This is not a pond. This is a large muddy puddle, a swamp, a damp dump of stagnant water. It smells. It's brown. When I reluctantly step in it, warm mud oozes between my toes.

Sylvain loses it. "What the fuck is this? You said a lake. This is a shithole. Merde. It stinks. I'm not going in there. It's disgusting. We came all this way for this? Calice de Tabernac, esti."

Sylvie is unfazed. She wades in a few feet with the inner tube. "Come on, Jacquie."

I am just as repulsed as Sylvain is, but we are here now. I try to put Emmanuel's toes in the water, and he shrieks instinctively. It's bad. But I put him in the Snugli baby carrier and wade out to Sylvie. I can feel grass and/or something touching my legs. Oh god, please not snakes.

I mount the tube with some difficulty, and we paddle around the tepid puddle. After awhile, I get used to the smell and don't notice it anymore. For years, when the memory of this day surfaces, I smile to think of Sylvain's rage and our disappointment with the lake. I actually enjoyed paddling around with Sylvie and the baby, especially her smile and our hot legs occasionally bumping each other.

Sylvie was a free spirit. She'd been married and had a little boy, whom she left with the father when she decided to leave the corporate world. I think it takes a strong woman to leave her child. She thinks it's a better life for him with his dad.

She prefers to travel and enjoys the outdoors. Her eyes are the colour of the sky and clouds. She is cute. One night at a party we are invited to, she seems high on something. She takes me to a bedroom to talk where it is quieter.

"I love Stephan, but sometimes mid-month when my drive is high, I need a lot of sex. One time I was at a party and I had sex with a guy, but it didn't satisfy me, so he sent in another guy, and another one. The rest of the time, I don't really care. But when I need it, I need it. That's when I like to have a woman, too."

Oh.

She acquires some bamboo blinds from somewhere and says,

"Jacquie, can you please help me hang these?" Her English is excellent, her accent very slight. She is standing on a chair. My face is near her crotch. She suddenly looks down and giggles. I giggle, too. I begin to wonder about the possibility of having a rendezvous with Sylvie.

One night, I get up to go to the bathroom and take my Bible with me. It falls open to Romans 1:25-26: "They exchanged the truth about God for a lie, and worshipped and served created things rather than the Creator, who is forever praised. Because of this, God gave them over to shameful lusts. Even their women exchanged natural sexual relations for unnatural ones." I feel like God is saying *No* to my lifelong hope, wish, dream, and desire.

Our little home life falls apart one day, after Sylvain and Stephan have a big fight. Sylvain's adoptive dad, whom we got in touch with because of the baby, comes and picks up our stuff in his station wagon at month's end, including a large white plastic bucket of diapers waiting to be washed. I remember the water was green and smelling when he took them. They should have just gone to the dump. I felt terrible that some other woman would have to deal with them. It's not how I was raised. I could hear my mother's voice as if they'd been dumped on her: "A bucket of dirty diapers, can you imagine? Ugh, the colour and smell of that water was enough to turn your stomach."

We hitchhike back to Montréal and begin the depressing task of looking for shelter once again.

"I can't believe we're back here in this position," I say. "I liked living with Sylvie and Stephan. We had a home, help, company. Fuck, Sylvain."

"Fuck them. I know my brother. He is an asshole, always taking the best for himself."

"Yeah, but now we're on the street with a baby again. I hate this."

"Don't worry, my love. We'll find something."

"We'd better and fast."

As we walked, I wondered how I got into this position and thought about my old life in Vancouver. We tromped along until we got to rue Sherbrooke. We found mercy from a nice couple managing a building there. We got Sylvain's dad to drop off our stuff, mostly a mattress and a baby swing he bought us at a real flea market. The building managers kindly rummaged through the basement storage of items left from other tenants and produced a small dresser, kitchen table and chairs, and deathtrap wooden crib.

I am grateful. We settle in. The bedroom window overlooks a cement square below surrounded by the other apartments. Everything is grey. I sometimes hear people screaming and fighting from behind other open windows, so I know they hear us when I rage at Sylvain.

He spends as little time as possible indoors. The real life for him is out on the street where he makes friends with the young male and female sex workers that populate Sherbrooke night and day.

I become a homebody, not wanting to expose my baby or myself to the sights and sounds outside the front door. Emmanuel swings. I can't remember what I did in that lonely, empty, ugly apartment. No TV, very little stuff. I just don't know.

One day, Sylvain wets Emmanuel's hair up into a baby mohawk, puts a spiked black leather bracelet around his neck, and takes pictures. He looks adorable.

Then Sylvain invites Giovanni and Aruni up to our apartment. Giovanni is Italian and worked in a pasta restaurant in Old Montréal once. Now he works as Aruni's pimp. She is a tiny thing, brown skinned, and from Cambodia, she tells us. Her mom was mean to her, so she got kicked out or ran away, I forget, and became Giovanni's girlfriend. He suggested she get paid for all the sex she was having with guys anyway. Soon Giovanni and Sylvain hatch a money-saving plan. Giovanni and Aruni will move in with us. We throw a dirty, stained, rescued mattress on the living room floor, and now we have roommates again. One day, I hear Aruni reply in response to a question in French from Giovanni, apparently about how she likes the new arrangement after she's spent most of a day with me and the baby. "C'est plat." It's boring. I kind of understood what she meant, but it was easier for me because I had breastfeeding to enjoy, and it was my baby. I didn't like the environment, but I loved my baby.

The three of them naturally speak French most of the time. I feel like an outsider. The one good thing about the arrangement is that Giovanni makes the best tomato sauce I've ever eaten. We pick up some pasta at the Boni Choix and wait. He won't tell me his secret, and he won't rush the sauce, no matter how hungry we are.

The worst thing about the arrangement is that Aruni brings a client into our home one day, and Emmanuel and I have to stay trapped in our bedroom quietly until she's finished, which is remarkably quickly. It's awkward, though. I'm wondering what they're doing out there. Once

Emmanuel makes a sound, and I hear the guy ask in English, "Is someone here?"

Aruni replies, "Oh no, we're alone. That was nothing."

When Sylvain comes in later that day, we are alone. "Sylvain, Aruni had a client up here today. What's with that? This isn't going to work if she's going to bring clients up here. I don't want to feel like a prisoner in my own home, and I don't want to imagine what's she's doing with them. This isn't a proper environment to raise a child in. I know he's a baby now, but it's not right. I shouldn't have to leave my house so she can blow guys in it."

"Okay, okay. I'll talk to her. But it's easier for her if she can bring them up."

"But this is our apartment. What did she do before? If that's what they want, they have to get their own place. This isn't going to work out, much as I'll miss the sauce."

The situation is soon resolved when Aruni comes home one day in tears. Her English is limited, but she tells Sylvain in French what happened, and he translates for me. The cops picked up Giovanni and took him to jail.

"Don't worry," he tells her. "We will go visit him. But you have to have ID." They have a little exchange in French, and he says to me, "She's not sixteen; she's thirteen." "Oh my god." No wonder she's so tiny. Poor little thing.

How long has she been working the street? A child prostitute is in our living room. I pass people with needles in their arms on my way to the creepy laundry room embedded in the basement bowels of the building, and my husband is on the street with the riffraff, inviting people in to use our bathroom.

"Come on, Sylvain. This is bullshit. I want out of here. The baby does not belong in this environment. It's not safe. Besides that, it's getting cold, and I don't have a proper coat or footwear. The squirrels in Sherbrooke Park are as fat as I've ever seen them. Winter is coming. We're not ready. Let's make our escape and go back to British Columbia, where it rains but you don't need boots and a parka." I work on him day after day, wheedling and whining, weaving my case.

At last, he agrees. We get our 850 dollar welfare cheque at the end of October, and we tell Pierre he can have the next cheque for helping us out. I write a thankful, apologetic note to the building managers, and we do a midnight move to a Greyhound bus, which we ride for three days and nights to the Wet Coast, like Jonah in the belly of the whale.

We arrive in Vancouver at 6:00 a.m. and go straight to the welfare office to wait until it opens. It's pouring rain. I have no socks. My shoes are soaking wet, and my feet are ice cold. But we're back on familiar ground. I feel safer here somehow. A woman in the welfare office gives us vouchers for a room and food.

By the end of the month, we have found an apartment in Chinatown over an Italian grocery store. Welfare has given us money for a crib and some basic furniture. But Sylvain and I are not getting along. We have a huge screaming fight in the street outside the welfare office.

"If you want to go, go. Fuck you. But I'm taking my son."

"Don't be stupid. You can't take him. He's breastfeeding."

Sylvain is trying to undo the umbrella stroller to get Emmanuel out. We're literally on the verge of pulling the poor child limb from limb. I manage to grab the baby and go running into the welfare office, shaken. They put me up in a shelter that night.

A tearful repentance ensues. Oh God, I'm sorry I've made such a mess of my life again. I can't stand it. I have to get away from Sylvain. He's crazy. Please help me. I promise to serve You if you'll just help me escape. I need a miracle. Only You can make this happen for me. Please help me, Lord. In Jesus's name, Amen.

The worker and I discuss options. I think the best thing would be to bribe Sylvain with the Québec welfare cheque to have a trial separation, where I would stay in Vancouver and he would return to Montréal for a month. Welfare will supply a bus ticket for him to leave. The hard part will be convincing him. He is extremely stubborn and will not want to leave the baby. I really believe it will take divine intervention for him to agree.

When I return to the apartment in the morning, he is livid and vents at me for getting the system involved in our business. He rages on and on and then breaks down crying about how sorry he is. It is an emotional rollercoaster, and I feel like I am playing a volatile chess game, always having to stay one step ahead but not being allowed to show what I'm doing, or I risk forfeiting the game. It takes several hours, but by noon, I lock the door behind him, and he is on his way to pick up a bus ticket and return to Montréal. I lean against the door after double checking that it is locked, breathe a sigh of relief, and say out loud, "Thank you,

Lord. Thank you so much."

The place is too quiet. I call Jim, the Iranian who'd taken all my belongings when we left Vancouver, to see if I can get my stereo system back.

"I don't have it," he said. "But I can bring you something. Where you live?"

He brings an old radio, and I can feel his lust as he looks at me. "You want a job?"

"Well, maybe. I don't know, with the baby."

"I buy a restaurant. You can work there. Baby in back."

"I could try it and see. Where is it?"

"Davie Street, near Burrard."

"Oh, over there. It's kind of far, but I guess I could figure out a bus. Okay, I could use some cash."

Jim's restaurant is tiny, about four or five tables, and serves Jamaican food. Goat, roti, things I have no experience with. I take Emmanuel's little walker and leave him in the back with Jim, who cooks, along with his mother sometimes, or his girlfriend, Shannon. Emmanuel's eight months old now. I work about three shifts. The place isn't busy, and the tips are negligible. During an empty spell, I go into the back to see Emmanuel.

"Hi, baby, how are you?"

He looks at me, and I know something is wrong. His eyes don't look right. He looks like he is stuck inside, wanting but unable to respond to me. I suddenly remember that feeling, the night Jim drugged and raped me.

"Jim, did you give him something? What did you give him?"

"No, nothing."

"Don't lie to me. I can see there's something wrong. What did you do?"

"Just a little. Tiny, tiny." He tries to show me with his fingers. "Just keep him quiet."

"Jesus, Jim, what's wrong with you? You don't give drugs like that to a baby. Fuck." I pick Emmanuel up and hold him close. "Are you okay, honey? Mommy's here. It's okay. I love you." I start packing up his things. "I'm going to go now," I say to Jim over my shoulder.

"No, you stay. I have no one."

"I'll finish the day but that's it. I'm done."

At the end of the day, Jim pulls a twenty-dollar bill out of the till and gives it to me for three days' wages. All the way home I think about slashing his tires. If I'm completely honest, though, I'm not sure that was the last day I worked for him. Sometimes in my memory I play the scene the way I wish it had gone. But I remember telling his sister what he did, and she said, "He's stupid." I think that was the next day.

Why would I go back? This is the question that I'm ashamed to answer. Because I'm stupid. I can't say no. I have low self-esteem. I don't care enough about myself or my child to avoid a dick like Jim. Why didn't I report him to the police? Because I'd have to admit I was on welfare and working under the table, taking my baby to work with me. I might be declared unfit. And maybe I was, maybe I am.

It's evening. Emmanuel and I are alone in the little apartment. It's sparsely furnished, as usual. Emmanuel is ten months old, asleep on a foamy on the living room floor. I don't remember why he's sleeping there. I am on the couch, reading. We don't have a TV. Suddenly Emmanuel begins to thrash. What on earth? I go to him. He looks hot. I touch his face, and it's burning up. His eyes are rolled back in his head. I'm terrified. What's happening? What should I do? I remember my mom saying my sister had convulsions when she was a baby. I think that must be what this is. I grab the phone and call 911.

"911. What's your emergency, police, fire or ambulance?"

"Ambulance."

"Okay, what's happening?"

"I think my baby's having convulsions."

"Okay, can you confirm your address is 598 Union St.?"

"Yes, I'm upstairs, apartment #1."

"Okay, ma'am, the ambulance should be there shortly."

"Thank you."

Emmanuel is lying still now, still seemingly asleep. Soon, the paramedics knock at the door and look at him. "So, what's the problem?"

"He was jerking around. I think he was having convulsions."

"He seems fine now."

"What if it happens again?"

"Call us back."

Soon after they're gone, his head arches back and his arms and legs start thrashing again. This time the ambulance takes us to Children's Hospital. They shave some hair from the side of his head and keep him for observation. I'm scared. What's wrong with my baby boy? Is it because I did acid and smoked pot a few times when I was pregnant? Is it from Jim giving him part of a sleeping pill? Is this my fault? Oh god. I feel so guilty. I'm sickened to think he could be suffering because of me.

We are released. Two months later, Emmanuel has another seizure and again two months after that. Whenever he gets a cold or infection, his fever spikes, and he convulses. We go back to the hospital for an EEG to determine if he is epileptic or if the condition is infantile only. The test results are inconclusive, but he is put on an anticonvulsant medication.

Sylvain returns to Vancouver after three months. I hear a knock on the door. I open it. Sylvain is standing there. My heart lurches.

"I'm back."

"I see that. Sylvain, I'm not ready to live with you again."

"I want to see my son."

"Of course. But I think it would be best if you stayed somewhere else, and we can make arrangements for you to see him."

"Don't be stupid. You're my wife, and he's my son, and we're all going to live together. Please. Now, where is he?"

And he steps past me into the house. I thought afterwards, I shouldn't have opened the door, but he would have kicked it down. He gets back just in time for Emmanuel's first birthday in April and insists on staying. By July, I've had it with him again. I move out while he is out of the apartment.

He had gone with me to see a visiting prophet at my sister's church that I'd been attending. As usual whenever Sylvain went to any church, there was conflict, and he ended up taking off. The church had two pastors, Michael, who was married to Clara, and Hugo, who was married to Lisa. Lisa had a talk with me.

"You love the Lord, don't you, Jacquie?"

"Yes."

"Why are you with him?"

"I guess it's my karma."

"God doesn't hold our sins against us if we ask Him to forgive us. I think you should take seventy-two hours and really seek the Lord's will about what He wants for you and then do it."

"Okay, thanks, bye."

That night I run a bath and light a candle on the edge of the tub. As I soak, I think about what Lisa said. I'd be happy to do God's will if I knew what it was. That is always the issue. I pray, quietly. Lord, do you want me to leave Sylvain? The candle flickers. That is enough of an answer for me. Candle flicker means yes. The more difficult thing is to enact a plan, as he will certainly not let me go willingly.

I make the mistake of telling him that I prayed, and I believe God wants us to separate.

"Don't be stupid. God would never tell you that. God wants families to be together. You're listening to the wrong voice, my friend. And I don't want you talking to your sister or the people from that crazy church. They are brainwashing you. I mean it. Don't speak to any of them. I'm staying with you all the time to make sure you don't. Don't even think about leaving any more."

This is getting oppressive. I feel like I am a captive. Fortunately, Sylvain gets bored indoors easily, and soon he says he is going out to make some money.

"But you stay here. Don't go anywhere. And don't talk to anybody. I'll be back later."

As soon as he is gone, I call my sister. "April, I need help. I need to get out of here tonight. Sylvain's just gone out. Can you come and pick Emmanuel and me up and can we stay at Andrew and Karen's?" These are April's house parents—the couple with whom she roomed and boarded while studying to be an occupational therapist at the University of British Columbia.

"Well, I can pick you up, but you'll have to ask them about staying here. Just a sec."

I speak with Karen who informs me I need to repent of a bad attitude before I stay there. She is referring to something I'd said about them being judgmental of Sylvain. I apologize, and April picks us up. The next morning, I give my life to the Lord, again, during the altar call. You can never be too sure when you can never be sure at all. After the service, Clara, Pastor Michael's wife, approaches me.

"Now, Jacquie, I believe God told me that if you need a place to stay, you can stay with us."

"Wow, thanks, Clara, that's very generous."

I tell April and Karen and Andrew.

"Well, that's it, then. We better get you moved out of there today," someone says. A small team of people come to the Chinatown apartment. I am nervous. What if Sylvain is there? Thankfully, he isn't. We disassemble the crib, grab necessities, and scram. I leave a note and fifty dollars on the table for Sylvain. I feel bad, even though I believe it is the right choice for me.

9

Emmanuel

Emmanuel and I stay with Michael and Clara until Andrew and Karen, the couple April boards with while she goes to the University of British Columbia, move to a house in Kitsilano that is ideal for us to move into with them. It feels to me like God has put His hands together and made a nest for us. It is so perfect, living with family and friends, sharing cooking and cleaning responsibilities. Every day is lovely. Emmanuel and I take his stroller down to the beach and feed the ducks, or just play outside, or go to West Side Family Place so he can play with other kids. One of my favourite memories is standing with him in the dusty lane behind the house picking blackberries and sharing their warm sweetness. We all go to church a few times a week.

Sylvain isn't happy with my decision to leave, of course. He doesn't know where I went or have any way of contacting me except the church where he'd gone with me once. As I am singing and worshipping God with my eyes closed one Sunday morning, I feel someone slip into the space beside me and my stomach lurches. I open my eyes to see Sylvain standing there.

"I want to see my son. Where is he?" he whispers loudly.

I begin to shake internally. "He's in the nursery. I'll go with you."

After a second surprise visit again in the church two or three months later, which ends with a call to the police by my bodyguard friends at the church, he starts to talk about wanting visitation rights. Pastor Michael arranges for me to talk to a lawyer, who just happens to ask me if I am absolutely certain Sylvain is Emmanuel's father.

"Actually, I'm not 100 per cent sure because there was an incident." I tell him about Jim raping me and that the dates were close enough to render some doubt. When Sylvain is told a paternity test will be required before he will be granted access, he backs off. He wants to continue to believe that Emmanuel is his son. That's when I remember God telling me not to be angry about what Jim did. Turns out He was just planting an ace in the hole for me.

That church was very close knit. Read: well controlled. The expectation was that everyone attended all the meetings. I thought some of their ways were kind of extreme, especially at first, such as the no dating rule. The church was primarily composed of university students. The idea was that everyone socializes together. In order to get married, God has to tell either the man or the woman who He wants them to marry. They then tell the elders of the church but no one else. God has to then tell the other person, who tells the elders, who pair the couples up. Once the elders have informed the man, he then invites the woman for dinner, their first date, and proposes marriage. I'm not making this shit up.

One Sunday morning, I am up early and getting ready for an adult Sunday school class. I usually walk to church, and the rest of the family comes an hour later for the main service. I am standing in front of the bathroom mirror curling my hair when my sister April gets up and comes over to me.

"Where's Emmanuel?"

"Sleeping in, I guess."

"That's unusual," she says. She goes to his room and comes back to me. Her face is pale, and her voice is shaky. "Jac, there's something wrong. I think he's dead."

"Well, if he's dead he hasn't been dead long because I heard him coughing in the night," I say casually, but I set my curling iron down and go to his room. He is lying face down in exactly the same position I saw him lying in when I looked in on him a few hours earlier after using the bathroom. At the time, I thought to myself that's an odd position. I hope he can breathe. But I didn't check.

I lower the side of his crib and reach in to touch his shoulder. It feels like cold clay. I flip him over and realize he is gone, but a hideous body remains: His eyelashes are bent, his nose is flattened, and purple-and-blue blood has pooled in the skin of his face. April comes into his room and screams until Andrew and Karen are crowding the tiny bedroom. April clings to Andrew. Karen is a nurse, and she instinctively grabs the body, puts it on the carpet, and begins to do artificial resuscitation, but within a few breaths, we all know it's too late. Someone calls 911, and soon two uniformed men are in Emmanuel's room. One scoops the stiff body from the floor, and they tell us they're going to Children's Hospital.

I am in shock. Everyone has left the room to get ready to go to the hospital. I look into the empty crib and see Emmanuel's beloved soother. I pick it up and put it into the pocket of my skirt. He may need it later when he wakes up, I think to myself. But somewhere deep down, like a shadow at the bottom of a swimming pool, I know he won't need it.

Karen comes in and says, "Jac, Michael and Clara are coming over. They're going to follow us to the hospital. We'll go as soon as they get here."

I go into the bathroom and look in the mirror. My hair looks awful, partly flat and partly curled. But I don't bother to try and fix it. I am a robot. April is rocking hysterically, mumbling, at the end of my bed.

Finally, we get into Andrew and Karen's van and drive to the hospital. April is crying and trembling. I sit dry eyed, imagining that perhaps God will do a modern-day miracle and Emmanuel will be fine when we arrive. The newspapers will run articles about what happened, with headlines like "Dead Baby Is Resurrected." It may start the promised revival of people believing in God that we hear about every week at church.

Andrew lets us out near the entrance and goes to park the van. April, Karen, and I link arms and walk toward the entrance doors, which open automatically. We approach the reception desk. Karen says, "We're here about the little boy that was brought in." The receptionist looks at us, then down and away. This is when I realize there's no miracle. He's dead, still dead. We're asked to sit and wait.

A doctor soon arrives. "Who's the mother?" he asks.

"I am," I say.

"Would you come with me, please. You can bring someone with you."

I look at April. She's a mess. "Karen?" She nods, and we follow the doctor into a small room.

"I'm very sorry to have to tell you this, but your son is dead."

Now the tears flow of their own volition. "I can't believe it. I can't believe it." I feel stupid, but I can't stop saying, "I can't believe it."

"Did he have any medical history?"

"He had infantile convulsions and was on an anticonvulsant medication. He's had a cold the past few days. We both have. I heard him coughing in the night."

"Based on the condition of the body, he appears to have died in the wee hours of the morning. We'll perform an autopsy and let you know our findings."

"Okay, thank you."

"Would you like to say goodbye?"

I'm not sure about that, but I don't want to leave without seeing him again. We get the rest of the group and are led down a hallway to a curtained room where Emanuel lies in the blue fleece pajamas my Grandma Kaiser sent him for Christmas. I loved them so much I had his picture taken at Sears in them just after Christmas, a couple of months before this awful day.

Clara says to me, "You can kiss him if you want to." I sense this is in case I have reservations about breaking Old Testament rules about touching the dead. I don't want to kiss him, but I want to stick my finger in the space created by his curled fingers. Out of a sense of expectation because of what Clara said, I lean over and kiss his forehead. His hair feels different. I take a deep breath.

"Goodbye, little one. I love you," I whisper. I move away from the bed, letting the others do their things. I continue to weep, unable to understand the implications of this event for my life.

We pass the reception desk again.

"What do I do now?" I hear myself say, meaning, are there forms to sign or anything, but I hear the other meaning. What on earth do I do now? My purpose is gone. My joy is gone.

We drive home. By now it is lunchtime, but I can't eat. The police come to walk through the house, just procedure. They take Emmanuel's medicine, say sorry, and leave. Members of the church begin to arrive. They all stay all day. The last one leaves about 11:00 p.m. One of the other pastor's mothers pulls me aside. "Oh, Jacquie, I'm so sorry to hear what happened. I prayed. I asked God to give me something I could tell you. And I saw a picture of Jesus, and Emmanuel on his knee, and he wasn't smiling, but he was okay."

"Thank you, Hazel. That's comforting." Later, in my grieving, I would sit on the floor and put my head on the couch and pretend it was Jesus's knee and Emmanuel was on the other one and we were all together.

I decide to move into Emmanuel's room for a little more privacy as

I've been sleeping in the living room area of the downstairs. I put my single bed where his crib was. The first night I sleep there, I have a dream that I can't breathe, and I can't wake up. When I finally do wake up it is 3:20 a.m. After that, I often awaken at that time. I think that's probably when he died. He was not quite two years old. The autopsy revealed the cause of death was asphyxiation. I think he probably had a seizure. I heard him call out "Mama" that night, but I just listened and waited, hoping he'd settle. I didn't hear anything after that. But if he had a seizure, he might have been in the aphasic state after, which would have made him unable to lift his face. Imagine my guilt.

I'm remembering a time a few weeks before Emmanuel died. Karen comes downstairs to talk to April and me. Karen is a pretty, soft-spoken Christian woman who takes her role as Andrew's wife and the head of our household very seriously, even though she is only a few years older than us. As well, the church we belong to, Maranatha Christian Church, is part of the Shepherding Movement, which was popular in some Christian circles at the time. Therefore, Andrew and Karen have a spiritual obligation to watch over us and boss us around, kind of.

Karen says: "Hey, April and Jac, I want to speak with you. You know, you two should be praying to God about getting husbands. April, you'll be finished school soon, and Jac, Emmanuel needs a father."

Good thing Sylvain wasn't around to hear that. He'd flip. Unfortunately, I didn't trust him to see Emmanuel on his own. I was afraid he'd take him, sort of like I had. But I was the mother and was taking good care of him. Sylvain liked to live in the street.

"Yeah, okay, I guess." I don't really have any use for a husband. Things are perfect as they are, in my opinion. But in obedience, I pray: "Lord, I pray you'd direct me toward a husband. Please make Your will known. Thank you."

Lying in bed later, I began thinking about Fred. Fred is a member of the church, of course. He is fairly good looking, with a nice smile and blue eyes. He seems more interested in my friend Cassandra and her little boy, Mason, but I know he likes kids.

There are two problems I have with Fred. I always think of him as "Poor Fred" because he is prematurely bald. Also, he has club thumbs, a genetic anomaly that causes the thumbs to be unusually wide—"like little chicken drumsticks," as he likes to say. I am going to say something right now. I suffer with perfectionism. I am attentive to detail, and little things bother me. I sometimes feel embarrassed to be seen with certain people. These are a few of my myriad faults. Call me shallow, call me vain, call me picky. This is how I am.

I begin to feel like Fred must be the man I am supposed to marry. Why? Because, one, I keep thinking about him, and, two, he'd be God's choice, not mine. I am not happy. However, I am being trained to be obedient to God. If He is telling me to marry Fred, I have to. I am supposed to tell the elders that I believe God is telling me to marry Fred. I do not want to marry him or tell them. I think I'll tell them Sunday morning after church. But I am going to be seeing them the next night at Bible study. If I am going to be obedient, the sooner the better. So, I say to Clara, Pastor Michael's wife, after the meeting: "Can I talk to you, please? I've been praying at Karen's urging, and I believe God wants me to marry Fred."

Clara purses her lips for a second and says, "Okay. Don't mention this to anyone else. I'll tell Michael and the rest of the elders. Don't do anything. Just wait on God and we'll see."

I nod. That was Wednesday night. Four days later, on Sunday morning, we find Emmanuel dead in his crib. So, besides being sick about the death, I am sick about the word from God. I suddenly feel sure I've made a mistake. I don't need a husband now, nor do I want one.

"Clara, I have a problem," I tell her the next time I see her. "It's about marrying Fred. I don't want or need a husband anymore. I just went along with it because I wanted Emmanuel to have a father. I don't want to marry Fred. I don't know if that was God or me. I'd like to retract it."

"Hmm. Well, as I said before, don't say anything to anyone, and let's just wait. If it's God, Fred will get your name. If he doesn't, it's not."

I nod, but I don't feel good about it. Emmanuel died March 5, 1989.

Sometime in the next six months, I have a horrible dream in which one of the elders is whispering my name in Fred's ear. It seems so real. One day in September, the phone rings.

"Hello?"

"Hi, Jacquie? This is Fred."

My body goes cold with instant nausea and anxiety. I am freaking out on the inside. I know what this call means.

"Hi, Fred."

"I was wondering if you'd like to go for dinner with me this Friday night."

"Uh, okay, I guess."

"Yes? Alright. That makes me very happy. I'll pick you up at 6:00 p.m."

"Okay. Bye."

I hang up the phone, and tears sting my eyes. Oh no, dear god, no. This can't be happening. I don't want to go. I run upstairs to tell Karen and April. They start squealing and clapping, jumping around.

"You guys, stop. I don't want to go. I'm scared."

"What do you mean?"

"I don't want to marry Fred. I don't need to. Emmanuel's gone. I think this is a mistake. Also, I had a dream that one of the elders hugely hinted to Fred to ask me."

Karen said, "No, Jac, that wouldn't happen."

"How do we know? The elders are the only ones with the names. It could happen."

"But then it wouldn't be God's will."

"Exactly. It isn't. It's a flawed system, people just choosing who they want."

"Just calm down. You're not committed yet. Just go on the date and relax."

But I can't. I feel sick from the moment Fred arrives in a borrowed convertible until he takes me home. We drive from Kitsilano to Queen Elizabeth Park, where we walk from the parking lot to the top of the hill. It is sunset. Fred looks into my eyes. "Jacquie, will you marry me?"

"Uh, I guess so."

He looks hurt. "Say yes."

"Yes, I guess so." He tears up. I am swallowing vomit.

"Let's go to dinner now."

We drive to Richmond to the Abercorn Inn. We are seated at a table for two.

"Fred, what made you choose this place?"

"I had a two-for-one coupon."

"Please excuse me."

I go to the bathroom and explode with tears and snot. Oh, God, I can't do this. I don't love poor Fred. I blot my patchy red face with toilet paper. I want to stay in there, but I know it is getting on, so I take a deep breath and go back to the table.

"Are you okay, Jacquie?"

"I guess so."

"All right then. Let's order."

Driving home, Fred reaches to take my hand, which I keep clasped in my lap.

"You don't seem too happy."

"I'm sorry, Fred. I'm just not sure about this."

"What do you mean?"

"Well, I submitted your name four days before Emmanuel died. I was going to submit it on the Sunday, but I forced myself to do it sooner. If I'd waited, I never would have told Clara. I don't need or want a husband, Fred. And this whole system scares me. I don't love you, and I don't know if I trust God to give me love for you after we're married. What if He doesn't?"

"God doesn't make mistakes, Jacquie. You just have to trust Him. Anyway, we're here."

Karen comes out onto the step. "Fred, come in."

We climb the stairs and enter the house. "Congratulations!" Karen says, giving each of us a big hug. April and Andrew are there. Everyone is smiling except me.

"You two sit on the love seat. I want to take your picture," Karen says. Then, "We've got some champagne. Come have a glass." Champagne? I am impressed, but I might as well have been drinking unsweetened grapefruit juice.

Soon Fred leaves, and the girls want a rundown of the details of the evening, which I give them. They soon have the cringe look clinging to them, too.

"You know what, Jac, God's in control. Just pray and leave it with Him to work out."

I try. Fred and I are allowed to hang out together alone now that we are engaged. He takes me to Spence Diamonds to choose a ring. I don't want a ring. They all look the same to me. I don't care. Every time I see Fred, he ends up feeling bad. I am miserable. I keep asking God for a sign one way or the other. I am at the beach begging Him one day and suddenly, seemingly out of nowhere, a huge rainbow fills the sky. Is that a yes? I'm still not ready to accept it.

For Christmas, Fred buys me a silver watch. I buy him a shirt and sweater from a consignment store. I am in anguish. Most of our church goes to a conference in San Antonio, Texas. I am able to go, thanks to gift money people gave when Emmanuel died. It is there I finally decide

I can't drag this on into the new year. I find a couple of scriptures to back up my decision. I tell Fred. I feel sick. He is devastated. What a fiasco.

Two years later, I marry a man named Boris. Unlike Fred, he had plenty of hair but was fairly heavy. Three weeks in, I wish I'd married Fred. In between Fred and Boris, I was engaged to a man named Harold I met at a Granville Street bus stop. We fooled around a bit, even though I was still living with Andrew and Karen, and April. I dragged Harold to church with me. He was Jewish but got saved and baptized at my insistence.

Despite that, I had some reservations. I don't know why I find it hard to trust men. When I called off the wedding four days before it happened, he was pissed off. His ex-girlfriend came to Vancouver from Winnipeg to make havoc of my life. They stalked me, made hang-up phone calls at all hours, slashed the tires on the van I drove at work, stole my mail, including the Bible my mom had carried in her wedding, and went through my garbage.

I've never wished I'd married Harold.

In one of my grieving sessions after Emmanuel died, I went into his room and sat on the big stuffed dog on the floor across from his crib.

"Oh God," I said aloud. "How can this be...allowed?"

"Why would You take back from me the gift that You had given me?"

"Why would you," He asked me then, "refuse the ones I tried to send?"

Ouch. Those words pierced my heart like an arrow, but in my mind's eye, I saw a hand grab the arrow and remove it before it could fully penetrate. I heard in my head "Your son didn't die for your sins. My Son did." Bam. Forgiveness.

I didn't have to live with the guilt of feeling like Emmanuel's death was a punishment for the abortions I'd had. After this experience, the dreams in which he kept dying over and over in different ways stopped. In one, he is holding my hand, walking beside me, and I look, and he has drowned in a puddle. Stop. It's not my fault. He just died.

Three days before Emmanuel died, I had a dream. I stood before a glowing figure I took to be Jesus, God, the Lord. I didn't see his face, but I knew who He was and quickly discovered that I could communicate with Him, not through speech but by thought. I was forming questions about all kinds of things, and I could perceive His thought answers. I asked a lot of questions that He answered to my satisfaction, or at least to my understanding. At the end of our exchange, I felt everything was okay because I understood.

Later, I thought perhaps God had kindly prepared me for the dreadful day He knew I would soon face. Even though upon waking I couldn't remember some of the details, the memory was vivid, and there was the feeling of an implied acceptance of my life. Of course, I missed my little guy. There'd be no more teaching him the alphabet, reading books warm and cozy after a bath, or picking blackberries in the lane. Emmanuel was an exceptionally beautiful child, and I'm not saying that because he was mine. His skin was a soft nut-brown, with curly brown hair; he had large brown eyes that glittered under arched brows and sparkling white chiclet teeth. He really was a gorgeous little boy. He loved to run through the house naked after his bath, squealing with delight.

The day before he died, we were praying. Emmanuel said, "Fava (Father), peese help me be bedent." As we humans are wont to do, we ascribe particular significance to things especially after someone dies. An almost two-year-old's prayer to be obedient could have been because I was trying to train him that way. Or it could have been an indication that he knew his destiny and was asking for strength to fulfill it, just like Jesus in the Garden of Gethsemane before his crucifixion. Yeah, okay, maybe mom was right when she said naming our child after God was a bit pretentious.

One thing that gave me great comfort was the thought that I'd have a two-year-old for eternity, if we both went to heaven and he didn't age there. Who knows, but I could hope.

Andrew and Karen were wonderful with driving me around to funeral homes and helping with the arrangements. I don't really know how it all came together. Dad and Bunnie, my stepmom, drove from Yahk to Vancouver. Thankfully, he didn't show up with a moose carcass to dispose of, like he did at my wedding years later. At least, that's how I remembered it. When I questioned him about the details, he told me he'd been the cook for some American hunters who had shot two bull moose and gave him four hindquarters, which he kept in icy cold water for a week before the wedding. He arrived in Vancouver with the hindquarters in the back of his truck. He butchered and wrapped the meat in our backyard, saving one large roast for the wedding dinner, which was apparently delicious. Unfortunately, the rest of the meat didn't freeze fast enough and went sour, and it had to be disposed of, along with the bones—a bit of an inconvenience in the city.

Mom flew in from the closest airport to Creston, which is Cranbrook. On the day of the memorial service, April was falling apart. Dad sat beside her with an arm around her shoulders, which is as much affection as he'd ever shown either of us. He said to me, "I'm proud of you."

I didn't want him to be proud of me. I wasn't crying because I was so numb and anxious simultaneously that my emotions were jammed. I noticed the little white casket at the front of the church didn't look like the one I'd chosen from the catalogue. It looked tacky.

I did cry as it was lowered into the ground, however. April and I stood clinging to each other, sobbing under an umbrella on that grim, grey day. It was one of the worst moments of my life, with many more worst moments to follow.

10

Becoming Wifey

Since I have no little boy to look after now, it's time to reenter the work force. I was a single welfare mom living in one of Vancouver's most affluent neighbourhoods when we lived with Karen, Andrew, and April. I get a job at a school-aged childcare centre and attend Langara College in the evenings to receive a ten-month certificate course in working with school-aged children, including being trained in first aid and getting a class-four driver's license.

One of the children that attends the summer program requires a nurse to clean her breathing machine occasionally. That's how I meet Vicky, the nurse. She is delighted when she finds out I am a Christian and invites me to her church. By this time, Maranatha, as well as Andrew and Karen's household, has disbanded. Some leaders from other churches were questioning some of the teachings of Maranatha, and it was suggested they were extreme enough to be considered cultish. You can get the full story online. Bob Weiner, the head of the ministry, continues to work under other banners now.

April and I have moved to southeast Vancouver to be close to my job, as I don't have a car. So, one Sunday morning—according to my journal I "wore my beret at a jaunty angle," gad—I go to Vicky's church. It is a nondenominational storefront church called Liberty Christian Fellowship, tucked in between a restaurant and a produce store.

I enter the room. There are about three people in the chairs and about five onstage. Where is everyone? I see Vicky and approach her.

"Oh, Jacquie, you came. This is wonderful. Come and meet everybody. This is Pastor Dan."

Pastor Dan is in his late fifties, I'd guess. His hair, thinning on top, is dyed black. This immediately makes me suspicious. What are you trying to hide, grey hair? Are you vain? What else do you try to hide? As he shakes my hand, I notice his hands are unusually soft, from lotion? Next, I meet his wife, Dani, mother of five grown children, who now looks permanently pregnant. There is a handsome young man in a suit and tie named David. This guy is a hunka hunka burnin' love. I am so overwhelmed at his handsomeness I am unable to speak to him directly for many months.

The service starts. Vicky, David, another girl, as well as Pastor Dan and Dani lead the worship. They're all strong singers. The music is good, familiar Christian choruses and worship songs. This is important to me; it's my favourite part of church. Pastor Dan plays guitar, and his wife Dani plays the piano. I used to sing in choirs at church and at school and love singing, but I'm never sure if my voice is all that good. My other favourite part of church is judging the backs of hairdos, of which there are few here. After the service, there is a fellowship time, with coffee, tea, and potluck food. As we are enjoying this, a heavy fellow, also in a suit but with no tie, begins to give his testimony, right there, to the few people sitting nearby: "Oh man, when I first felt the power of God, it nearly knocked me to the ground, yup. I was opening the bay door of my shop, and I saw this light, and, wham, it came right into me, and I fell backwards. I knew God had touched me. Right then He delivered me from my addiction to cocaine, yup. I cried in that shop every day for eight hours a day in repentance. And God started to turn my business around and prosper me, yup. Yes, He did, He certainly did. I started getting jobs left and right, and I didn't even have a phone!"

"Excuse me, but what do you do and what's your name?" I ask.

"Cabinets, I build cabinets, and my name's Boris."

"Okay, thanks. Sorry for the interruption. Go ahead."

"Yup, I was living in that shop then, too. I started going to church fourteen times a week, Catholic churches, other churches, prayer meetings. I didn't care where. And then God delivered me from cigarettes. This Christian girl I knew prayed for me, and I felt something on my tongue, and I knew I was delivered. I called my mom and said, Mom, guess what? I quit smoking. And she said, 'When was your last cigarette?' and I said, 'About an hour ago.' Ha ha, yup. God just started doing miracles, yup. And I moved out of that shop and into a bigger shop, and God brought me tools, and then He even brought me a wife."

"Is your wife here?"

"No, no, she died. She had cancer, but we believed God was going to heal her. She had it before I married her. Her name was Sarah. She was ten years older than me. I was twenty-nine; she was thirty-nine."

"I'm sorry. When did she die?"

"Six weeks ago."

"Oh, that recently. That's too bad."

"Well, I'm praying to God for another wife. He took her to heaven, and she's okay but what about me, God? When You gonna bring me another wife?"

At this, his eyes and hands are raised, imploring the Lord. Pastor Dan smiles and says, "Boris calls me every day asking when God's going to give him another wife. And I say, 'Soon, Boris, soon.'"

I know one thing for sure: I don't want to be his wife. I look around at the rest of the women. Slim pickings in the wife department, it seems to me. There is one lovely girl who comes to church with her also attractive mother. I can see Boris may have a bead on her, but she is not interested. He's dreaming, deluded if he thinks he has a chance. I've observed this throughout my life. If I am attracted to someone, they aren't attracted to me, and I'm not attracted to the people who are attracted to me. What is this annoying phenomenon? Why is it so hard to find someone who wants to find you?

I go to church the following week and hear more of Boris's story. He fills in details for me, as I keep asking him questions, such as "Where did you shower when you lived in your shop?"

"I had a little sink in the bathroom where I could wash a bit. Once a month, I rented a motel room." Yikes.

Then I say, "I lost someone, too. My son died about a year and a half ago."

"Oh, is that right? Yeah, it's hard, eh? I installed seven bathrooms the day after my wife died. Yup, just kept workin'."

That doesn't sound healthy to me. Poor guy. He doesn't seem to know how to grieve.

I continue to hang out with this ragtag little group of Christian soldiers, although I feel a sort of sadness that we aren't a more successful church. One Sunday after church and fellowship, Boris offers me a ride home. I usually take the bus and the Skytrain to get there, so I appreciate the offer. I climb into his mustard-coloured pickup truck, and we visit a bit outside the house I share with my sister, in his parked truck.

Life has gotten kind of boring. We live in the burbs, go to work, come home. My sister says: "What do you want for supper tonight, Jac? Cereal or popcorn?" I don't have any friends nearby, not any friends at all really, now that Maranatha's broken up. I attribute this boredom and loneliness to my next disastrous mistake.

I become Boris's wife six months after I meet him. For years, Boris calls me Wifey until I finally assert myself and say, "My name is Jacquie. I'd appreciate it if you'd call me that." So, he does, but he turns it into a joke where he says "Jaaaacquie." I suppose I should I appreciate that he is making an effort, but it also seems to minimize or belittle my request. I attend Sylvain's wedding in February 1991, and he attends mine in March a month later. We became reconnected as friends for a brief time. When Emmanuel died, I didn't have any way to contact Sylvain other than his last known welfare office, so I asked them to pass on the information and my contact information. He called me but didn't believe me at first when I told him Emmanuel had died. He thought it was a ruse to keep him away. So, I took him to the cemetery to see the grave marker. It had a metallic coating on it, and I let him scratch the picture of a bird on it with something sharp, but I can't recall what it was now. We cried together. Emmanuel's death felt like the end of a chapter in Sylvain's and my story. He drove me nuts as a partner, but he's a special individual whom I value as a friend.

After Boris's and my wedding ceremony, in a moment of typical frankness, Sylvain looks at Boris, then looks me in the eye, and says, "He's fat," as though this makes him unsuitable for marriage. I'm not really concerned with his body. I am more interested in the way he proudly strides around his little 1500-square-foot cabinet shop, showing me his saw, edge bander, spray booth, and 5T truck for delivering kitchens. Surely this business is meant to support a family. I want a little girl.

Ours is a homemade wedding in our storefront church. Then comes the wedding night. Boris's best man, his cousin Joe, leans over during dinner and says to me, "I don't know what plans you have for tonight, but I've heard the Sheraton on Canada Way is very nice, if I may suggest that." We haven't made any plans. I couldn't think that far. My nerves were shot just doing this cheap little shindig. I'd bought roses at Safeway and made corsages, but they were forgotten in the fridge because I was too overwhelmed to delegate responsibility to anyone for them. As I was driving to the airport to pick up my grandma, I screamed as loud as I ever have, making my own ears ring. It was temporarily cathartic.

We take Joe's suggestion after the ceremony and the mid-afternoon meal, which was partially prepared and donated by the congregation. One of the women from the church made and decorated a lovely cake with fresh roses on it. My Aunt Liz and a cousin had flown in from Calgary and helped my mom cook moose roast and a ham or turkey or something. Honestly, I don't remember many details or when it all took place. What I remember is the way I felt. As though low-grade electricity had replaced my blood or like the little Dutch boy with his finger in the dyke. Oh, no, that might be how Boris felt. Or like there was a ticking time bomb strapped to my chest that would detonate if I stopped smiling, and my cheeks were getting tired. Also, I was very thankful for the thirty or so guests, including friends and relatives that came, and I kept telling them so. By now, my mom and dad were both remarried, but they came without their spouses and I was glad they were able to set aside their differences, although it was probably pretty hard for my mom. I think my dad will always love her in his own way. When it was over and time to leave, we went to the Sheraton. As he did for our wedding rings at a jewellery store in a mall, Boris begins to barter for the honeymoon suite. It's been hours since we've eaten, and I'm hungry.

"Are you hungry? Can we have dinner here?" I never have to twist Boris's arm to eat. I feel a bit conspicuous in the dining room in my white wedding dress, even though it is cocktail length and nonrefundable—bought for my called-off wedding to Harold.

After a delicious meal of medium-rare prime rib, baked potatoes with butter, sour cream and green onions, and tender-crisp carrots and green beans, we go to the room. It's lovely, two floors with a spiral staircase to the bedroom.

"Oh, what a waste of this beautiful downstairs. We should invite everybody over," I say, although, of course, that isn't going to happen. But my thriftiness is inherited from my mother, and I can't avoid the thought.

We ascend the stairs to the bedroom. I am nervous. Boris and I have managed to wed with no premarital sex, with each other, that is, except for a blow job I gave him on Valentine's Day. (Speaking of blow job, my whole adult life I've wondered why it's called a blow job because it's a suck job. But I finally discovered the answer in a book I read, historical fiction, I think it was, and originally it was "below job," as in below the belt.)

There is a round jet tub in the bathroom.

"Oh look, let's have a bubble bath," I exclaim. I leave Boris in the bathroom to run it while I open the complimentary champagne and down a shot. A nice touch. We're going to need this. I am wearing a backless dress with crotchless pantyhose. I undress alone in the bedroom, champagne glass close at hand. This is weird. Doesn't he care about seeing me undress? I wore this pantyhose for him. Naked, I grab the bottle and glasses and go to the bathroom. When I return, Boris is under the bubbles. I slide in and pour us each a glass of champagne.

"Cheers!" Clink, drink.

I would have to say anxiety was the prevailing mood throughout the preparation and ceremony of this wedding. Now, the warm water churns around me, the foam tickles my neck, the champagne bubbles in my belly, and I am still nervous.

The first time Boris and I kissed, a peck, really, he told me I had bad breath. "Sarah always had bad breath because she was sick," he said.

We haven't kissed since. I don't know what to expect or what to hope for. I hope we'll emerge from our bath warm and fragrant and slip between cool, clean sheets. His arm will be under my neck. I'll lie sideways, my hand on his chest, hopefully his hand on mine, my leg draped across his. He'll gaze into my eyes and say, "Jacquie, I can't tell you what it means to me to be here like this with you now. You are so beautiful. I love you so much, and I'm so thankful God brought you into my life." Or some such thing.

What happens is that I hog the champagne, without experiencing any of its relaxing effects.

"Do you think we could order another bottle of champagne from room service?" I ask.

"Well, I guess so, but just this one time."

This is similar to his thriftiness coming into play after he put our bartered wedding rings on my credit card.

I've had my second glass from the second bottle by the time we're dried off. He goes to the bed and gets in the left side. Then he says, "Sit on my face." Clang, clonk, quash.

Oh my gosh, really? What? Did he just say that? Is this how we're starting our sex life? Don't get me wrong. I don't have a problem with oral sex. It's just the bluntness, the awkward timing. I can perceive that he is trying to please me with this command and that he thinks this is the ultimate for my pleasure, and this is why he's offering it, particularly knowing how clean I am. But my insides shrivel, and I want to cry.

What about foreplay or is that what we did be*fore* we got married? Even though we really didn't. Nobody ever talks about their wedding night. I suppose because it's a sacred time between the newlyweds. Therefore, I don't know if my horror story is common or not. My next book will be on that subject. Send me your stories. Change your name.

All I know is that any sexual desire I may have had cannot be buoyed up by all the champagne bubbles in the world. Now I'm just drunk and sad and deeply disappointed. "You know what? I'm exhausted. Do you mind if we just go to sleep? Let's try this again tomorrow." Maybe I gave him a blow job, I don't remember. Probably.

The picture that someone takes of us the next day speaks volumes. I look totally hungover—eyes half mast, skin blotchy. My gorgeous hair from the day before is a limp echo of its former beauty. I am wearing the pleated dress pants Boris bought me because he didn't like my clothes. They make me look like I stuffed a ham in my pants. My collar is crooked. Aunt Liz is in the picture, smiling broadly. She cleaned out Boris's camper so that it would be ready for our honeymoon.

Ah yes, the honeymoon. Driving, driving, driving, for Boris, sleeping, sleeping, sleeping for me.

"It would be nice if you'd stay awake and talk to me, yup."

"Sorry. I'll try, but driving makes me sleepy."

We are travelling to Anaheim, California, to see Disneyland. I have a rash on my face and have seen a naturopath about it. He recommends a special diet that eliminates all the foods I usually eat, including cereal and popcorn, for a diet that is mostly vegetables and carbohydrates or vegetables and protein but never carbs and protein together. Oh, and no sugar or alcohol. Great. I give it a try while Boris keeps on eating whatever he wants, every couple of hours. It is annoying.

We finally arrive in California to discover the song is wrong. It does rain in California. We park the camper in a Target parking lot, and I assess the situation. Okay, I can't eat. I can't drink. And we can't go to Disneyland. What else could go wrong? And then I feel it—that warm surge between my legs that means I can no longer have sex. Boris's late wife Sarah's cancer was ovarian, and she bled a lot. I've had sex with my period before, but it's messy. I don't think Boris and I are up for it. If our honeymoon is an indicator of our marriage, it is going to be rough.

Upon returning home to Vancouver after ten days and nights, specifically to Burnaby, where we've rented an apartment, I soon realize I am still bored. Boris comes home from the shop and lies on the couch all night, every night. I take him snacks and drinks. He can talk at great length on two subjects: God and his business. He isn't interested in having sex with me much. He masturbates beside me every morning and enjoys the blow jobs I give him regularly. We never use birth control other than the rhythm method of me knowing when I'm most fertile and avoiding sex then. One night a couple of months after we're married, I mount him and get pregnant. I want a little girl for company.

I don't recall whether we discussed a possible pregnancy that night. I'm not sure he really wanted children. He wanted me to work for him in the cabinet business, which I did for ten years, without and with children. When he found out I was pregnant, I think he was happy to tell his parents but maybe not thrilled overall. I don't recall him having sex with me while I was pregnant.

Nine months later, just as we are going to bed one night, my water breaks. Off we go to Royal Columbian Hospital, where our little girl arrives about eight hours later. She is nameless for three weeks while we debate possibilities. In one brainstorming session, our friend Vicky, the nurse who takes credit for matchmaking us, suggests Shiloh. The name sticks with me, and I do some research. In the Bible, Shiloh is the name of the city where the Israelites keep the ark of the covenant, which represents God's presence. So, Shiloh is where the presence of God dwells. Her middle name, Delight, comes from the joy she brings me as I gaze on her perfect self, in particular her adorable little ears, in her bassinette in the hospital.

Shiloh's first challenge in life is her health. She has eczema, an itchy skin rash, all over her body. She spends her first birthday in the hospital with an asthma attack. I think Boris changes one diaper in her first year so I can't say he never did. I do pretty much everything for Shiloh. He goes to work and comes home tired. He gives me money to run the household, and I spend it as frugally as possible.

After a year, Boris moves his shop to a bigger shop in Coquitlam. He wants my help to pick up material for his kitchen and bathroom cabinet jobs. We pay the bills together once a month. I soon find myself parroting my mother when my dad ran his travelling seafood business: "I hate debt!"

Two-year-old Shiloh stops me dead in my tracks the day she leans against the fridge and says, "Mom, stop it. You're making me drive crazy!" Oh dear. How many times have I told her she is driving me crazy? Too many. It isn't her fault. I just can't cope with all the things that are expected of me. Shiloh's poor health, asthma, eczema and food allergies have us running from one doctor to another in search of cures. We are prescribed special diets whose efficacy is hard to see. I can't seem to maintain any kind of order in terms of medications and restrictions. It is all too much.

She is cranky, and I am cranky. And worst of all I'm not getting laid, even though I followed the rules and married a Christian man. He has no interest in sex. Mutual sex, that is. He'll take all the blow jobs he can get and is enraptured by the exquisite sight of squirt on my face. But in twelve years, he kisses me about three times. I cry myself to sleep almost every night for the first year of our marriage.

"Boris, I think we should see a counsellor," I say.

"What for?"

"You know what for. We don't have regular sex."

"I don't have a problem. Why do you want to talk to a stranger about our personal business? Everything's fine. We don't need to go."

"It's not fine. It's not normal. I want to talk to someone."

"You shouldn't go against what your husband says. I'm the head of the house. God made it that way."

"Well then, will you at least agree we'll read the sex book that you and Sarah had?"

"Sure."

I should have got him to agree to read it more than once for a few minutes before bed. He tells me he and Sarah didn't have sex because her cancer was ovarian, and she bled a lot. I bet she could still give blow jobs, though.

I get a certain amount of pleasure from making sure my partner is satisfied. But there's a limit. After several years, I have to see a chiropractor for my sore neck. I've had enough. We sometimes have sex together, but it has become relegated to the status of a bargaining tool. Too bad, because according to the Bible, there's no sex in heaven.

Eventually, as we drift away somewhat from God and the church and look for stress relief in other places, we do a bit of roleplay and watch some porn, only it is usually what he likes, which is Asian girls getting cum shots, and I think we both felt a bit guilty. Overall, I think he's selfish, and I tell him so.

We have only two children, using no birth control, only the withdrawal and the rhythm method, carefully avoiding sex during my most fertile time of the month. Both times, I get pregnant deliberately and conceive on my first attempt.

11

Cracks in the Cradle

For years, we host a weekly home-group meeting at our house. A homegroup is a designated group of Christians from a church who meet in a home or homes on a weekly basis to encourage, support, and pray for one another. The leaders of ours are a couple called Tim and Tam. They have two daughters, a few years older than Shiloh, who is almost two and a half. I am eight months pregnant. Their daughters, Morgan and Madison, hatch a plan to have a sleepover at our house one night after homegroup.

Tim and Tam and the rest of the group leave. Boris goes straight to bed. I tidy up the dishes, letting the girls play for a few more minutes. "Okay, girls, time for bed," I say. "Morgan and Madison, you'll sleep in the guest room here. Come on, Shiloh, bedtime."

Morgan says, "Aww, but Mrs. Johnston, if Shiloh doesn't sleep with us it's not really a sleepover." Grrr. I knew this was not a good idea.

"Well, I don't think she'll go to sleep in your bed."

"Please let us try it, please, pretty please."

My heart sinks as I prepare for this disaster. It's late, and Shiloh's overexcited. "Well, we can try it. But Shiloh, listen to Mommy, if you don't go right to sleep nicely, you have to go to your crib."

"Yay. Thank you, Mrs. Johnston."

"Uh huh. Okay, everybody into bed now, quietly. Mr. Johnston is sleeping. I'll pray. Father, thank you that Morgan and Madison could sleep over. Please give us all a good rest, in Jesus's name, amen."

I turn off the light and am almost at the end of the hall when I hear Morgan saying, "Mrs. Johnston, Shiloh is bothering us." Fuck, although I didn't use to swear then like I do now. I tried to keep my mind clean. That is the feeling, though. I spin on the carpet and shoot back to the guest room.

"Shh, please." Shiloh is jumping over their heads on the pillows.

"Okay, Shiloh, that's it. I'm sorry, but you have to sleep in your crib now. I warned you. Let's go." I grab her with difficulty, and she starts to wail.

"Shh, be quiet, Daddy's sleeping. We don't want to wake him up. Shh, please be quiet."

She continues to wail, wriggling and squirming to show her discontent with my decision. I drop her gently into her crib. "Quiet, honey, please stop crying."

The more I beg, the harder she yells in rebellious defiance. Then I hear it. Our bedroom door opens, and Boris appears in his underwear. I step out of the way as he grabs Shiloh, flips her, and gives her diaper a few good swats. Then he disappears, snapping the light switch down on his way out. She goes into shock, whimpering and hyperventilating in the corner of her crib. The bars create shadows from the light in the hallway. Her face is blotchy red, wet with tears and snot.

I stand looking at her, horrified for a moment, then walk out to the living room and sit on the green couch, pulling my legs up under me. I am in shock, too. Oh God, I whisper into the dark room, I'm sorry. My tears are suddenly flowing. I'm sorry for poor little Shiloh. Jesus, please comfort her right now with your Holy Spirit. Please let her feel your peace. Please help her understand and learn from this. And please forgive me for causing this to happen by not saying no in the first place. Why is it so hard for me to say it? Oh God, I pray Shiloh won't experience any permanent damage from this. Please forgive us for not being good parents. Eventually, she calms down and falls asleep while I am in the living room, praying.

I feel overwhelmed by hopelessness. I feel I can do nothing but damage the innocent souls given to me. Oh God, why on earth would You give me another child when I don't know how to take care of the one I have? I'm a bad mother. I tell my daughter she drives me crazy. I can't maintain routines. I can't stand up to Boris. I'm a horrible mother. If it's Your will, please take this unborn child from me so I don't screw up another life. Or take my life and kill two birds with one stone. By this time, I'm crouched on the beige carpet sobbing. I want to die.

I sense a shadow pass over me, and I look up. It's Boris in his underwear again. "What are you doing? Come to bed."

"I'm praying."

"It's bedtime."

"Boris, I feel sick about that spanking you gave Shiloh. She's only two and a half. She was totally freaked out."

"Don't be silly. Come to bed now."

"I'm not ready. I'll come soon."

"Well, hurry up."

I feel surprised and happy that he leaves. It makes me feel better. I bask in that feeling for a few minutes. I get a Kleenex, wipe my face, blow my nose, sigh, and go to bed.

The next day we have breakfast, and I have an errand to run before I drive Morgan and Madison home. It's about 11:30 a.m. when I pull up in front of their house. Tam opens the front door, smiling and waving. I open the car doors to let her girls out, and they go running to her.

"Aren't you coming in?" she calls.

"I wasn't planning on it," I yell back.

"Come in for a bit," she says.

I release Shiloh from her car seat, and she holds my hand as we enter the house. The kids play quietly around us as Tam says, "So how was the sleepover?"

"Don't ask. It was dreadful. The girls wanted Shiloh to sleep with them, but she was goofing around. So, I put her in her crib, and she screamed so loud she woke Boris up, so he gave her a spanking, and I felt horrible about it. What am I doing having another child? I felt suicidal last night."

"What? Are you kidding? That's terrible. We need to pray about that. Why don't you stay for lunch and we'll pray after?"

"I dunno. I didn't bring Shiloh's diaper bag or anything. I was just going to do a quick drop off and go home."

As if on cue, Shiloh says, "Mama, I have a poopy diaper." I groan.

"Are you sure?" Stupid question, as kids know.

"Come to Mama, let me see." She squeezes in between the couch and the coffee table, backing toward me. I pull the stretchy waistband of her diaper to reveal it is full of peanut-butter poop, the smell of which makes me turn my head away instinctively.

"Oh, no, Tam, it's full. We have to go."

"I was just going to make some grilled sandwiches. It won't take long."

"I can't leave her in that diaper. She's bound to get a rash."

"Oh, hey, you know what, I may have some of Morgan and Madison's old cloth diapers downstairs. Let me check." She reappears a few minutes later with a few diapers in her hand.

"Look, I do." She lays one out on the carpet.

"Now if I can remember how to fold it."

"Try this, Mommy." Tam's daughter takes over with the cloth.

"Tam, you don't know Shiloh like I know Shiloh. She doesn't take well to new things. I highly doubt if she'll let me put that on her, even if we can figure out how."

Tam and I continue to chat, and soon we find ourselves in the kitchen making grilled sandwiches as planned. After lunch, Shiloh goes with the girls to their room to play.

"Let's pray," Tam says.

Just then, the ice cream truck comes by. We hand the girls some money and run to Tam's room, sitting side by side on the floor with our backs against the bed. Tam is a serious Christian. She wasn't raised with religion like I was. As we start to talk to the Lord, we pour our hearts out about the difficulties of parenting and asking forgiveness for our shortcomings.

I have been to lots of meetings where the leader says, "Oh, the presence of the Lord is here. Can you feel it?" But I never feel it. Boris sits in his recliner every morning with his Bible open in his lap, eyes closed, palms ups, saying, "I feel the presence of the Lord ever so rich." Again, I never feel anything, but maybe that's because I am too busy making his scrambled eggs and toast.

But this particular day as we humble ourselves, I feel something. I feel like God is there hearing our prayers.

When the girls finally knock on the door and us out of our reverie, it is late afternoon. Crap. I still have to drive home in rush hour and have dinner on the table at five o'clock when Boris gets home. Tam pulls a casserole from her freezer and says, "Throw that in the oven."

I give her a hug. "Thanks, Tam. I really needed this. Thanks, girls, for watching Shiloh all day. See you soon."

Shiloh is cranky, having missed her nap. I get her into the car seat and drive. When I pull into the carport, she is sleeping. I think guiltily of that filthy diaper she's been in all day, but I hate to wake her. It will be so much easier getting dinner on the table if I don't have to deal with her. I leave the windows open in the car and prop the back door open so I can hear her if she calls and go about getting dinner ready.

When I am done, I go back out to the car and undo her car seat. "Come on, honey, out we go. We're home. Let's go change your diaper." I take her to the guest room near the bathroom where I keep her changing station. I put her down and undo her diaper. I am dreading what I am about to find. Gingerly I pull the front of the diaper down and gasp. The poop is gone. Gone, I tell you. Completely and totally gone. No shit. Her bottom is fine, not red, no rash. I can hardly believe it, except I saw and smelled it earlier. I run to the phone and call Tam, leaving a breathless message on her answering machine.

I finish the diaper change, tearing up with the realization of how much God cares for my little girl. Even if I am a terrible mother, He will protect her. Obviously, He can remove the worst mess we can make. This incident becomes an anchor, a marker in my walk with God. As an aside, it makes me realize why God doesn't do many miracles: They're just too hard for people to believe and create more doubt than faith.

There are many, many times I cling to the memory of that miracle. It keeps me from giving up entirely on the dark days ahead.

I am in the parking lot of a local wholesale building supply company in Burnaby when Shiloh is still a baby. Winter rain falls on me as a young employee and I load four-by-eight sheets of melamine into the back of Boris's pickup truck. Shiloh is in her car seat up front, crying her head off.

I say to my work partner, "How do you like your job?" At that moment, I hate mine. I decide to get pregnant, so I can stay home with my children. So, I do.

"Shiloh, we're going to have a baby, so you have to go pee and pooh in the toilet now. The baby will have to wear diapers. We can only have one kid in diapers at a time."

I buy a training potty and some nonallergenic treats, and we get to work. I have to give her the bulk of the credit. She is trained by the time Keziah comes along.

Keziah, pronounced kee'-zee-uh, is another Biblical name. We have somehow likened Boris to Job, although Boris has only lost a wife. Job lost everything but his wife, who suggested he curse God and die. Maybe it is because Boris is a bit of a sad sack and feels like Job. I don't know. But after Job loses all his children, flocks, and fields, God restores his family and gives him three daughters: Jemimah, Keziah, and Keren-happuch (which was a close second choice). According to the Bible, Job's daughters were very fair and had favour in the land along with their brothers. Keziah can also mean "a pleasing fragrance" and someone who makes other people happy.

I think Shiloh and Keziah both exemplify their names. Shiloh is a devout little Christian. She prays the sinner's prayer with Keyz when Keyz is about two. Shiloh is also concerned about her Grandma Johnston's eternal destination. She grows up to write and illustrate a children's book about the gospel to take to India to give to children there and to work in her church as a youth leader. Keyz is a spa unto herself. She wears perfume and lotions and potions, always smelling wonderful, with incredibly soft skin.

They are two and a half years apart. Shiloh loves her little baby sister. I remember clearly putting Keyz in the Jolly Jumper, much to her delight while I make dinner and Shiloh crouches beside her, smiling and cooing, saying, "I love my baby."

I do get a reprieve from most of my responsibilities at our cabinet shop now that I have two children to look after, but some days I'm not sure I've traded up. Every mother knows the drudgery and isolation of caring for young children. In general, though, I am happy with my little family. Except when I'm not.

One morning, Boris and I have a fight about something before he leaves for work. I feel my back is up against a wall, and it is either change, die, or flee. After he leaves, I run back to bed and bawl. Two-year-old Shiloh follows me into our bedroom. Through tears I say, "Oh, Shiloh, what should I do?"

She dispenses her first bit of child wisdom when she looks me in the eyes and says, "Obey God." I am startled. How can this tiny person show such grown up responsibility at such an early age?

Soon enough, Boris wants me back at the shop. He creates a playroom, meaning he dumps a bunch of toys on the floor in an empty room and closes the door, so I can work with him. I feel guilty but assuage it by thinking of all the immigrant kids that grew up in corner stores. Still, I don't like leaving them unsupervised. In *Uncle Arthur's Bedtime Stories*, a large book of morality tales that used to be found in our dentist's reception area, a lack of supervision almost always led to disaster when it came to children. When the girls start Christian school, I have to pick

them up, hit McDonald's, and then go back to work. I always tried not
to go back and to instead go home and make supper, but the truth is my
kids ate a lot of McDonald's growing up. I wondered later if it contributed
to Shiloh's Crohn's disease that was discovered when she was sixteen
years old and in high school.

> Journal entry, October 17, 1997:
>
> These are the times in his conscious mind
> that my husband fears and dreads
>
> These times alone in the bowels of the morn
> when I really should be in bed
>
> asleep, and still, the tongue is dead
> with no more arguments to form
>
> Instead, I'm awake my stance to take
> in the light of the coming dawn.

Boris is in his usual position in his recliner when I return from putting the girls to bed. "We have to do something about the girls'
bedroom," I say. "Keziah's four years old and still sleeping in a crib.
There's barely enough room to walk between the crib and Shiloh's bed.
I can't take it anymore. This house is too small!"

Even though we live in a three-bedroom house, we had taken Shiloh's
baby room and made it into an office, so Boris could work at home as
well as at the shop. I want to move, after seven years of paying off
Stephen Chu's mortgage. I've never liked this house. We took it in
desperation when Boris's negotiating tactics on another house and the
limits of our income left us with little choice. The living room has wood
panelling and yellow gold drapes. It is old and ugly.

To my surprise, Boris says, "Okay, let's move."

"Really? I'll grab the paper and see what's for rent."

Boris calls, "Shiloh, Keziah, come here." Seconds later, they appear
in their pajamas.

"Let's pray as a family that God will give us a new house."

So, we hold hands and Boris prays, "Father, we ask you to give us a
new house and we thank you in Jesus's name. Amen. Okay, back to bed.
Run."

I open the local paper and start circling ads.

"Ooh, listen to this one. Four bedrooms, two full baths, jet tub, gas fireplace, large kitchen, fenced yard. 1,075 dollars. No smokers or pets. That sounds good."

"Call. Ask them if we can go see it tonight. Right now."

"Okay, hang on." Surprisingly, the landlords agree to show us the place as soon as we can get over there. I run downstairs and ask the tenant, who rents the basement suite, if she'll watch the girls until we get back.

Twenty minutes later, we are in front of the house. It is beautiful, fairly new, on a cul-de-sac, and in a neighbourhood with a playground in south Port Coquitlam. Boris rings the doorbell. The current tenants answer the door and let us in. On the main floor is a bedroom, perfect for the office, and a storage closet, coat closet, and hallway to the garage.

Upstairs there is a living/dining room with a gas fireplace, a big, beautiful kitchen, and a family room with gas fireplace and a patio door that leads to a private backyard. The house has high ceilings and crown moulding throughout. There are two decent-sized bedrooms, a full bath with skylight, and a sixteen by twenty master bedroom with walk-in closet and a full en suite, including a jet tub. Boris is saying, "Yup, it's nice, yup," trying to keep a poker face. The landlady comes and says, "What do you think?"

We simultaneously say, "We'll take it." I pull out my chequebook. We are home within an hour of our family prayer. We move the following month and live there for seven years. Every day of those years, I was thankful for that house.

After unpacking, we have fun decorating the house and building dressers, entertainment units, and a U-shaped office desk. We buy a big-screen TV and home theatre system. I am proud of our new home. It is a sanctuary, pleasing to the senses. I host my writing group here, church homegroups, family dinners, and my fortieth birthday party. It's a happy home for a family prone to depression.

Once we're settled, Boris strives toward his dream of having a production shop, selling cabinets wholesale, and acquiring large expensive pieces of machinery and equipment. His mom and dad give us fifty thousand dollars when his grandma dies for a down payment on a house. But Boris buys a sixty-eight-thousand-dollar saw instead and later a seventy-eight-thousand-dollar dowel inserter. Before we had Shiloh, Boris believed God told him he was going to have a son made of metal. I never really understood what that meant—born with braces on his teeth and/or legs? Boris thought it meant he'd be strong. We'd chosen possible names of Steele or Sterling. Everyone gave us baby gifts in blue. But we had two little girls. We decide the prophecy was fulfilled when Boris purchased a 105,000 dollar CNC machine called Rover (by the manufacturer), to cut, bore and drill panels according to specifications entered in the fridge-sized computer. I realized that Boris himself was Rover's Data (Dada). The overhead climbs, eventually reaching twenty-three thousand dollars a month, as does the demand for more money and time. He moves the business into a ten-thousand-square-foot shop. This takes a toll. Money we could use for family living is being spent to retool and set up. Plus, he keeps rearranging things.

Our upwardly mobile ascent reaches its zenith but then begins to unravel. Boris has suffered from depression throughout our marriage, but his mental condition reaches a crisis when he starts calling me from the shop several times a day in tears. He is melting down. I send him to see a doctor, a fellow Christian, who prescribes him antidepressants.

Boris experiences a seemingly miraculous recovery, but the doctor keeps increasing his dose. He starts smoking cigarettes again. He soon is talking about building million-dollar yachts instead of cabinets, and he drags us out to marinas to look at boats.

What is going on? My best guess now is that he was overmedicated into a manic state. He starts making poorer and poorer decisions.

After ten years of working with Boris, I say no to him, "I don't mind working, Boris, but I don't want to work with you anymore. It's too much. I spend all day every day and all night with you. I need a break. Normal businesses hire people if they need help. Hire someone."

In retrospect, I think that's what set him adrift, unsettled him. That's when he started smoking cigarettes again and stopped consulting me about large purchases for the business. I start smoking with him a bit, too. For my part, taking care of all our stuff— the house, yard, and van as well as the cooking, cleaning, laundry, and helping at the church and Christian school, not to mention providing Boris with more and more taxing emotional support—wears me out. I feel burned out.

I seek relief in acting and join a community theatre group. What a delicious escape— fun, cool people, teamwork, and parties with alcohol. My favourite remedy. Boris isn't much of a drinker. One of the moms from the Christian school works at a u-brew, and I make a batch of wine.

Boris may have a glass with dinner, but inevitably by the end of the evening, I've finished the bottle.

We usually go on a vacation once or twice a year, and I drink wine then or maybe a cocktail or two, piña coladas, or Caesars, or margaritas. In my memory, we drank little if at all for the first ten years or so, but now I'm remembering some date nights where we'd have one or two drinks. It was a treat. I am only allowed out of the house two nights a week, in which Boris is too tired to get out of his leather Lazyboy to tuck the girls in bed, so I have to do it before I leave the house. The more I am away from my family, the less I want to go back. Everything and everybody at home bugs me.

"You know, Jacquie, what you're doing is not right. No, it isn't. The drinking, being away from your family. The Lord's not pleased."

I can't remember what I said back to Boris. I know that I am cutting loose, and I don't care. This is self-preservation. One day, Boris calls me at home. "Why don't you come and have lunch with me today?"

"I'm sorry, I can't. I have to go meet Caroline who just moved out of the suite downstairs and get her share of the hydro bill. It's already arranged."

"Oh, that's too bad."

"Why, what do you want?"

"No, nothing. I just want to have lunch with my wife, but she's too busy."

"Well, yeah, I am. I want to get that money. Another time, okay?"

"Yeah, if you're too busy..."

That evening, I put dinner on the table at 5:00 p.m. as usual. "Your dad's late tonight, girls. Let's eat."

When Keziah pushes her feet against the base of the glass table, I ask her to stop, or it will break.

"Keziah, stop pushing your feet on that glass. It'll break."

While furnishing the house, Boris wanted a shiny black lacquer dining table. We were looking in the Buy & Sell and found an all-glass table. The glass top sits on four legs also made of glass. The table's hard to describe but basically the entire top and base is glass with a couple of hinge connectors. We buy it. Then he finds a black lacquer one he really wants, so the all-glass table with pencil back metal chairs becomes the kitchen table. Stupid, totally impractical. We have school-aged children and a glass table. Come on. Every time those chairs tip, I grow horns.

I beg Boris to find a buyer for it so we can replace it with something practical. I end up buying a large plastic tablecloth to save cleaning, but I can't stop Keyz from pushing against it.

When Boris isn't home by 6:00 p.m., I call the shop. No answer. Must be on his way. I am somewhat distracted wondering where he is.

"Where's Daddy?"

"I don't know. He'll be here."

I put the girls to bed and call the shop again. No answer. I am beginning to worry. What if he had an accident at the shop and couldn't get to the phone? What if he was sitting in his truck having a smoke and had a heart attack? What should I do? I dial the RCMP.

"Hello, this is nonemergency, but I'm wondering if it would be possible to have someone go by our business. My husband hasn't come home. It's extremely out of character."

I give them the address. They call me back shortly. "No, Ma'am, the door is locked. There's no vehicle of the description you gave us."

"Okay, thank you so much for checking. I really appreciate it."

Where could he be? Where would he go? He doesn't have any friends. What on earth would he be doing? What if he's dead? He's not. He could be. What would I do? From out of nowhere a thought comes to me. What if he's doing drugs? I would pack my stuff in the van and drive away. Oh God, please protect him. Please bring him home.

I stand at the living room window, watching the lights of every vehicle that turns onto our street. I feel panicked and calm at the same time. I check the clock. Those batteries must be almost dead. Where is he? And then, at 1:30 a.m., the phone rings, startling me.

"Hello?"

"Hi, Jacquie."

"Boris, where are you? I've been going crazy. I was so worried about you. Where are you?"

"I'm downtown."

"Downtown? Why? Doing what?"

"Okay, just listen for a second, okay? I'm sorry. I messed up. I need you to come and pick me up."

"What?! What are you talking about? What do you mean, messed up? What happened? What do you mean me pick you up? Where's your truck?"

"It got stolen."

"Stolen? How? When? What's going on?"

"I'll tell you about it later. Just please come and get me."

"Are you crazy? The girls are sound asleep in bed. Take a cab."

"Yeah, all right then. See you soon."

"This better be good or I'm going to kill you. I've been worried all night. Hurry up and get here."

An hour later, he comes in the house and heads for the Lazyboy. I assume my position on the black leather couch to his right.

"All right, start talking."

"Okay, so I went to North Van to pick up a cheque from a customer. On my way back, I was driving through downtown and I saw this girl, and I stopped to ask her where I could get some cocaine."

"Why?"

"Just listen. So, she said she had some rock. That's what they call it now. She asked if I wanted to smoke some, so we went to this room, like a motel room, but there was no sex or nothing like that."

"Yeah, right." But knowing Boris, I more or less believe him.

"No, we just smoked this crack, and there was another girl there. And I went to go the bathroom because I had these pasty things in the corner of my mouth. And when I came back, the girls were gone. They must have taken my keys out of my pocket when I was in the bathroom."

"Oh my gosh. Unbelievable. So, while I am sick with worry, you are doing drugs with hookers who steal your truck."

"Yeah, I'm sorry. I messed up. Please forgive me, Jacquie. I'll never do that again." He is teary.

"You got that right. But the fact that you did it tonight concerns me. It's hard to believe. Something's wrong, and we need to fix it."

"No, no, nothing's wrong. I learned my lesson. I'm never touching that stuff again."

When Boris reports his truck stolen at the police station, he tells them he was with the hookers for sex because he doesn't want them to know about the drugs. The next day, we go to ICBC, the provincial government vehicle insurance office, and he repeats that story to the nice man who is going to give us a loaner vehicle. I sit beside my husband, smiling and nodding.

The ICBC guy seems suspicious. "You're okay with this?"

"Well, we're Christians. Forgiving is what we do."

"Okay, sign here, and here's the keys."

"Thank you, bye now." I can see him shaking his inside head.

We drive the loaner truck downtown to the area Boris was in the night before. With his extra set of keys, I hold my arm out the window as he drives and press the remote honker. Sure enough, we find it in Drake's Towing yard.

It costs eighty-six dollars. As much as the taxi cost. This is turning out to be an expensive blunder. I don't ask how much he spent on crack. Because the truck has been reported stolen, it's supposed to be checked by the police before it is released. As usual, Boris puts on his nicety-nice duh-yuh charm and cons his way out of it. He doesn't want the cops to find crack crumbs and fingerprints or anything incriminating, so he gets in his truck and I follow him home in the loaner. We agree he's received a lot of grace.

The following Friday, Shiloh's friend Ellie is over, and the girls are in the family room watching TV after supper. Boris is late again, not a good sign. The front door suddenly bursts open and he bounds his three-hundred-pound frame up the stairs, heading straight for our bedroom. "Come here," he says.

I follow him into the bedroom and close the door behind me. He has a bottle of red wine in one hand and a large bag in the other. What's going on? First of all, if he's buying me wine, he's buying me.

"What's in the bag?"

"Here, this is for you." He sets the wine on the dresser. "And these are for you." He pulls a large box out of the bag and opens it. He is sweaty, agitated. The box contains a pair of black leather thigh high boots on five-inch heels, with a lace up on the back at the top. "Put them on. Put them on."

"What the hell? What's going on? Why are you sweating? What... Oh my god. You went downtown again, didn't you? I hate you. You lying, fucking piece of shit. So now you're high and you want me to be your hooker. Fuck you. Get away from me." I start pushing him out the door, lean on it, and lock it.

"Jacquie, come on, please. Don't do this. Come on. Please. Let me talk to you. Open the door."

"No, I'm not. You can talk to me under the door."

"Come on, Jacquie. Open the door. Talk to me."

"I don't want to talk to you. I don't know who you are. What the hell are you doing? This hurts me."

"I'm sorry. I know but I just wanted us to have some fun together."

"Sucking your dick in high-heeled boots isn't fun for me."

I stand up from my sitting position by the door and go to see if the wine has a screw top. Excellent. I crack it and have a glug. I have to make a plan. I don't want to spend the evening locked in the bedroom, nice as it is. I have another glug and call Neil, my gay friend who directed a couple of plays I'd been in. "Hey, Neil, what are you doing?"

"I'm at the space." This is the community theatre rehearsal space where he works when he's preparing shows.

"Are you? Great. Can I come and talk to you?"

"Sure, see you soon."

I go to the room where the set for the play currently in rehearsal is located. This is at the Riverview Hospital, a group of buildings that formerly housed patients with mental health issues. One of the empty rooms that is off the same hallway as the theatre rooms has a door that's always open a few inches and has an ice cold draft coming from it. It makes the hair on the back of my neck stand up every time I walk by. Also, the building is believed to be haunted. I've seen lights on in upstairs empty rooms more than once. Scary as hell. The buildings and grounds are a popular movie location. One time in the winter, I drove up to see a bunch of caribou fenced in on the side of the building where we met. Turned out they were filming *Elf*. I find Neil in a corner, at the director's table.

"Hey, Beautiful, what's up?"

"My husband's doing crack. What should I do?"

He nods, as though familiar with the situation. "You tell him he has to go to rehab, and you can resume your relationship when he's been clean a year."

"Really? That's a long time. What if he doesn't want to go?"

"You have to set boundaries. Be firm. Tell him he has to."

During this chat, while I give him the details, Neil and I are enjoying our usual glass of wine from his supply. He makes his own and usually has copious amounts in his trunk. I thank him and go back home.

Boris is in his chair watching TV. I go and sit beside him. "Okay, listen. You have to go to rehab. When you've been clean a year, we can resume our relationship."

"Don't be silly, Jacquie. I don't need rehab. I'm done with that stuff."

"Yeah, that's what you said last week. Bor, this is serious. You need to get some help. I'll support you, but we have to work on it together. We'll get the homegroup to pray for you."

"No, no, no, don't go telling people, especially not them."

"You know what? This has to come out in the open. It has to be exposed to the light."

So, I tell the homegroup and get a referral from one of the members for counselling. The night of our first appointment, Boris is late again.

I call the counsellor. "I don't think he's going to show."

"Well, that's okay. But I think you should come anyway."

"Really? Okay, see you shortly."

I am angry. We are doing this for him, and he doesn't even show up. I tell the girls, who are about eight and ten, where I'm going to meet some people for counselling and that their dad will hopefully be home soon. I realize they're young to be left alone, but I have a cell phone, and I tell them not to answer the door. I get in the van and open the garage door with the remote before starting the engine.

Boris is standing in the driveway. He comes and gets in the passenger side. He is rushed, sweating.

"Oh, you made it, just barely. I was going without you. Seems like a good strategy to go to your counselling appointment high, I guess, eh? Yeah, that really makes sense. Like everything else you're doing lately."

"Come on, Jacquie, okay. Just relax. I'm here. I'm going."

We get onto the highway to Abbotsford. I turn on the radio so I can seethe with rhythm. Boris is fiddling in his seat. I look over and he has pulled a little clear glass tube and a lighter from his pocket. He takes a puff and says, "Wow."

I lose it. I start screaming and swearing, hurling curse words like hailstones. My yelling gives me a sore throat, nothing more. We get to our appointment, and I like the intake guy immediately when he says, "People can only take so much, Boris."

That was Boris's only appointment with a counsellor, but I go back for nine more sessions. We try a Christ-based twelve-step program at our church, but he bails, and I continue with that, too. I am amazed that I struggle with pretty much all the dozen or so issues in the workbook people had tried to overcome. Choosing just one to work on is difficult, but I choose low self-esteem because I can see what a crippling effect that has on my life. The unconscious belief that I am unworthy is the root of my boundary problems. I don't think I have the right to say "no." I always feel that the other person's feelings are more important than my own and that I am less than.

Once, my typing teacher in high school, who was usually one of the nicest guys ever, snapped. He completely lost it on me because I'd forgotten to bring typing paper again. His anger terrified me. He sent me down the hall toward the principal's office, yelling several steps behind me, "Who do you think you are?"

I puzzled over his question for years. I guess he was implying that I thought I was someone special—someone who could charm her way through life, borrowing from others more responsible—and that I assumed the world owed me this privilege, whereas in truth, at the time, I was just basically a bit scattered and forgetful. I meant to get paper, but the only time I thought about it was when I needed it, like replacing an old toothbrush. He missed the mark, but as I said, he did get me to think, which is a teacher's job.

After three months of trying and being lied to constantly, I can't take any more. As far as I know, Boris has only been using for this long, but maybe he's been doing it for much longer and hiding it. I'm suddenly remembering a customer of ours who was into coke. Maybe Boris started chipping away then. I'm not sure when he first used cocaine before I met him. He told me he smoked ten joints of marijuana a day for ten years. I know he was smoking and selling pot in high school, giving an otherwise unsociable person some status among his customers. I also found out after we were married that he left Vancouver Island on the floor of the back seat of his sister's car because he was skipping town due to drug debts to some heavy dealers. He was very paranoid when I first knew him, checking the lock on the shop door repeatedly, and that was a few years later.

Some friends and I stage an intervention, before it was called that, letting Boris know that if he chooses not to accept our help, he'll have to leave the house. We wrangle over the details of the contract for four hours. Finally, he signs it. Our friends leave, we go to bed. When I get up in the morning, he isn't there.

He comes stumbling up the steps just before 7:00 a.m. I open the door and say, "Give me your keys, please."

"Oh, come on, Jacquie, not now. I have to go to work."

"Give me your keys."

"Stop it. I can't deal with this now. Come on."

"Boris, last night you agreed that if you continued using, you would leave the house."

"You guys all ganged up on me. What was I supposed to do?"

"What am I supposed to do? Stand at the window for three days when you tell me you're going outside for a cigarette? Worry about your dealer coming by to shoot at the house because you stiffed him? I can't. You're breaking my heart. I can't, and I won't live like this anymore."

"I have to go now. We'll talk about it later."

I follow him to work and sit across from him at his desk and say, "Give me your keys" until he does, although not until I've insisted for a few hours. By then I'm exhausted, but at least I have the keys.

I'm remembering a Sunday morning a couple of months before the intervention. The girls and I are in our usual scramble to get ready for church, only today more so than usual because it is the Christmas concert, and we have to go early. We are all in a dance with the other kids that is going to snake through the sanctuary. We have simple costumes to wear—belted robes and towels tied with rope for head coverings like Biblical shepherds.

"Okay, have we got everything? Shiloh, did you take your puffer? Good. Okay, let's get in the van."

"Where's Dad?" Errch. Time stops. Boris did not come home last night. I am tired of covering for him and angry that he is missing our performance. I am sad, too, that my little girls are going to have to know the truth and that their lives will be shattered as mine is.

"Girls, come here, listen to me. I'm sorry to have to tell you this, but your dad has a drug problem."

"What are drugs, Mom?" asks Keziah.

"Drugs are things people use to help them feel better when they're not feeling good, like medicine only not from a doctor."

Shiloh wants to know what kind of drugs.

"Your dad's using something called cocaine. He goes out to do drugs, sometimes all night. I don't know where he is, but we're just going to carry on, okay?"

"Is he ever coming back?"

"Of course, he is. This is his home. I just don't know when, and I'm sorry he's missing your show. Just pray for him."

Did I actually say that? Did I pull a Myra Morton on them? That's my mom's name, and once in awhile, I find myself behaving like she would have done, even though it's not what I want to do. One time when I was a kid, she gathered us kids together and made us pray for our dad because his drinking was out of control. I was annoyed. I thought he should be praying for us. I'm not sure. I don't remember, but it's possible I did something like that with my kids in this moment, just like she did.

In fact, I'm realizing now I was repeating the pattern my parents played out when I was growing up and it makes me sad. For some reason, I thought I'd avoid that by marrying a Christian man, but Christians are human the same as everyone else, and cycles repeat themselves.

"Okay, let's go now. I don't want to be late. It makes me nervous. Come on."

We go to church and do our show. I am a wiseman, dressed in a comical wig and beard and funny glasses, leading the hands-free conga line and inventing silly movements for the kids to follow at certain points in the music. It is supposed to be fun, and I can hear the congregation laughing, but there is a tangle of emotions in me, giving me a sour stomach.

I am hiding inside a costume, and inside me, I am hiding the sickening knowledge that our family ship is going down, Titanic-ing, surrounded by all these nice church people, who are mostly hiding their own problems, too.

Looking back, I realize how the difficult things I faced in my life became the learning ground for some necessary self-improvement. As previously mentioned, discovering how to set boundaries when I was married to Boris became a game changer for me. Self-esteem is related to boundaries because in order to set boundaries, you have to believe you deserve to have your feelings respected and protected. Eventually, I came to recognize the damage low self-esteem was causing in my life and realized I could change the way I thought of myself: I was worthy of making self-saving decisions. One day, my sister said to me after I'd told her a few of the crazy things I was going through with Boris that "Once an addict, always an addict." That gave me the impetus I needed at that point to resign from the company, to stop taking responsibility for problems and debts I didn't cause, and to begin the complicated process of emotionally separating from Boris.

The counsellor Boris and I saw together in Abbotsford that one time gave me an audiotape about codependence. I listened to that tape repeatedly during the time I was making these changes in my life. A male voice on the tape told the story of a man who was walking. He was happy, satisfied, living a good life, and excited for his future. He came to a bridge, on which another man was approaching him, with a rope tied around his waist and coiled over his shoulder. The man with the rope stopped on the bridge and said "hello" to the other man, who returned the greeting. Then the man with the rope said, "Would you mind holding this end of the rope please?"

The other man didn't really want to because he was on his way somewhere, but he thought it would be rude to refuse so he took it, whereupon the other man jumped off the bridge, almost taking the other guy with him. But the rope holder managed to hang on to the rope and stay on the bridge deck. "What did you do that for?" he yelled at the guy dangling at the end of the rope.

The man replied, "Please don't drop me."

The other man said, "I can't stand here all day. I have things to do."

"But if you let go of the rope, I'll die."

"But I can't hold it forever. My arms are getting tired."

"You'll be responsible for my death if you let go."

"I'll tell you what. I will stand here and hold the rope while you climb up it."

"I can't. It's too hard."

"Well, then, I'm going to tie the end of the rope to the bridge railing and be on my way. It's up to you whether or not to climb up."

And the man resumed his journey.

That story helped me immensely to realize it was okay to let go of Boris and that my own life was important. That counsellor recommended I buy some books about anger, work on replacing "I should" with "I would like to" and wanted me to do ABC [actual event, belief, consequence] analysis on my feelings every day. In the twelve-step group at our church I attended while separating from Boris, I worked hard on my low self-esteem issues. One particularly difficult week, I lost my shit during our meeting, ranting, raging, yelling, and crying. People were kind and gave me hugs and verbal encouragement as well as flowers, a card, and some money the following week. It was a group setting, and the woman leading it liked to talk. I often wished she'd allow more time for sharing from the participants, as I wanted and needed to unload most weeks, but she was a volunteer doing her best, and you can learn from listening, too.

When Boris returns from his forays into the underbelly of society, he sleeps excessively to make up for the nights he's lost. He sleeps through the homegroup Christmas party at our house. "Long nap," I keep saying, when people ask where he is. He finally crawls out to the kitchen after everybody leaves to scrounge for some food and that's when I realize why he's always so tired. The drugs keep him going and going until he finally crashes.

As I'm reading a journal from that time, I notice how many times I had to say no to him during that turbulent time. After he left the house, he kept trying to get back into it, or see the kids at crazy times, or have them sleep over, or get me to do his laundry, or cook him food. I realized that even though it was a painful time, there was little about him that I missed, and I believed God had better things ahead for me. I was ready for a change.

I decided I'd be better off without him if he wasn't willing to work on his addiction, and our friends helped me confront him.

"Girls, your dad is no longer going to be living with us."

"What? Why? Where is he going?" Shiloh asks.

"He's going to live at the shop. It's too hard for me to live with his drug problem and he won't get help."

"Will we still see him?"

"Yes, I'm sure you will. He loves you very much."

Boris's mom, Eileen, comes to town for a visit. She is aware I've asked him to leave the house. "Kicked him out" is his version and therefore probably hers too, but she is a good person and tries to keep the peace.

"Would you like me to take you over to see him?" I ask. She doesn't drive.

"Oh, yes please. That would be real nice."

We all get in the van and drive to the shop. "I don't know if he'll be here, but we'll take a chance."

I unlock the main door, and we go to the office he has put our bed in and knock. When no one answers, I open the door. He is slumped in a chair in the corner of the small room, sleeping.

"Boris, wake up. Your mom's here."

"Huh?" He startles awake, groggily. He blinks his eyes, which I see are mucky with greenish goo. His half-open eyes roll around in his head as he mumbles and fades in and out. It is shocking. I shouldn't have brought the girls. It's hard for all of us to see. We don't stay long. Eileen doesn't say much—raised in the school of thought that if you can't say something nice, don't say anything at all—and we don't discuss Boris's condition on the drive home, turning the conversation to more pleasant things. I've always gotten along well with her, perhaps partly for that reason. She's never spoken to me of Boris's drug use in the past, but I wish she'd said something about it before we got married or even during the ceremony when the pastor asked if anyone knew just cause that we should not be joined in holy matrimony. But that's hindsight seen through lenses tinted with regret.

At this point she doesn't appear to be blaming me. But blood is thicker than water, and as the years roll on, we don't maintain contact for a time because I'm not as good about keeping my mouth shut as she is and Boris believes my making him leave the house makes his addiction worse and tells her so along with some other things he thinks about me. She is the one who bridges the gap five or so years later by sending me a get well card when I have my breakdown, and we maintain contact casually until she dies.

A few months later, the phone rings at home late at night. "Hello?"

"Is this Mrs. Jacquelyn Johnston?"

"Yes."

"I'm Dr. Albright. I'm calling from RCH emergency department. Is Boris Johnston your husband?"

"Well, we're separated but, technically, yes."

Is this the call I've been waiting for, telling me that he's dead? How many times do you say "Fuck off and die" before it works? This is basically what I've been saying in my head for a long time now. He's tried to get back in the house countless times and has been difficult in wanting to see the girls.

"We have your husband here. He was brought in by police. A city bus driver called them because he was slurring and incoherent. We've determined he's had a cerebral hemorrhage."

"He's a crackhead. Sounds like he's finally blown his brains out."

"He needs to have surgery, as his condition is life threatening. We need your consent."

"I'd rather not give it. Could you ask his mother?"

"Well, the spouse is preferred."

"What if I say no?"

"As I've explained, the situation is life threatening."

I pause. Can I live with Boris's death on my conscience? No matter how angry I am at his betrayal, abandonment, and rejection, no matter how much I hate him for destroying our family and leaving me with all the responsibility, and no matter how many times I've wished him dead, I can't live with knowing I could've prevented his death but didn't. He is still the girls' father.

"All right, go ahead."

"Thank you. Goodnight."

A couple of days later, Boris's cousin Joe comes to pick up the girls to take them to visit their dad in the hospital. I refuse to go.

Apparently, when they work on his brain, they remove the gloomy, depressed loner Eeyore gene, and he has a shiny new sociable personality. Lo and behold, he's found his Tigger gene. He talks to everyone he meets, Forrest-Gump-like. He quits doing crack and goes back to his ultrareligious life. He meets a woman named Paula, a psycho Barbie gold digger who becomes his puppet master, who helps him fill out court documents to battle over custody of and access to the children.

I am in a highly agitated state of mind by this time, a walking powder keg. I can't afford a lawyer. Boris sweet talks some poor woman he meets in a mall to represent him pro bono. He's a good con, top of the class, a veritable idiot at everything except building cabinets and manipulation. And I don't qualify for legal aid, for some reason I've forgotten. I have no job, no income, no money. Everything we made went back into the shop. My mom is paying my rent. He and Psycho are taking me to court to get custody of the girls. He has no clue he is going to end up paying child support.

As anguished as my soul is, I do derive a little satisfaction at playing the role of legal beagle, drawing on the years of crime TV drama shows I watched while Boris held the remote. Call me Mary Mason. A guy I go out with after Boris and I split up tells me randomly about a phrase lawyers use in court: "May I suggest?" It's strange what minutiae lodges in your brain only to resurface much later like a popcorn hull in your teeth.

"You may question the witness," the judge says to me.

I stand and approach the podium. Paula, aka Psycho Barbie, sits nervously on the stand, with her long, blonde, and overprocessed hair bugging the shit out of me.

"State your name for the record, please."

She leans towards the microphone. "Paula Sicobicz."

I begin. "Can you please tell the court what your relationship is to the applicant, Boris Johnston?"

"Well, I help him and advise him about his problems."

"You called me at home and told me you are a counsellor. Is that correct?"

"Well, Boris wanted me to talk to you about your relationship with him."

"Are you a counsellor? Do you have training in that field?"

"I went to school."

"Where?"

"Ontario."

"And what was your course of study?"

She shrinks a little. "Business."

"All right. So, we have established that you took a business course. *May I suggest* that, in fact, you are not a trained counsellor, nor do you demonstrate any particular qualifications to dispense information or advice on the subject of relationships. *May I further suggest* that, in fact, your association with Mr. Johnston is purely for financial gain. And *may I also suggest* that you do something about that awful hair of yours. No further questions. I rest my case."

The whole court thing was horrendous, emotional, time consuming, and frustrating. A court date was set. We (Boris, Paula, his lawyer, and I) appeared before a judge who got the basic story from us, which was that Boris was a crack addict according to me, and I was an alcoholic, according to him. Paula didn't look at me, and I tried to give her the evil eye. Boris ignored me too, but we were both highly aware of each other's presence in the court room. Then another date was set, and we appeared before a different judge and did it all again. But with a third judge, I lost my shit and talked loud enough to be just this side of the border of contempt of court: "This is ridiculous. We've gone over the same facts multiple times. This place is like a walk in clinic when we need a doctor that knows the history." Thankfully, that day the judge was a woman, and she seized our case, meaning we would deal with her only from then on.

One day, the judge asked if the girls had any pets. I said, "No, not anymore. Keziah had a hamster, but it died, and I've been too overwhelmed to have the funeral for it she requested so it's in a Ziploc bag in the door of the freezer for now. I keep thinking it's a chicken breast." She smiled. It was the only smile I saw from anyone in court in those many, many months.

At one point before the female judge seized our case, Boris and Psycho Barbie sought an interim order for access to the girls. I can't cope with my kids, my ex and his crazy woman, and my crazy alcoholic, crack-using boyfriend Curt, so I ask my mom if the girls can stay with her.

"Sure they can, Jacquie. You just do what you need to do." Which is get drunk and stoned every day and try to deal with the frustrating insanity of fighting over our children. Thanks, Mom. I drive the girls the five hundred miles to Creston in September 2005, just as school is starting. I feel sick and scared and guilty and relieved, very relieved. As I drive across the flats on my way out of town, I start praying in tongues, something I haven't done for years, praying for my children, crying as I drive, begging God to take care of them. Praying in tongues is praying in a sound language that makes you feel like you're speaking directly with God on a level that's deeper than words. It makes me calm down a bit. Then I turn up the music and listen to Stevie Ray Vaughan wail the blues and chain smoke for the twelve-hour trip home.

Shortly after I get home, we have an appearance at court. Boris whines to the judge that he can't get a hold of the girls. The judge gives me a stern warning that I am not to deprive him of access before the case is settled. Fuck. Fuck, fuck, fuck, fuck, fuck. That fat asshole just ruined his daughters' best chance for a decent life. So, Mom brings the girls home on the bus. And I carry on with my oh-so-shabby job of caring for them. They have food, clothing, and shelter, but I'm distant emotionally. I am unable to recover from my feelings of betrayal, of abandonment, and of being used by Boris, who is tormenting me with this court bullshit.

It seems to take forever to accomplish anything, but we finally wrestle through to an agreement in which we have joint custody and joint guardianship. The girls will live with me and spend alternate weekends with Boris once he has suitable accommodation. Plus, he has phone calls and email access as well as two nonconsecutive weeks in the summer. There is plenty of room to add access if we agree on it. He is only allowed access if he is in a clean and sober state. I insist on the right to demand drug testing if I am concerned. I also reserve the right to appoint a guardian other than Boris should something happen to me. It is an unusual stipulation for which his lawyer doesn't understand the need.

"Why is that important to you?" she asked.

"Because I feel like I'm going to die."

Boris called my cell phone forty-three times one week and left lengthy messages, which I had to pay for, about how God's judgment was going to come down on me. He often sounded psychotic even in court, referring to himself in the third person, as the father. I transcribed many of his calls to use as evidence in court, but they were never listened to. To me he sounded crazy, talking about how I was in the darkness and about how I was a disobedient and rebellious wife whom he wouldn't divorce but who needed God to burn some stuff off of. I felt tormented by him. He'd been raised to expect submission and service from a wife and wasn't prepared, as with many men of his generation, for the changes that occurred as women tried to reestablish boundaries and ideals and work toward a fairer balance of power.

In retrospect, he was a desperate man who'd already lost a lot and feared losing his children, who'd suddenly become far more valuable in light of the circumstances. I understood his fear when he and Psycho Barbie had the girls and didn't return them at the agreed time and didn't answer my calls for a few days. Sheer terror would describe it better than simple fear.

I didn't think I'd survive if I didn't find some way to release all the horrible feelings of anger, blame, rejection, abandonment, and hatred that I felt toward Boris. I'd been told that we don't forgive for the other person; we forgive to release ourselves. I spent most of a day in bed crying, looking at the baby pictures of Boris and me in the little family display in my room. The only way I could let go was to look at that cute little boy, who was given up for adoption, who was raised by a harsh father and a mother who couldn't stand up to him, and who never meant to hurt us. In that picture, he was innocent. It was to him I whispered through my tears: I forgive you.

Here is an example of the kinds of messages he was leaving on my voice mail:

Hey Jacquie, I'm just not willing to pass my kids over to the darkness, okay. You know you've chosen to go that route. You've chosen to be disobedient to your husband. You did it your way.

You paid your price for it, but you're not taking the kids into darkness. And what I see on Keyz right now and what I hear, you know, coming just, you know what? I'm going to break that darkness over those kids, and I'm going to pull them back into the light like they have never seen before. You can wander off into the darkness though. It's not about you; it's about the kids. I mean, I love you, too, but you're a little bit too damn rebellious for me anymore the way you are. You've always been rebellious. You've always been blaming. You've always twisted. You've always done your stuff. But I don't deal with that stuff no more. And no, I won't divorce you. Maybe one day you'll come to the end of yourself and maybe we can talk. But you ain't coming in easy. I'm sorry to say that. You've got some stuff to deal with. You're going, we're going, the Lord's going to burn some of that stuff off you because you can't walk in the way you're at right now. I would not even want to be around you right now 'cause all you've done is put me down and badge me to the ground and I've never done that to you. So, who's a Christian and who's not? We know that, and we see that, and that's your choices. The kids aren't going with it. You got it right? Okay, let you go. Bye.

He lied about his income and was ordered to pay 239 dollars a month for child support and fifty dollars a month for spousal support. Whoopee. He was also supposed to contribute 56 per cent of all extraordinary expenses, including but not limited to school fees, based on my supplied receipts and other documentation. He refused. It wasn't worth the fight. And that's the thing about court. You wrangle out an agreement that soon becomes meaningless because most rules get broken in the course of living life. He paid child and spousal support for a few years and then quit. The BC Family Maintenance Enforcement Project (FMEP) was supposed to ensure mandated support payments were made. At least they kept track of any lapses and consequences, such as loss of driver's license and inability to leave the country, could result. However, when his mother passed away, I made a claim on his inheritance for the amount owing, through FMEP, and he had to pay up in a lump sum. I felt awful, mind you, when his sister said FMEP had called her, the executrix, the day after the funeral, which Boris asked me not to attend.

By the time the money came in (it was about fourteen thousand dollars), I was on disability and not allowed to have more than five thousand dollars in assets, so I split the rest between the girls. Life is strange. I'm still getting my fifty bucks a month spousal, though I'd be willing to give it up so I wouldn't have to see Boris. (He likes to pay me cash, but we've made an agreement that he pays me annually instead of monthly so that we don't have to meet so often). The thing is that the annual payment doesn't benefit me because it comes off my disability cheque. But neither of us has the wherewithal to go back to court to terminate the order.

One day as I am pulling into my garage, after dropping off the girls at school, I remember that I have to decide whether or not to keep a watch I've bought myself for Christmas, which is my last credit card purchase before I declare bankruptcy and is possibly my last good Christmas present for a long time. I have it in the van for possible return. I decide to have another look at it. I take the box from the bag and admire the silver bow on the blue box. I lift the lid to see the silver watch resting on a grey velvet pillow. As I adjust the angle of the box to see the face, the overhead garage light reveals something I haven't noticed before. The face of the watch is black, but under the light, there is a pattern of diamonds embossed on the surface.

In that moment, I understand a message. I don't know how to explain it. Simply, I'd say I heard a voice inside me say, "On the face of things, this time seems very dark. But there are diamonds hidden underneath." Shortly after, I see a jewelry store flyer that has a picture of a woman who looks remarkably like a younger version of me. She is admiring a diamond on her finger, with a caption that says, "What you've always wanted." I keep that picture on my fridge for many years; in fact, I still have it to remind me that good things will come out of the dark times. And they have—diagnosis of bipolar disorder and medication, solitude, self-actualization, good relationships with my children, and employment enjoyment, to name a few. Fast forward. The other day I realized I have a diamond pattern decorating the little empty nest apartment I live in now, quite literally. Somehow, subconsciously, I have purchased and been given furniture items with diamond patterns in them, right down to a Kleenex box. I find it quite remarkable, now that I see it.

I kept the watch and wore it for years until a battery change couldn't keep it alive. I declared bankruptcy. Before the business crashed completely, Boris had two people working in the office and three guys in the shop. My mother bought a kitchen from him that miraculously arrived in Creston complete. She told me to get our minivan put in my name (which involved a high speed chase downtown after an uncooperative Boris), made the last few payments on the loan and insured it for me until I got on my feet. I have to say her generosity kept me alive sometimes, particularly in this instance. With everything else I lost and everything I went through to keep the little I had, not having a vehicle would have been the tipping point. And when the van was done, she gave me her five-year-old car, a black Chevrolet Impala with forty-eight thousand kilometres on it. I could always depend on the Bank of Mom.

12

Bye Bye Birdie

I met Robyn at a church in New Westminster that Boris and I attended for a few years when Shiloh was a toddler. Robyn—a lovely, petite blonde, and single mother of teen daughters who didn't attend church with her—was assigned to our meeting group, a gathering of eight or so people who met weekly to encourage each other in our Christian walks and our praying. The group was led by Tim and Tam, and it became a core of more or less regulars, including Boris and me, for about five years. It was comprised of couples and singles, ranging in ages from twenties to forties. I'm not sure who decided how the groups should be organized; church leadership, I guess.

In retrospect, I think the pastor was abusive in the way the church members were pressured to give financially and verbally chastised if they didn't. Boris was always attracted to churches that preached prosperity. He gave generously, believing it would come back to him multiplied many times over—a case of a manipulator being manipulated, in my view. He gave a TV evangelist ten thousand dollars for his wife's healing. She died, but there was no refund. I wasn't comfortable with the pastor from our first visit on, but my vote didn't count.

Robyn had been married to a pastor, and they had a small church in Saskatchewan. She was trained as a schoolteacher. They had twin daughters and adopted a third. Then her husband was diagnosed with a brain tumour.

Robyn and her husband took a sabbatical after a difficult three-year period involving a church split. They went to the States to a place reputed to help people recover from burnout. That place's belief system was "word faith," otherwise known as "name it and claim it" or "blab it and grab it." Basically, it was a movement within Protestant Christianity, which was based on prosperity and the idea that God wants us all to be rich, healed, and successful. According to the idea, God's work was already done, Jesus had secured it all for us by His obedience on the cross, and now it was our job to individually appropriate these things for ourselves by confessing the word of God and claiming what we wanted or needed. Similar ideology is present in the popular teachings of The Secret and other new age philosophies.

When Robyn asked for prayer for her sick husband, she was told she just needed to believe he was already healed. When he died under her care—the horrendous details of which included watching him hemorrhaging blood—they blamed her for not having had enough faith. Such is the twisted nature of what some people think is faith. She sold their house and moved her three daughters and herself to British Columbia to be closer to her dad, who was going to help her out but who got a cancer diagnosis and died within days of her arrival.

She got a teaching job at a Christian school, which was run by villains who underpaid her, promising a raise the following year. By the following year, she had married a man, Ervin, from the congregation, out of a sense of obligation to a prophetic word, which is the technical term for a message from God, so to speak, given by someone in the church. She was then told that because she was married, she didn't need a raise. The guy had an anger problem, and she didn't love him. Her elderly mother came to stay with them. One evening she was out grocery shopping, and Ervin was at home with the girls. She came home just as a police car and an ambulance were arriving. Neighbours had heard yelling and crying and called 911.

Ervin was in a rage, screaming and out of control. The two girls were asking him to please stop yelling and didn't he care that Grandma was dying. He grabbed one daughter by her hair, to pull her back into the kitchen. Robyn's elderly mother had stepped in to stop the fight and got shoved as well. She slipped in her sock feet, fell, and suffered a broken hip bone. Her daughters were terrified as their grandma looked as if she was dying, and, in fact, she did nearly die, when her blood pressure dropped very low due to pain and shock.

The police told Robyn that she could press charges against Ervin, but she didn't, at the time. She took the girls away for two days to calm them down, and then she told Ervin he had to pack some clothes and find somewhere else to stay until he got some counselling. This happened in March, 1994. It took this incident for her to come to her senses and begin to recover from denial. They remained separated after that.

Later, her mom had a stroke at the kitchen table, and Robyn's daily routine included a care trip to the hospital, until her mom passed away a few months later. She had separated from her husband and changed jobs to become an office manager for a small carpet company in Surrey. Her boss there, Harold, was an alcoholic. She spent years agonizing over her second marriage and eventually acquired a hard-won annulment. Her teenage daughters were rebellious, and one was showing signs of mental illness.

Robyn and I become prayer partners, and she shared many of these personal things with me only, not the whole homegroup, as she knew how judgmental Christians can be. Her house needed a new roof and other repairs, but she was only earning ten dollars an hour and was trying to save money to help with her children's postsecondary education, so she couldn't afford house repairs. Her situation was unbelievably depressing.

I was still with Boris at this time and had my own troubles to deal with. But, thankfully, my mom and dad were both still alive, divorced and remarried, living thirty miles apart in the Kootenays, in Creston and Yahk, enjoying their lives. Mom came out to Vancouver to visit us once a year or so, while her health allowed. I could always count on her to help me out financially for special needs. I realize, listening to her story, that Robyn is much more alone than I am.

I help however I can, listening, praying, giving. She then changes churches to one closer to where she lives, and I don't see or hear from her so much anymore. She joins a singles walking group and has been seeing a nice guy for a while, but is vague when I asked about a possible permanent connection. Some time passes, and my own life as I'd known it begins to unravel. My godly husband of twelve years has started to use crack, and we are going to lose our cabinet business. Soon we will separate and embark on the turbulent legal experience of custody and guardianship of our children.

In 2002, I call Robyn to pray for me. When I dial her number, a male voice answers the phone. "Hello, I'm not sure I have the right number. Is Robyn there?"

"This is the right number. I'm her husband, Russ. Who's calling?"

"My name's Jacquie. I'm a friend of hers, although I haven't talked to her in a while. So she did get married. Congratulations. She told me about you."

"Yes, well, she told me about you too. We couldn't find your number. Robyn's not here right now. She's in a care facility. She has brain cancer."

"What?! How can that be? What happened?"

"Well, she was actually having symptoms for some time."

"Yeah, the last time I talked to her she had self-diagnosed ADD."

"Yes, and she had extreme fatigue and other things. We got married on November 3 and went to Victoria for our honeymoon. She wasn't feeling well there, had a severe headache, and was slurring her words. We returned home early, and she had a brain scan, which showed three large tumours, nine days after our wedding. They removed one to do a biopsy, but they can't get the others. It's just a matter of time."

"Oh my gosh. How much time?"

"Typically, with this type of cancer, about eight months or so. She'll just continue to lose functioning until she reaches a full coma, and that's it."

"Oh, I'm so sorry, Russ. I can't believe it. It's so awful. Can I go see her?"

"Yes, I'm sure she'd like that. She wanted to contact you."

I get the address, it's in Cloverdale, and stop in after my counselling appointment in Abbotsford. This is the same counsellor that Boris and I went to see when he smoked crack on the way and never went back. It's basically talk therapy. I make my appointments to coincide with the girls being at school. At this point, I'm still living in the happy house in Port Coquitlam, a suburb of Vancouver, British Columbia. I'm driving about an hour each way for subsidized counselling, at a church recommended by someone in our homegroup.

When I enter the building, the odour of old bodies accosts me. I ask for Robyn at the reception desk. I am told she is in the dining room. I round the corner and scan the room of aged and ravaged bodies. How can my lovely, healthy, petite, blonde fifty-two-year-old friend be among these damaged human relics? And then I see her, a white wrap covering her scarred, patchy scalp, her pretty face now swollen almost unrecognizable by the steroid drugs. I approach her with trepidation.

"Hi Robyn. It's Jacquie. Do you remember me?"

"Of course. I couldn't find your number."

"How are they treating you here, okay?" She nods, maintaining eye contact and a smile.

"I talked to Russ. He seems like a really nice guy. I'm so happy you found him."

She is wearing a bib and has to use a walker when we go to the music class across the hall. All the participants are given hand bells, and a young man calls out and points to their notes on a flip chart. Oh, dear god. I am in kindergarten again on the dark side of the moon.

On the inside, I want to run out screaming, "No, no, this can't be happening," but I have to remain calm and cheerful for her sake. When the visit is over, mainly because I can't take any more, I give her a hug and then go and sit in my van and turn on the ignition. But I can't see past the sudden blur to drive, so I turn off the van, put my arms over my head on the steering wheel, and bawl. I don't care who hears me. I can't help it. For fifteen minutes, the emotional torrent rages. What the fuck is going on? If God wants to pull someone out of the game, why wouldn't He take a sinner like me instead of someone like her?

Or is that the deal? The best students graduate first. This earth in all its splendour is just a dank piss tank compared to the coming glory. That's what the Bible tells us. But why so much suffering? Why is that necessary? The questions swoop in my head like squalling seabirds.

Exactly as predicted, Robyn's condition continues to deteriorate. One day when I am on my way to visit her, my ten-year-old daughter Keziah calls me on my cell phone. "Mom, where are you? Can you come home?"

"I'm just going to see Robyn. Why, what's the problem?"

"There's a bird in our house, and I'm scared."

Of course, she shouldn't be home alone, but sometimes there's no other choice in a stretched household like ours. We do keep in touch on the phone, in case anything happens.

"What? What kind of bird? Where is it?"

"I dunno, a small bird. He's in the fireplace."

"Okay, don't worry, Keyz, I'll be right there. Just stay away from it."

I turn around and quickly head home. When I get there, I put on a pair of gardening gloves, open the small living room window and screen as wide as I can, and approach the fireplace. Sure enough, the little bird is flapping around in there, and we are equally nervous in each other's presence. I part the mesh fireplace curtain and try to grab him gently, but he flaps and flies, and I scream and jump back. He lands on the metal curtain. Slowly, I get my hand in position over him, but instead of flying, he keeps crawling away, until he's inched himself into the very corner of the curtain, upside down, with his head cocked to one side. There is nowhere else for him to go.

Carefully I cup my hands around him and I can feel the rapid beat of his heart as I walk the few steps to the window. I stick my arms through the small opening and slowly open my hands. For a split second he reorients, then with the realization that his freedom is close at hand, he tears off into the sky with relief turbo-charging his ascent.

It is a strange little event that I dismiss until I see Robyn later. When I arrive she is sitting outside in a wheelchair with Harold, her boss, who goes to see her every single day, even more than her husband. He sits with her for hours, not saying much, just keeping her company.

Toward the end of her life, a few months later, it is difficult to say how cognizant she is, but everyone treats her as though she is still with us. I share my distress with her about her worsening condition. Somehow, no matter how limited her ability to communicate becomes, she finds some nearly imperceptible way to indicate her acknowledgment.

So the day of the bird incident, she is sitting in the sun with her head cocked to one side. It is just one of the many freak things that her body does as the tumours crowd the brain. As soon as I see her, I think of the little bird and tell her the story. She is the little bird that will soon find herself in the hands of God, and experience the exhilarating flight to heavenly realms.

I remember asking her to tell me what it is like on the other side if she can, once she passes over, or at least keep in touch. Today, as I began to write this, my entire body erupted in multiple waves of goose bumps for a few minutes. That's my personal indicator of spiritual presence.

Now the twist in this story is that I begin spending time with Russ, just because we are two hurting puppies licking each other's wounds. Boris and I have recently split up, and Russ and Robyn are anticipating her imminent passing. I feel like I have to tell Robyn that Russ and I have become good friends, so I do. I know she understands. The next day, July 22, which happens to be my birthday, and which I had also mentioned to her because she had been at my fortieth, Russ calls me at about 11:30 a.m. "They called. It's time," he says. "I'll meet you there."

When we arrive in Robyn's room, we are told by her daughter that she's just passed. Russ bursts out of the room sobbing, and Pamela, the daughter, leaves. I am alone in the room with Robyn's yellowed corpse, now departed by her spirit. I go and stand by the window, and the dark shadow of a bird flies across the pavement below. I don't see the bird; I only see the shadow.

After that, Russ and I keep seeing each other off and on for several months. He is a kind and sensitive person, and a great support for me during the brutal court proceedings with Boris. He's also a good lover, and we have some wonderful times together, even though we're both in a state of deep grief and mourning over our lost spouses and marital lives. How can I help falling in love with him? Alas, Russ decides, after an appointment with his church counsellor a few months later, a woman no less, that I'm not marriage material. Maybe the term was "couple material," but it comes to the same thing. She was no doubt thinking in practical terms, about the children we each had and how much additional responsibility there would be for him, and for me too, if we got together permanently. But did she know about our spiritual connection, and how we gave each other happiness in a dark time? Was she jealous of that, maybe? Russ took her advice and broke my broken heart, despite having enjoyed some wonderful sex and many good conversations with me.

"You're too much fun," he said.

"There is no such thing," I said.

13

The White Ghetto

I've been separated from Boris for a couple of years now. Russ and I have stopped seeing each other, after spending weekends together for several months, consoling each other for our recent losses and upheavals and having fun together in the process. I'm back to being on my own but with two growing daughters to look after. Keyz is ten, and Shi is twelve. One evening, I decide to go see my brother Gary, who lives nearby in a ground-level basement suite with his Fijian wife and deaf son.

"Sissy, how're you doing? Come on in. Long time no see."

"Yeah, eh? Hi, Luba."

"Luba, make Jacquie a drink."

"Make it yourself. I'm tired. I've been working on my feet all day."

"Okay, bitch, have it your way," Gary says good naturedly. He quickly produces a rum and coke from the makings already on the counter. "Let's go outside."

We put some distance between us and his grumpy wife by stepping onto the patio and closing the door. There is a guy sitting in a lawn chair.

"Hi," I say.

"Hi."

"Jacquie, this is Curt."

"Oh, hi there."

"I'm his neighbour," Curt says. "I just live down at the end of the street."

"Oh, yeah."

We chat, smoke, and drink for awhile. Somehow, I get onto the subject of needing a job. Curt says, "You should apply where I work."

"Where's that?"

"It's a seniors' residence called Darkwood Manor. I'm a cook, but we might be hiring servers. I could talk to my manager for you. I think servers start at about fourteen an hour."

"Really? That's decent. Yeah, I think I'll apply. Give me the info, please." I get a casual position when I am hoping for full-time, but at least it is something.

Shiloh and I are at odds. She's eleven and doesn't like my drinking. So, she steals and stashes the small amount of wine and the few wine glasses in the house in some low, rarely used cupboard. The girls are getting subsidized counselling during this time from a local community organization. One day when I go to pick Shiloh up after her appointment, her counsellor asks to speak with me privately. Shiloh told her that I pushed her up against the wall. "Did she also tell you she smashed one of my glasses?" I asked. The counsellor said "no," but she was obligated to report the incident to social services. "Go ahead," I said. "I can't have an eleven-year-old destroying my property."

I never heard a thing from social services. I know my children are suffering the breakdown of our family, but I don't know how to deal with it in my own state of brokenness. Shiloh feels particularly betrayed by me when her cousin finds a package of cigarettes in the van cubby. They confront me, and I admit I smoke. She screams as though she's been stabbed. She misses seventy days of school in grade five. I take her to a doctor who prescribes her antidepressants.

Shiloh goes to live with my mom in Creston for grade seven. I am so thankful that Mom is willing to take her. I know that she is safe and well cared for there. I think Mom is a good surrogate parent now, better than when she raised us—because she doesn't have the stress and distraction of dealing with Dad's drinking. Shiloh, Mom, and I talk on the phone. The five hundred mile distance seems to help. When she returns ten months later, she is seemingly transformed. She is weaned off her antidepressants in Creston and doesn't seem to need them anymore. She thrives at school. My mom's second husband, Hans, likes her, and he hardly likes anybody. My mother's love has healed her wounds.

But whenever I get a call to work, I have to scramble for childcare for Keziah, who is nine years old. It is stressful. After a year and a half of casual employment, I fight my boss for a more regular part-time position.

However, six months after I start working there, I get involved with the cook. This is Curt, who got me the job. He is a nice looking guy but has a missing front tooth from falling drunk off his bike or something. It turns out he is forty-seven years old, living in his mom's basement down the street from my brother. He's lost his driver's license. He is a hardcore alcoholic. Perfect. It takes me awhile to realize he is also doing crack.

Pretty soon, he's moved in with me. Actually, I think that happened on our second date. However, to his credit, he is good in bed, one of only a few men out of the umpteen I've fucked over the course of my life who actually makes me orgasm, mainly because he likes the idea of two women together as much as I do. He is an unusual lover but effective because he verbally creates a fantasy about two women while playing with himself and then just penetrates me when we're both turned on. I don't have to do much of anything to him, which I like, and apparently, so does he.

Also, he is a cook. I sort of lost all my housekeeping skills when our family fell apart. He cooks in the kitchen and the bedroom. You can see my dilemma in whether to keep or get rid of him. Eventually, I hatch a plan to oust him. But now I am loath to disclose this, lest he read this and hunt me down like he promised he would, when I am least suspecting. He was mad because I broke up with him and wouldn't let him in my house. I opened a police file. They said it was probably just drunk talk. But he had a charge of uttering threats from an incident with a former lover. I think threats are a weak person's weapon, a desperate attempt to control with fear because they feel powerless. That's why I use them, anyway.

After I separated from Boris, I was with Russ, then Ace, then Curt, then Laird, then Screwy Louie, then Art, then Drago, then Van with several one night stands or brief hookups scattered throughout, involving an assortment of big cocks. An endless series of unsavoury companions. I started smoking pot with Russ for the first time in about twenty years. I hadn't done any since I was with Sylvain. He smoked very little, but it was a nice relaxing treat. Most of the other guys I was with after that also smoked. I tried to hide it from my kids, but it has a pretty distinctive odour. I think Keyz tried it with her cousin when she was about twelve and was chronic by the time she was fourteen. I don't think Shiloh used it other than to try it out a couple of times. I tried to stay in a sexual, alcoholic, and/or marijuana haze to prevent me from feeling the pain that threatened to consume me daily.

Shame follows me like a shadow. I try not to think about what it is like for my children to see me with all these different guys. This goes on for about five years. I'm in my mid-forties. The girls are young adolescents. They learn to cope, avoiding the unpleasant scenes as much as possible by going out or retreating to their rooms. I withdraw from involvement at the Christian school as much as possible. The couple of times I attend awards ceremonies in the chapel, I cry the entire time and worry the people beside me can smell my booze breath. I quit attending church also. I no longer belong.

Nine-year-old Keziah is jealous of my boyfriend Curt. She thinks I like him more than her and announces to me she'll kill herself if I don't quit seeing him. "Keyz, come on. Don't be ridiculous," I say. But I know that whenever someone talks about suicide you should pay attention. It's a cry for help.

"I'm serious, Mom. I can't stand him. I don't want him in our house."

"How would you kill yourself?"

"I'd put a plastic bag over my head."

This rattles me. She actually has thought of a plan, a method, a tool. Dear god. And it is one that I would never have thought of. I feel out-matched.

"Keyz, I can't tell you how it would break my heart if you did something like that. I love you and I would miss you so much. But it's normal for adults to want to be together. And you can't grow up threatening me because you don't like the way I do things. Sometimes you just have to accept things and try to find a way to deal with them, even if they're unpleasant. What is it you don't like about Curt?"

"Everything. I hate him. You like him more than me."

"No, I don't."

"Yes, you do. You spend all your time with him."

"Well, I want you to spend time with us, but you won't. You just go up to your room and refuse to participate."

"That's because I hate him." In verbal acrobatics, this is the loop de loop. It makes my head spin.

"Well, I'm sorry, but please let's try and work this out some other way than you killing yourself. Please don't ever do that." And I probably added, "I've been through enough already. I really can't take any more carnage."

I think I call 911 or the crisis line to get some advice. They tell me to keep an eye on her. I ask Curt to go back to his mom's to give us some space. One day not long after he's moved out, Curt is over, as he is most evenings, before walking back to his basement room in his mom's house. Suddenly I notice Keziah has left the room and been gone for a while. I say, "I'll be right back. I'm just going to check on Keyz." When I get upstairs and poke my head into Shiloh's bedroom where the computer is, Keyz is sitting with a plastic bag over her head tied loosely around her neck. I run to her and frantically rip it off.

"Keziah, what are you doing?"

"I told you I was going to kill myself."

Sweet Jesus. I send Curt home and call the hospital. They tell me to bring her in to Royal Columbian Hospital Psych Emergency. I tell her that's where we are going. She brightens immediately, asking how long she'll be there and what to pack. I feel I've been duped, but you just never know, right? So you have to go through the whole rigmarole. What a lovely way to spend an evening, going for a nice drive across town, sitting on a hard chair next to Keyz, who says nothing, just sits there. We wait, my favourite thing in the world, as my mind tells me awful things about how this looks to others. Thanks, Keyz; it's great spending time with you. I'm more exasperated with her than worried about her state of mind just now.

They finally speak to Keziah, first alone, and then they call me in. A panel of doctors and experts has determined that Keziah is not, in fact, suicidal but rather highly manipulative. She got that from her dad. They tell her all the things I've already said to her myself about my right to have a life and send us home, with an aside warning to me not to keep plastic bags in the house. Are you kidding me? At that time, plastic bags came into our house on a nearly daily basis. That's what you used to carry food home in. Everything you bought came in a plastic bag. They proliferated in the plastic bag holder my mother-in-law had made me. In fact, we had two of those.

Ironically, in the decade since, it seems the whole world has recognized the deadly potential of plastic bags, and we are now encouraged to use cloth bags, no bags, or to pay for them. The environmentally friendly black cloth President's Choice bags I get from the Superstore would make a lovely and appropriately coloured death hood, symbolizing the return to the earth the wearer was about to make. For heaven's sake. It just seems like such a ridiculous and impossible suggestion at the time. And if someone wants to kill themselves that badly, they'll find a way. That's the terrifying thing; it's the motive, not the means.

My life feels hopeless. I am lost in a desert with no food or water, and the sun is going down, and the vultures are circling overhead, and the coyotes are howling nearby. I am stuck in my mucky misery, plodding through life in cement shoes. The most awful part is how guilty I feel about how my addictive behaviours, which have accumulated since Boris and I split up, are hurting my kids. I'm still pretty heavily into drinking, smoking weed, and fucking wantonly and randomly. I don't know how to turn things around. I'm not really there for them or for myself emotionally. I don't know how to change any of this.

What happens next is we plummet to an even lower socioeconomic status. There is only one wage earner. No one is at home most of the time during the girls' formative years, and no one is cooking meals or running the show, really. I'm a separated, bankrupt, underemployed, and suburban single mother teetering precariously on the verge of a nervous breakdown. How do I keep ending up with men to whom I seem to be attracted but then end up disliking and discarding? Honestly, it's as much me as them that's the problem, I think. I have a mood disorder and alcohol and drug problems; I have also lacked parental guidance in my life about relationships. But how could I be offered any when my parents didn't get any? You can't teach what you don't know. I wonder if I'm trying to punish Boris by being with so many other men, trying to show him that even if he hadn't wanted to fuck me, other guys do. Or maybe I'm just trying to learn how to recognize my patterns of dysfunction in attractions and relationships and have to repeat them often to be able to see them and change.

Way back at university in Lethbridge when I was nineteen, I developed a crush on a stunning female student in my English class named Tanis. She was perfection to me— blonde, blue eyes, long lashes, gorgeous long slim muscular legs layered with soft skinned curves, slightly imperfect beautiful smile, nice boobs. Really pretty. Typically, I'd say I prefer brunettes, but the blonde was natural, and it totally suited her. I never got to touch her gorgeous legs, but, hey, I could imagine. I was jealous when she told me a guy had asked her out for dinner. He didn't deserve her. She was so hot. He was so white bread. Her silly delight about going on a date with him made me decide I would never tell her I was attracted to her.

There were a couple of girls in the drama department who shared a place and were together all the time at school. I wondered if they were gay, but I never heard anyone suggest that. I was shy to ask because what difference did it make? I wasn't going to do anything about it anyway. But I guess I was curious enough to want to know what gay women looked like and how they lived. If these women were lesbians, they looked just like everyone else, so how would a person tell? I'm in my fifties now, and I still don't really know the answer to this conundrum. I guess I never really pursued my interest in other women seriously enough. Still, at the point when I decide that the men I'm meeting are a bunch of losers and I'm not going anywhere I want to go with them, I do start thinking about opening the door to the possibility of woman-to-woman love ever so slightly. I start looking around.

14

Breakdown

It is the long weekend in September 2008 in the white ghetto in Port Coquitlam. I am forty-seven years old. The booze/pot fog has lifted, now that I've cut ties with the endless list of loser men I'd been hanging out with. I am energized, feeling good, insightful, and creative. I wake up, grab a sketch pad and pencil, and begin to draw, ideas coming too fast for me to capture them. I called in sick at Darkwood Manor yesterday and do so again today. I just can't face that place anymore. We've been short staffed, and I have been working overtime. I am burnt out. I feel bad letting the team down, but I know I'm not well somehow. I can't go to work.

After drawing a bit—which is a rare activity for me but one in which I engage occasionally when feeling inspired, usually creating somewhat abstract designs that I don't show anybody—I bounce down the stairs to get some breakfast, when the phone rings. It is my friend Linda from my comedy group. Linda has bipolar disorder and a great mental health team that offers all sorts of perks, free classes, and passes to different events.

"Hi, Jacquie. Do you want to go to the PNE with me? I have two free gate passes."

The PNE, short for Pacific National Exhibition, is a huge fair and amusement park with rides galore. There is also a vendors' building where various wares are hawked. There is musical and other entertainment as well as specialty food concessions, a petting zoo, a dog show, and equine events. It's a two-week event every summer in Vancouver that's been going since 1910. There are nine hundred thousand visitors each season. I haven't gone for years. Boris and I did take the kids once when they were really little; in fact, I think Keyz was a baby in a stroller. I remember Shiloh getting itchy from the petting zoo.

"Okay, sure. Is it okay if I bring my daughter?"

"Sure, that's fine. You'd have to pay for her though because I only have two passes."

"Yeah, I know, of course. Okay, do you just want to meet there?"

"Sure, how about 2:00 p.m. at the main gate?"

"Sounds good. See you later."

"Hey, Keyz, come here," I holler.

Keyz is fourteen years old and is a sweet, petite young woman, with long hair that she dyes black and sometimes adds extensions to. She wears pounds of mascara from under which her greenish eyes glitter. She's wearing short shorts and a teeny t-shirt.

"What?" she asks.

"Where's Shiloh?"

"With her friends."

"Do you want to go to the PNE today?"

"Really?" She smiles, hoping this is for real. Such a thing has never happened before. I don't like crowds or having fun.

"Yeah, really." It feels good to make her happy. "Linda has some free tickets."

"Well, could I invite a friend?"

"Yeah, but invite someone that can buy their own ticket, okay?"

"Well, yeah, but what if they can't?"

Oh, screw it. I'm always cheaping out. I can afford it. "Yeah, okay, I'll pay for your friend."

"Thanks, Mom. I'm going to call Jessica."

"Okay, start getting ready. We're meeting Linda at 2:00 p.m., so we have to leave by one-ish."

"Okay."

We get ready and have some time to kill. My mind is humming with all sorts of thoughts. I start talking to Keyz, and in the ensuing conversation, I realize it is the first time I have ever had a conversation with her like this, where she tells me how she thinks about things, what her favourite colours are. I feel like I am talking to someone else's child because I realize I don't really know her at all. She is going into grade nine, the high school, yet she seems so young and suddenly precious.

As it turns out, she has to bring two friends for some reason. Oh well, what the hell. My generosity is rarely shown to my children. I always have money for beer, though. Let's splurge. Still, I am shocked when I have to fork over 240 dollars right off the bat for basic admission and ride tickets, plus extra for snacks. How do real families do it?

"Okay, Keyz, listen. I'm going to give you my cell phone and Linda's number is in it. We'll keep in touch through the day this way, okay?" The girls run away from us.

"You wanna smoke a joint?" Linda has a prescription for medical marijuana. She is chronic. She smokes all day, every day. She only takes a break to sleep. We go over to a secluded spot by a pond I didn't even know was there, and she rolls a joint, lights it, has a toke, and offers it to me.

"Uh, I don't know, Linda. I've been trying not to smoke. I felt kind of weird the last couple of times I smoked."

It's an understatement. I had taken a week off work to attend a class in memoir writing at the University of British Columbia. The class went from nine in the morning to three in the afternoon, every day for a week. Rather than ride the bumper of rush hour all the way back to Port Coquitlam, I decided to have a local holiday and go to the beach every day after class and then go for dinner somewhere before driving home. One day, I'd had a toke or two at the beach, then chose a long, dark, narrow restaurant on West 4th Avenue that had a couple of patio tables. The patio was crowded at that time of day, so I was seated at a barlike ledge with a view into the cooking area. The server asked, "May I bring you a beverage?"

"I'd like a glass of white wine. What do you recommend?"

"I've got the perfect thing. It's called Blasted Church."

Did I hear her right? Soon my glass appeared, and I had a sip. Good. I noticed a man with a large movie camera balanced on his shoulder. A prickle of apprehension suddenly swept over me. I looked into the kitchen where orange flames leapt from the grill and the chef, and an Asian butch lesbian, it appeared, dictated instructions to her two male assistants. What is going on here? I felt confused, troubled. Have I accidentally somehow stumbled into hell? Did I die and not know it? Is that camera man recording my life that God will judge? How could I die and not even feel it? Are all these other people dead too, then? Did I have an accident?

I slid off my stool and went outside to check. The van was parked where I left it. Everything appeared to be normal, but in my head, nothing was normal. I tried to ignore my crazy thoughts long enough to eat my dinner. I quickly paid my bill and got in the van and started driving home. I remembered my children. Poor Shiloh and Keziah. If I am dead, what will happen to them? Oh my gosh, I didn't get to say goodbye. I miss them.

Now I'm crying and I pull off into Granville Island so I can call the girls. I dial, wondering if they can receive a message from me now that I'm dead. Ring, ring.

"Hello?"

"Keyz, is that you?"

"Yeah."

"Can you hear me, sweetheart?"

"Yeah."

"Is everything okay there, honey? Where's Shiloh?"

"She's with her friends."

"Are you okay?"

"Yeah. What's the matter? Mom, are you crying?"

"A little, but it's okay. I'm on my way home. I'll see you soon, okay, honey? I love you."

"Love you too. Bye."

I smoked pot the first time with Uncle Ron when I was fourteen. It made me feel horny. I liked it. I didn't smoke it much again until I was in my early twenties, when I was living in Lethbridge, going to university, and working. Hank and I smoked there and in Vancouver regularly. Sylvain was also a regular smoker. But when I married Boris, I was doing the Christian thing and didn't smoke for about twelve years. Once I got back into it, I smoked pretty much daily. Once in awhile, it made me feel paranoid and a little crazy, but most of the time, it just made me feel mellow. After the restaurant vision of hell, though, I was leery about trying it again.

But I reason that since Linda gets medical marijuana, it could be better, so I have a puff. I realize soon after that it was a mistake. I feel strange again. The noise and lights and smells as we walk through the grounds overload my senses. I am glad Linda is with me. We go past a booth with people handing out free samples of a yoghurt drink, which we drink.

I feel like Alice in Wonderland. After the drink, I feel myself shrinking into a little girl again. Linda becomes my mother. It is a flashback of the time my mom took me to the Calgary Stampede when I was a young child. The sounds and smells of the PNE meld with the sounds and smells of the Stampede in my childhood memory.

"Do you want to go see the horses?" Linda asks.

"Okay."

We go and find seats in the only occupied section. Shortly after we arrive, people begin to leave, one by one, two by two. I am paranoid that Linda and I smell bad. But could we smell worse than horse poo?

"Do you have to use the washroom?" she asks me.

I shake my head.

She goes. Right after she gets back, I say I have to go. When I get inside the washroom, there are two women in there, one around my age, one a little younger. The younger one is freaking out.

"I just had an incident with security. I accidentally knocked over an umbrella stand, and I don't know what they thought, but they started chasing me, and I had to run in here to escape them." She is extremely agitated, pacing erratically, talking quickly, about to cry.

I go over to her and put my hand on her arm. "It's okay. Calm down. You're okay."

She stabs at the buttons on her cell phone hopelessly. "I'm trying to call the police, but I can't get them."

"I'll stay with her," I say to the other woman who is watching this. "Can you go for help, please?"

She nods and leaves. With my hand on this crazy woman's arm, I feel as calm as an angel. In the Bible when angels appear, they usually say, "Fear not" or "Don't be afraid." I guess they're pretty calm. I begin to wonder if perhaps I am an angel. Or if she is me, and I am my own angel. Her behaviour seems familiar.

I hope Linda will wait for me. I am in there quite awhile. Finally, some uniformed men come, and they start talking to her. They are calm, too. I leave her with them and go to find Linda. She was worried about me.

"Sorry, I had to help a lady in there. Let's go."

We share some fries and look at some stuff, then go back to the pond for another toke, which I take because I am already messed up. I figure it can't hurt. Then we go to get a spot in the outdoor arena for the Spirit of the West concert. While we are sitting on the grass waiting for the band, I call Keyz with Linda's cell phone.

"Hi Keyz, how are you doing?"

"Okay."

"Are you having fun?"

"Yeah."

"Okay, good. We're just waiting for a concert to start. Talk to you later. Bye."

When the band starts playing, we all stand up. We are packed in like sardines, but I cannot help feeling that the music goes through me. As I dance, people move back a bit. I dance like a dervish until sweat is flying off the ends of my hair. I hear someone behind me say, "Never underestimate the power of alcohol." But I'm not drunk, haven't even had a single drink that day. I am fuelled by some other chemical concoction coursing through my brain. Linda dances beside me but not with the same intensity. I sense she may think I'm acting strange, but I don't care. I can't stop. She doesn't say anything. I hope she's enjoying herself as much as I am.

After the concert. we walk over to the marketing building, where vendors of every description hawk their wares. Linda heads straight for the massage devices. They are strapped to the backs of chairs that we sit in while the units massage our backs. A woman approaches us.

"How does that feel, ladies?"

"Good."

"Isn't it wonderful? Six stainless steel heads rotate and vibrate against your body, loosening sore muscles. You can use it on your back as you are now, or you can put it on the floor and do your feet, or you can stretch out your legs and put it under your knees. It's very versatile. You can take it with you wherever you go." She smiles, nodding. She is attractive. I like her haircut, her eyes. I would like to fuck her.

"How much is it?" I ask.

"We have a special show price of 199 dollars."

"What? Oh my gosh, that's a lot. Is there any wiggle room on that price?"

"No, I'm afraid not. It's already fifty dollars off the regular price." She looks like an angel.

"Okay, if you throw in a bag to carry it, I'll take one."

"Well, the box has a convenient carrying handle. How's that?"

"I guess it'll have to do. Just keep flashing me that pretty smile while you take my money, okay?"

Ka-ching, ka-ching. Done. Let's move on.

Linda says, "I already bought a ticket on the PNE prize home, but I think I want to buy another one. Maybe you want to buy one. It's a nice house."

"How much are the tickets?"

"Twenty-four dollars."

"Ooh, that's a lot. I don't know. What are the chances of winning?"

"Well, someone's going to win. You can't win if you don't buy a ticket. Oh, there's a ticket booth. I'm going to get one."

I sit on a nearby bench to wait while Linda makes her purchase. Minutes later she comes and joins me.

"It closes at ten o'clock. You better decide soon if you're going to get one."

As we sit, I notice people are beginning to come up the wide path. Remnants of my religion surface like debris on the ocean after a plane crash. An old song begins to play in my head:

I've got a mansion just over the hilltop
In that bright land where we'll never grow old.
And someday yonder we will never more wander
But walk the streets that are purest gold.

I've got a mansion in heaven, but maybe I need a ticket to claim it. I better get one. Just as I approach the booth, the lady sadly says, "I'm sorry, you're too late." Too late. Too late for heaven. I turn and look at the path again. *Wide is the path that leads to destruction. Narrow is the way to eternal life and few there be that find it.* Doomed, I'm doomed. No heaven or mansion for me. Might as well go home. It's closing time.

"Are you ready to go, Linda?"

"Yeah, I think we've seen everything. The park closes soon anyway, I think."

I borrow Linda's phone and call Keyz.

"Hi Keyz."

"Hello?"

"Can you hear me?"

"No, barely, sorta."

"Okay, come meet us at the exit. We're here waiting."

"Okay."

We wait and wait and wait. Twenty minutes later, I call again. "Keyz, where are you?"

"We're here."

"What do you mean? Where? I can't see you." My anger and anxiety began to dance with each other. Eventually, I have to hand the phone to Linda. She determines that we're at two different exits. We finally converge. Keyz has about three extra kids from our neighbourhood in tow.

"Can we give my friends a ride?"

"Sure, I guess." We head for the van, which has a seventy-five-dollar parking ticket on the windshield. This has turned out to be an expensive day.

Suddenly, it's as though someone has removed all the air and light from my brain. If I'm not going to heaven, it must be that we're going to get killed on the way home, and I'm going to hell. It wouldn't be right to take all these children with me. Linda can see there's something wrong. The kids are all in the van, buckled up, and waiting to go. I can't get in. I have to sort this out first.

Linda says, "Are we going?"

I don't have words to explain what happens next. It's as though God and Satan are having a tennis match in my head, and my brain splits down the centre to form the net. Everything Linda says sounds like the devil. Everything has a double meaning and keeps flipping. I can't make a decision because I don't know who is going to win the argument. I just keep standing beside the driver's side of the van but don't get it. Linda stands on the passenger side, waiting for me to get in.

I don't know what the kids thought about my sudden immobility. I think Keyz was embarrassed. Linda gave them all bus tickets, and they caught the bus together. I drove Linda home and dropped her off, but then I feared the kids were going to die in a bus crash. I miraculously made it home, parked in the underground, and climbed up the stairs into the house.

Here I am in my messy house after my weird day at the PNE. Keyz isn't home yet, but fortunately she returns soon after, before I have time to really go off the edge worrying about her. We get into some silly scrap upon her return home. We're both tired and have eaten too much sugar and then got ourselves worried about not finding each other again and not making it home together. For the 687,453rd time I feel like I just can't go on. I want these awful times to end. I want to die.

I try to send the girls to bed, as it is late and the next day is the first half day of school for the 2008 fall semester. Shiloh is going into grade eleven, and Keyz will be in grade nine. Shiloh doesn't want to go to bed as she is in the middle of a creative project, making collages on the covers of her notebooks, and Keyz is talking to her friends on the computer. In my experience, getting kids to go to bed is one of the hardest jobs in parenting. Shiloh still claims that my early bedtimes for them were unreasonable and she'd have to lie there for hours, waiting for sleep. I encouraged them to read until they felt sleepy, or worst case, do whatever they wanted in their room, just as long as they were out of my space. It was especially hard in the summer, when it was still sunny out at 8:00 p.m., their bedtime. I understood, as I'd been a nighthawk my whole life. I often felt a strong compunction to listen for burglars as a child while my unprotective parents slept. I used to count ceiling tiles, try to meditate, or have one-sided conversations with my sleeping sister.

But the best way to fall asleep I've ever discovered is to pray. I don't mean asking God to help you fall asleep; I mean asking Him for help with your shopping list of needs and wants and explaining why He should fulfill them. Then, change your focus to those around you and ask for general blessings for all you hold dear. After that, go in for some spiritual warfare in the fight against carefully executed Satanically inspired evil in our world. I guarantee that a few words in, you'll be slurring in your sleep. That's because Satan himself will cast a spirit of slumber upon you to stop you from opposing his diabolical plans, according to the Bible. Works every time.

The particular night I'm trying to tell you about, however, none of us slept. Somehow we all end up in my room where for several hours throughout the night I rant maniacally about how I can no longer remain on earth. I have to go and be with my other children that need me, those being my departed son Emmanuel and my three aborted children, all living as orphans in heaven. I feel I've neglected them too long, and Shiloh and Keziah are old enough to take care of themselves, at fourteen and sixteen. But I know they aren't really, and I feel so bad and guilty for the miserable life they've had with Boris and me as their fucked up parents. I just feel I've done too much damage, and the little children need me more.

I begin dividing up my meager possessions for their inheritance, which amounts to about one thousand dollars in cash I've managed to save, three handcrafted collections of poetry I've written over the past few years, and my wedding ring as well as Boris's, which he inadvertently left behind when we separated. The girls are understandably confused and concerned, distraught actually, tearfully trying to talk me out of my plan to leave them. But I am determined. I have to go. I cannot stand to spend another day on this miserable planet where we've all experienced so much pain. My heart is breaking, though, thinking of leaving those two little girls alone here. I am afraid our family will be permanently, eternally divided, that somehow dear little Shiloh will merit heaven and Keziah and I will go to hell. It is a night of tears and torment. Keyz is begging me to stay, looking so incredibly vulnerable with her wet cheeks and pleading eyes, which get no sleep that night. Shi crawls into my bed and drifts in and out as the drama unfolds. She is the one who finally, at 6:00 a.m, suggests I call someone, perhaps my mom.

It makes sense to me to let someone know I am moving on and leaving my children behind. So I wake up my mother, sleeping some five hundred miles away, to tell her of my plan to leave this dark world. She is alarmed, asking if I've taken anything. I say "no," just smoked some pot at the PNE. But it makes me realize I have no means to carry out my plan. I made a reservation for a jet to heaven but forgot to buy a ticket, and now my kids have all my money. Shortly after speaking to Mom, the doorbell rings. Shiloh goes and answers it and the next thing I know two police officers are crowding my bedroom, putting me in handcuffs, and escorting me out to their car. My mom called 911. I didn't know it worked long distance.

Humiliation is the strongest emotion I feel while wondering how many neighbours are watching. I don't understand the need for the handcuffs. I'm not violent or resistant in any way. In fact, I am almost robotic. Even I realize how flat my voice sounded on the phone with my mom. Embarrassment. That's what I feel when I have to call my boss at work and tell him I am in the psych emergency ward for an indefinite amount of time and won't be in to work. Stupid. That's how I feel when I am questioned by doctors, and I can tell my answers don't make any sense. There is a brown stain on the linoleum floor. I keep staring at it, wondering if it is from my blood. I can remember dancing naked in the middle of the night at home recently and lying on the floor and flipping my legs over my head to stretch my back. That's when I heard a loud crack in my neck. Maybe I actually broke my neck and died, and now I am in the afterlife, which is kind of like a dream.

As I look around, the other people all look like or begin to represent people in my other life, people that I need to forgive and/or ask forgiveness from. The cops look like Keziah's friends. A workman looks like an ex-boyfriend I recently broke up with. One of the receptionist nurses looks like my partner at work. A security guard looks like Emmanuel's dad Sylvain, and a huge fat woman in an open cell looks like my ex-husband Boris. The slightest resemblance to people I've known previously makes these people morph into them. I am in a freaky place, increasingly convinced that I am now stuck in purgatory with all these people I have grudges against. Dear God, let me out. This is no better than where I was.

One disturbing image that remains with me is of an older man I saw who is lying face down on the floor and is naked except for what looks like a diaper. I wonder if he is dead like me, and I go to approach him, but I am told to stay away. Even in my current state, I can't help wondering how on earth a human being ends up in that condition. He was somebody's little boy once. No one seems to care. After several hours of waiting, wandering, and questioning, I am put on a stretcher. I realize it is time to go to sleep. I do not want to remain on earth or in this purgatory. I question myself. Can I entrust my life to Jesus Christ and believe that I'll be with him in heaven when I awake? He has my children. Honestly, I've been shaken to the core. I'm not sure anymore, of anything. I can no longer distinguish what is real, imaginary, or the difference between life and death. I am terrified to go to sleep, believing that it is final.

I think I am given an antipsychotic injection, and then I lie back and try to relax because we all have to die someday, and no one knows where we go. I hope if Jesus is real He'll forgive me. Then I just focus on breathing as my toes, and then my feet, grow cold. I close my eyes and wait for the inevitable chill to creep up my body and still my breath. Sweet, scary death.

I wake up on the fourth floor of Royal Columbian Hospital's psych ward in my own little room and join the rest of the pajama-clad inhabitants for a meal tray in the common eating area around a large table with chairs. I get scrambled eggs, a yogurt cup, an apple juice cup, and cold toast with margarine. I've had a couple of friends who were manic depressive and visited them in the hospital before, so the scene isn't totally foreign to me. I never imagined I'd actually be a patient, though. It is a strange experience because not only am I crazy but so is everyone else in there. Patients tell me their stories, and I never know what is true, and I am feeling pretty weird knowing I must look to them like they look to me. My doctor is Dr. Nanjee. When he drops into my room on his rounds the next morning and hears my story, he tells me that I have bipolar disorder. He also tells me not to make friends with anyone, to avoid men, and to go out for lots of walks on the grounds.

On my second evening on the ward, a large dark-haired, stormy-faced girl named Melinda gives me a thump on the back with her fist, as I'm putting some colouring pens back into a white plastic container at the table where we've been sitting and quietly doodling.

"She's not allowed to do that. No hitting," another patient shouts.

Two of the other patients run and get the nurse. Before she arrives, Melinda says, "I hate you. My brother's coming tomorrow, and he's going to punch you right in the nose."

The next night she follows me into the washroom and stands in front of the door with her considerable bulk, ready to make any attempt to escape an unlikely dream. Again, the hateful words come: "I hate you. You're a horrible girl, and my brother's going to punch you right in the nose." She makes other similar utterances, even mentioning her parents.

I feel a weakness in my knees and wonder how hard I'll have to hit her to take her down in one shot, which I'd really rather not do in my current induced state of relaxation. I try to counter her antagonism with some logic and honest queries, and I am relieved when the tense moment passes, and she moves away from the door. I go straight to the nurses' station and explain the situation. The nurse says, "Why didn't you push the red emergency button in the stall?"

I say, "I didn't know there was one. I must have missed the tour when I checked in. What other amenities should I know about?"

Apparently my nemesis is moved to seclusion while I ensure no further intrusion by moving my bed to block the door. I am truly afraid of her. I am told to put my bed back and that she won't bother me anymore. She doesn't, but I keep an eye out for her after that.

I am disturbed to find out I am certified and can be held for examination for thirty days. As it turns out, Dr. Nanjee releases me after a couple of weeks. In fact, he lets me go home for a weekend after a week. Too soon. At that point, I'm longing to become a permanent resident of Ward 2. First of all, my brother Gary has to dodge construction on the streets, coming to pick me up from the hospital. I have to direct him by phone for about fifteen minutes while he's circling around, lost. Super stressful. He finally finds me, and I sign out around 9:20 a.m. We go to my place, and I give Mom—who has come from Creston on the bus to help out and avoid social services taking my children—the biggest hug I've ever given her. I could squish her easily; she's so tiny. There are piles of garbage on the patio because the extra underground key is missing. I just thought of a joke. Mom said they'd all have to go underground when I wrote my book, but by the time I'm finished it, they won't be able to because someone will have lost the key. Anyway, I asked her to save it because the night I thought I was going to die, I threw out a bunch of stuff and want to go through it again, which I do with rubber gloves, later that same day. I was mainly looking for my pot pouch, which contained a nice silver lighter, but I didn't find it. The garden looks better than I remembered it, with lots of colourful blossoms.

Sonny, Gary's deaf son and my nephew, slept over, but he is up now and on the computer. Shi is sleeping on the couch. She wakes up to give me a sleepy greeting. After a bit, I go up to see Keyz, who is also asleep. Oh Keyz, she who gave me grief in her own unique way on and off throughout the day, including black balls of old mascara in the corners of her eyes right from sunrise, taking off without saying goodbye and leaving a lying note, coming back with grass all over her ass from a roll in the clover with a boy I've never met, wanting twenty dollars to take her and her friends out for milkshakes, before she's given back the money I'd given her, buying herself a ninety-five-dollar TNA hoodie, but that's okay because I spoil myself sometimes too, not admitting until my time is almost up that she took my pot pouch and lighter, that she'd already given to a friend, that I dug through the garbage trying to find, bugging me incessantly to go out with her friends, "sending" me to the store for milkshake supplies, saying how good Church's Chicken looks even though she's an avowed vegetarian right now, and telling me she doesn't get along with her grandmother, my mom, who is stressed to the limit putting up with all our bullshit after traveling fourteen hours on a Greyhound bus to be here with us in our hour of need. Keyz settles down and behaves generously toward me in the evening. She colours my hair, my favourite colour, #22 Cinnaberry, and cleans up the kitchen after dinner.

I forget to take my 5:00 p.m. antianxiety pill, and I am yelling at Keyz again, just before 6:00 p.m. Just thinking about her behaviour makes my heart beat faster in an angry way. If Mom hadn't been there, I think I would have thumped her like I promised to the last time she lied and stole from me. Bro Gary's solution is to kill them with kindness. Yeah, right. She cried all night before I went to the hospital. I spent about five hundred dollars on her in the few days prior. Now it seems she wants to punish me.

In retrospect, I suppose she was angry, upset, and embarrassed. None of us knew what was going on with me. She wanted to distance herself. I get it now. Too late.

For the many years I joked about teetering precariously on the verge of a nervous breakdown, I never really thought I'd actually cross that line or hit that bottom. There is a certain shame to being crazy. It comes from the uncomfortable feeling that sane people have around a person who acts irrationally. Basically, human beings feel most comfortable around people who are most like them. We have a strong need to belong. People who are different are instinctively threatening. Huge strides have been made in destigmatizing people with physical disabilities and variations in sexual orientation. Mental illness is still an up and coming area for destigmatization, but it is coming. I am an advocate.

I performed comedy for five years with a group called Stand Up for Mental Health, a project spearheaded by David Granirer, which has now become a world-wide phenomenon. I was in the first class taught by Granirer in 2004. I had recently separated from Boris and was feeling out of sorts and out of control. I heard about the project at a single mom's workshop I attended. Through this group, I met some really great people, all of whom struggled with diagnoses, such as bipolar disorder, depression, and schizophrenia, just as other people may have to deal with diabetes, epilepsy, or chronic fatigue. Most people have to deal with some health issues in their lives, be they physical or mental. It's not so strange. Dr. Nanjee told me that 80 per cent of admissions to psych emergency are related to alcohol and drugs. But my observation is that many people who suffer with mental illness have experienced abuse or trauma. Sometimes it's just organic, some structural weakness in the body or mind that leads to debilitation.

As I write these words, I am now happily medicated and have been clean and sober for the past three years, since I left the hospital. I see my psychiatrist on a regular basis, and we tweak my dosage as required. I feel so much better. I feel like normal people must feel. I'm so thankful for the effective way the medication works and helps me live a good life. Shiloh said, "Mom, now you're funner and funnier." That's good.

At some point in that crazy night when I was in psych emergency, I thought that if I had the choice, I would be willing to come back to my life and do my step four, if it would save me from going to hell. Even though I attended a twelve-step program and got a graduation certificate, it was a set number of weeks, and I didn't actually complete all the steps. In fact, I struggled with them all, but to do a searching and fearless moral inventory, as step four recommends, and then admit my weaknesses to a higher power and another person in step five just seemed overwhelming. My list of sins was long and personal. I knew I would be uncomfortable telling anyone. But I told Jesus that if He'd give me another chance and not banish me to hell, I would try and do it because it seemed like unfinished business. It just occurred to me this minute that this account I'm writing about my life adventures is my steps four and five. Now I can die peacefully. And live happily. I can give up counting my steps—although in reality doing the steps repeatedly is intended to be a continuous, life-long process so you don't forget or lose sight of the path.

That would have been a great way to end this chapter, but I have a couple more things I want to add. The first is from a piece of paper I found later, on which Shiloh had written a journal account of the long, dark night. I understand that after the police took me, the girls had to go somewhere temporarily or into the social services system. My mom jumped on the first bus she could and rode for fourteen hours to arrive the next day. Keyz went to Uncle Gary's and Shiloh went to her friend Nandini's until their grandmother got there.

Shiloh's entry reads:

September 2, 2008, Nandini's house

Whoa man.

Pretty much the first day of grade eleven tomorrow—woot!

I'm at Nandini's house 'cause Mom had a crazy episode last night/this morning. It was actually kind of terrifying. She kept saying it was too late, she couldn't be forgiven, and she split up all her keepsakes and gave us her poem books & five hundred and sixty bucks cash each. And she kept saying, "I wish it was more. Uncle Gary will take care of you. I've already talked to him. It's too late for me, now. There's no time. It's too late. Just going to go be with Jesus and my babies in heaven." It was crazy.

Later I asked Shiloh to write down what it was like to have me for a mother and included the testimonial she wrote at my request with my application for a disability pension. It was approved.

The other thing I want to add is a journal entry I wrote in the psych ward one morning.

September 8, 2008

I went for a walk. I felt like there was something in my shoe or sock, so I stopped by a rock and pulled my sock off, and as I was looking down, I noticed a bug, which on closer examination turned out to be a flying ant. It was squirming and struggling, and I guessed maybe it was about to die, like the little yellow fly that did the frantic death dance in my room last week. I noticed it only had one wing and that's why it was struggling, but once it got the remaining wing properly positioned on its back, it was okay. It couldn't fly, but it could walk in a straight line. The other wing was lying dry in the dust, and I tried to pick it up, but it was too fine. It didn't matter because I got the point. Don't drink booze and don't smoke joints. I can't fly with a broken wing, but with a little repositioning, I can walk a straight line and carry my own weight.

15

Down in the Hood

Little by little, as my sanity returns, our lives begin to stabilize. I go to AA meetings and quit smoking pot and cigarettes. The residents of Darkwood Manor notice I am different. "You don't look happy, dear," one of them says.

"I had a nervous breakdown and found out I have bipolar disorder, so I'm on some medication for that."

"Well, I liked you better before. You're not yourself."

Which, of course, is the whole idea. However, I know what she means. My bubbly, fun-loving personality has flatlined. I've become a zombie. I plod through my days and soon carry an extra thirty pounds, a side effect of the medication. I see my psychiatrist every month for the first few years. Dr. Nanjee is short, squat, and balding, with heavy-lidded eyes. He has a wife and two sons. He is a traditional family man. He keeps a close watch on me, tweaking my meds as required. When I tell him I'd always been attracted to women, his brows furrow. He says, "You're young enough. You can find a nice man and settle down."

At one appointment, after telling him some of my sexual exploits, he says, "Why don't you try to go for six months without having sex?"

"Really? I don't know if I can do it. You mean sex with other people, right? But I'm allowed to masturbate?"

"Yes."

So, the challenge is before me. Now I have a solid excuse when a guy who I've gotten reacquainted with online and dated once emails me fishing for tail.

"I'm sorry, my doctor's restricting me from having sex right now."

It was easier to say it from behind Dr. Nanjee's fence, and I never heard from the guy again. At the appropriate appointment, I say, "You must be proud of me. I did it—six months with no sex."

"Now do another six months."

"What, are you serious? I thought I was done. You said six."

"How do you feel now that you've done six months?"

"Pretty good."

"You'll feel even better after another six."

He is right. I felt good inside. For my entire life, I've gone from one relationship and bed to another, sometimes just bed to bed. I was never really conscious of what I was doing, as I took whoever came along. Suddenly, I feel as though I have control over my body and my decisions. One thing I know for sure is that I don't care if I never sleep with a man again. If I am going to have sex, it is going to be with a woman. It's too bad I have waited until my late forties to decide because my body isn't what it used to be, and I'm not likely to see the beautiful bodies I might have if I'd started earlier. I just know I don't want to wait any longer.

I Google "where to find lesbian women in Vancouver." I find a website called *Sounds & Furies*, which is looking for volunteers, and I sign up, thinking this will be a good way for me to break into the lesbian community. A woman called Nicole Logan calls me up and asks if I'd be interested in some same-sex dance classes, after I tell her my reason for offering to volunteer. I am and drive downtown for a class. She is a petite woman, older. I feel awkward.

I don't know if it's learning new steps and making polite small talk with strangers or the fact that I feel like an imposter or the twelve-dollar drop-in fee, but I don't go back. But Nicole calls and asks if I'd like to volunteer at an annual event she produces called BOLDfest. BOLD stands for bold older lesbians and dykes. What's the difference, I wonder? I say yes. It's held in September at the Coast Plaza Hotel in the West End of Vancouver. I live way out in the suburbs. The event is advertised for women who are over fifty, but any age is welcome. I am forty-seven.

I go to the venue and see more grey and white hair than in the dining room of the seniors' residence where I work. That's one thing I admire about lesbians: They accept themselves as they are. Most don't conform to the annoying, expensive, and time-consuming conventions of most straight women—no makeup, hair colour, eyebrow plucking, shaving, fingernail polish, pedicures, or bras. Just get a buzz cut, throw on a t-shirt and jeans and go, and in comfortable shoes. Oh, how I admire them for their lack of vanity.

Liking girls or not, I still dress to please men. It's ingrained after Boris's influence of twelve years, not to mention a thoroughly heterosexual upbringing, complete with artificial beauty norms. I'd like to find another lesbian woman more like me in this regard, but they are rare in the over fifty lesbian world. Call me a self-obsessed narcissist, but I'm looking for a woman who looks like me. Not exactly, but you know what I mean. Someone attractive. So I've been told. In the seven years I volunteer for Nicole Logan at BOLDfest, as well as women's dances and music concerts, I have yet to find a woman I'm attracted to who is also attracted to me. I've met hundreds of women beautiful on the inside and some I find attractive outwardly, but no one who I've connected with is interested in having sex with me. Needless to say, I'm disappointed and still feel like an imposter.

Despite that, I manage to get laid a few times. The first time is back before my breakdown, an unexpected encounter with a woman in a pub washroom who has just washed off all her makeup, and now is freaking out. She asks if I have any when I come out of the stall. "No, sorry, all I carry is cover up and lipstick. You're welcome to them if you want." I look at her face. She is pretty, with short strawberry blonde hair and nice features, a reasonable reflection of me, especially when I see her big boobs.

She says, "You have to meet my friend Rory. Come with me." I follow her to a high table where a man with penetrating blue eyes sits. "Rory, this is... what's your name?"

"Jacquie."

"Look at his eyes. Aren't they amazing?"

"Very. Almost scary. You remind me of a guy who used to be on TV when I was a little kid. I'm not sure if he was on *Star Trek* or some other show like that, but he always freaked me out."

Rory says, smiling, "Don't be scared of me. I'm a nice guy. It's her you should watch out for."

"Sorry, what's your name again?" I ask her.

"Trixie."

"Oh yeah, that's right. I'll try and remember that."

When the bar closes, Rory and Trixie invite me back to his place. I'm nervous, as I don't know them and we're all drunk, but as per my usual habits, against my better judgment, I go. Rory has booze, and I set my purse down and follow him into the kitchen to help with the drinks.

When I come out of the kitchen, Trixie is sitting on the floor with my open purse between her legs. I think, *What the...?* and go back into the kitchen. "Rory, Trixie is going through my purse."

"Yeah, I told you she can be a little scary. She scares me. One night she got mad about my decorating and started throwing my stuff around. But she's hot. Don't you think?"

"Yeah, totally. I've gotta check on her."

When I go back out my purse is closed and put back. We continue to drink and listen to music, singing along. At one point, Trixie wants to demonstrate the strength of her legs by giving me an airplane ride, the kind you give a kid. I put my stomach on her upraised feet, and she lifts and holds me. I am scared, not knowing if I can trust her, but she doesn't drop or otherwise harm me. In fact, it's kind of fun.

After a while, Rory says, "You can stay here if you want. Trixie too. In fact, we can all sleep in my bed or you can sleep on the couch, whatever you want."

"Thanks, Rory, but I think I'm gonna go."

"Are you sure you can drive?"

"Oh yeah, I can drive. I don't live far from you. Thanks for the drinks. It was really nice to meet you two. Hope I see you again some time."

Rory says, "You will. You're a friend of mine now. I'm always at the Golden Crown and you're welcome to sit at my table."

"Thanks again, see ya."

I drive away, leaving Rory and Trixie there, thinking how lucky I am that they were safe.

Days later, I'm digging around in my purse for something and find Trixie's chequebook. Hmm, is that what she was doing in my purse? There is nothing missing. She must want me to contact her. So, I call her, and we meet at the Golden Crown and sit with Rory again. We have several of these encounters before she calls and invites me to go to her place for dinner. I've never been there before.

"This is nice, I like it," I say.

She says, "Yeah, it's okay. The rent's pretty good, but the sink doesn't work right. I have two sons. They're not here now. One is autistic. He's my big boy." She shows me their rooms. This is the first time she's mentioned her children.

She looks awesome in a short skirt and t-shirt. She turns on some music, and we dance while she makes dinner, which we eat on her little patio. It's a beautiful summer evening. If she makes a pass at me tonight, I'm going for it.

After dinner, we sit on the couch and she brings up the subject of sex, telling me that she's bi and curious about me. I say, "I'd love to have sex with you. You're beautiful. I've always wanted to be with a woman."

"So, I'd be your experiment then?" She kind of sounds hurt.

"Well, not just my experiment, like I don't care about you. But yeah, I guess, in the sense that you'd be my first."

She settles whatever internal dialogues she's having in her mind and agrees. I use the bathroom first and lie down and wait in her bed. And wait. It seems like she's taking forever. I'm turned on, excited this is finally going to happen, I am happy it's her, and I feel almost high from the anticipation.

Finally, she comes to bed. I'm really sorry, I don't remember details other than kissing my way down her body until I arrive at her pussy. She opens her legs. I gently push apart her labia to reveal a pussy that could have played a stand-in for an apricot. Gorgeous. She is totally shaved, thank god, clean and sweet and pretty. You thought I was going to say juicy, didn't you? Best apricot I've ever eaten.

"Are you sure this is your first time?"

"Yeah, but I've thought about it a lot." A little moan comes out of her that sends shivers all over and inside me. She goes down on me, and I'm so excited in no time I squirt. She says, "You came in my face," not with delight.

"Sorry," I say, but it's the first time someone's complained that I squirted.

The next day, I'm supposed to pick up my daughter Shiloh in Chilliwack. She and my stepsister, Liana, are driving from Creston where she's been at my mom's. I get a phone call to let me know when to start driving to meet them. I get on the highway and all I can think about is that apricot pussy. I replay the scene over and over as I drive. I can almost see it in the sky. I drive and think pussy. And drive and drive, and suddenly I realize I've driven past my destination, almost to Hope.

I make a phone call, then turn around and find myself in gridlock. They end up waiting for me for two hours. I feel so guilty. I can't explain why I'm late. Why must they suffer for my pleasure? Why am I such an airhead? I've never before or since experienced such a compelling, time-consuming fantasy.

So that's Trixie. We hook up one more time, but she seems reluctant. The time after that she invites me to dinner but at the last minute invites other people. I never see her after that, but I do start dating the guy she invited to dinner sometime later. I think it's kind of funny that he and I have fucked the same girl. Neither of us know where she is anymore, but we're still friends, and so are Rory and I, although I don't see him often. He and I dated for about five months, but I wasn't sexually attracted to him and never gave the poor guy any affection beyond hugs for all the drinks and one lovely dinner he bought me.

Another night I drive into the city from the burbs for a lesbian dance that is cancelled. Another woman has driven in from Horseshoe Bay. We get talking, starting with our disappointment about the dance. She is pleasant enough looking, good features, a bit heavy; 190 pounds she tells me, which I deem a conservative estimate. I'm learning to appreciate all sizes of women. In my head, there's a cut-out figure of the perfect woman, over which I lay the real women I meet to compare. None of them fit exactly, nor do I, but to her credit, this one is a real lesbian with two grown daughters.

"My brother just got me a car," this Miranda woman says. "I call her Betsy. I haven't driven for a while, so I love her. Come outside with me, and I'll show you."

As we're crossing a mostly empty parking lot, we stop, and she gently places my back against a lamp pole. "I'm going to kiss you," she says. And she does, leaning in and placing her lips on mine. "What do you think of that?"

"Gee, I don't know. You kind of took me by surprise. Nice, though."

"Okay, good. Come on, she's right over there."

We get into an old but not cool Belmont, painted flesh colour. The dash is decorated with small toys.

"See, this is Toby. My cat died, and this was her favourite toy, so I keep it here to remind me of her. And this is..." My mind wanders as she goes on. She looks normal, but there's something about her that is different besides filling her dashboard with small toys. I can't quite put my finger on it. She says, "Hey, there's karaoke starting in the lounge at nine. You wanna sing?"

"Oh no, I don't sing in public. But I'd like to hear you. Are you good?"

"Yeah, I can sing."

We return to the lounge, and soon it is her turn. She has a great voice. Who knew? She gives a beautiful rendition of Shania Twain's "From This Moment On."

"That was really good. You've got a great voice."

"Yeah, I know." Other people who make statements of obvious self-confidence like this always freak me out. It seems like bragging, and that's not a good quality to have. So, I was informed by my best friend Peggy in grade eight when she decided to stop being my friend and join the popular group. It hurt at the time, but her honesty was valuable. I wasn't aware that I came off as a braggart.

Another woman I know that I met at BOLDfest who was coming to the now cancelled dance calls on my cell phone and wants me to meet her at another lounge about twenty minutes away.

"Well, I'm actually having a good time where I am. I've met someone, and there's karaoke. Why don't you come here?"

She insists. We drag our feet a bit, but Miranda and I end up driving over there, only to discover she has left. I am annoyed. We drive back to the karaoke lounge, and Miranda sings another song—k.d. lang's "Constant Craving"—and then asks if I'd like to go to her place. "You can come in Betsy, and I'll drive you back here tomorrow."

"Oh, um, okay, I guess." Once again, I am taking a risk, going off to a stranger's house. I'd prefer to be in my own vehicle in case things go sideways, and I need to escape, but I can't really picture her hurting me. In fact, I suspect her intention is to pleasure me.

I am right. It takes a bit of time as she shows me her incredibly tiny place; it is actually an extra building intended as an office but which is now crammed with her belongings. There is a small bathroom with a toilet, sink, and shower, a small room with a single bed and a chair, and shelves holding her stuff. Oh, and the one thing that justifies the six-hundred-dollar-a-month rent—a tiny window with a view of the ocean.

"How long have you lived here?" I ask.

"Two months. I love it. I do some cleaning for the owners who live in the big house in exchange for a discount on the rent. I use their kitchen, too."

Wow, I am thinking to myself, I would hate to live here. She offers me a dealcoholized "near" beer and eventually invites me to the narrow bed. I picture myself falling off, but, thankfully, she suggests I get on top of her, and she masterfully manages my clit with her tongue and her lips while I lean back a little and finger play with her wet pussy. I am excited, she is incredibly good at what she's doing, and what I am doing feels incredibly good to me. Against all odds in that narrow bed and somewhat awkward position, she brings me to orgasm. I am grateful and want to reciprocate. She says, "Nah, that's okay. I know enough about my pussy to know you probably wouldn't like it."

"Why don't you let me decide that?" I see she is used to being in control but allows me access. If Trixie's pussy was an apricot, hers is a beef steak. Every woman is different. Luckily, I'm not a picky eater, although I don't like hair in my food.

I have an actual lesbian girlfriend for several months. I meet her at a meet-up potluck through an online community site. I am sitting alone in the living room, away from the food and chatter—lesbians love to talk, just like straight women—and she comes in and sits across from me. She is big, tall, and heavy, not attractive to me until she smiles and starts talking: "My ex-girlfriend's here tonight. She's got tires for my car I was storing at her place that I have to get from her. She's got two kids. I miss them more than I miss her. She won't let me see them. On Christmas Eve, I always gave the kids pajamas. Her kid opens it on Christmas Eve and says, Pajamas again? I tell him, Yeah, I give you pajamas on Christmas Eve so you can look good opening your presents tomorrow." She smiles, revealing nice teeth and a good-natured sense of humour.

She continues talking and introduces me to her ex. Later, she comes over to where I'm standing around the food and says authoritatively, "I'm getting numbers. What's your phone number?"

Despite the fact that I see other women's eyebrows rise, I tell her. My experience is that no one ever calls when you give your number, and I never call when someone gives me theirs. A few weeks later, she calls. "Hi, it's Nella. Sorry I couldn't find your number for a while, but I just found it. You want to go to a movie with me? Cirque du Soleil's *Worlds Away* is playing downtown."

"Um, yeah, I guess so. When, where?"

After the movie she asks, "Wanna go for coffee?" We end up in a Tim Horton's— which some people call Timmy's, but my friend Amber calls T Ho's, which I like better— and chat. Apparently, I freaked her out a bit with some of my God talk, so she tells me, but then she asks, "Would you like to see me again?"

"Well, I enjoy your company, but we live on opposite sides of a toll bridge. I'm a night person, and you're a morning person, and you're looking for lifelong love, and I'm just looking for casual sex, so I don't know if there's much point."

"That's okay. I like you. I'll call you again." And she does, and I go, and I realize she overrides all my no's. She's good in bed and provides me with some dream fulfillment in terms of regular sex with another woman. But I am embarrassed to be seen with her. I find myself trying to change her—to get her to pluck her eyebrows, wear a support bra not a sports bra, and to buy some new, more feminine clothes. I feel bad about this now. I basically did to her what Boris did to me. She is a head taller than me and twice as wide. I think we look ridiculous together, unsuited. This is confirmed more than once when other lesbians ask me, "Are you with her?"

She is a good person, outrageously generous, loving. But I feel that she's needy, and I soon feel smothered. It's not the first time I've felt this. I hate the drama of relationships, having to consider the other person's feelings all the time. I can barely deal with myself, let alone somebody else. When I try to break up with her, she reacts with extreme emotion; she hints at suicide, cries, and throws our travel journal in the street in the rain. She ignores me and then suddenly shows up the next day. Oh god, I hate this shit. This is why I am alone a lot of the time nowadays.

Thankfully, another woman is attracted to her, so Nella reluctantly replaces me, and I escape. All in all, it takes a year to wrap it up. She maintains a relationship with my daughter Keyz, who calls her Dad, and to whom she gives driving lessons up until Keziah's death. Nella and the new girlfriend have Keyz over for Sunday dinners. If I speak to Nella, she always tries to arrange a get together. She makes me promise. I hate promising because I give my word in integrity, and I don't want to promise something I don't want to do.

Nella has a picture of herself when she is about ten years old that reminds me of me. She wasn't large then. She was just an ordinary girl who thought about other girls. That didn't stop her from getting pregnant at fourteen with a married man, whom her single mom then petitioned,

THIS LIFE I'VE BLED

successfully, for money, which funded Nella's abortion, among other things. One of her best lovers to this day was a guy, another guy, but she hasn't slept with a man since she was in her early twenties. Sometimes it's hard for gay people to come out of the closet because there's so much stuff placed in front of the closet door, meaning you may have to push through some hetero relationships before you are true to yourself. I'm still doing it.

I guess I've settled on being bisexual, although I will say I prefer women over men. But I also prefer getting laid to celibacy, so I'll diddle the odd guy if I have to. But he has to be really odd.

*

The girls and I are in the living room of our subsidized townhouse, shortly after my breakdown and recovery. Keyz is painting her toenails while Shi doodles, watching. "Girls, I want to talk to you about something."

They exchange glances, never knowing what may come out my mouth.

"At my AA meetings, they talk about a twelve-step program. The fourth or fifth step, I forget, is where you write down all your defects of character and then tell them to someone."

"I think we already know them all, Mom," Keyz says.

"No, I'm not talking about telling you. First of all, I did a twelve-step course at the church when your dad and I first separated. I didn't do that step because I was afraid once I started on that list I'd never finish, but I also wasn't comfortable telling them to a stranger. I'm still afraid of doing it. But one of the steps after that is to make amends to all persons you've harmed."

Emotion chokes my voice, and my eyes well up. I don't want to make a scene, but I can't control it, so I just push past it. "I can never possibly make amends to you for all the harm I caused you when I was drinking. I'm so sorry. But someone told me the best amends is not to drink." I wipe a tear off my cheek.

"Aww, Mama Bear," Shi says and she comes to give me a hug.

"Yeah, that's good," Keyz says, putting the lid on her nail polish.

"It's okay, Mama, we forgive you," Shi says. I feel humble, grateful for these two precious daughters. I don't deserve their love.

They are somewhat shocked when I tell them I want to be with women. I tell Shiloh first.

Shi says, "I thought you were kidding." I'd made references to it in my stand-up comedy routines in the years I was in the Stand Up for Mental Health project, and I'd occasionally tried out some of my jokes and routines at home. There's a seed of truth in every joke.

She suggests I wait to tell Keyz. One day, perhaps because she's tired of carrying the secret alone, she says I should tell her. Keyz gets a hurt expression on her face, eyes shining with instant emotion and says, "Just another weird thing about you I didn't know. It's okay to be bi, but just don't be full on lesbo. I couldn't handle that." Interestingly, by the time she was sixteen, she was bisexual herself.

I arrive home one evening at about 11:00 p.m., after visiting a friend in Vancouver. When I enter the house, I see sixteen-year-old Shiloh lying on the living room floor holding her stomach, with a pale face.

"Hi," I say as I walk in.

"Mrs. Johnston," Shiloh's friend Vivi says, jumping up and coming toward me, "Shiloh has a really bad stomach ache. She's been lying there for awhile."

"Why didn't you call me?"

"We tried. Your phone must be dead." I pulled it out of my purse. Of course, it is. Stupid cell phone. Never works when you need it. I go over to Shiloh. "Are you okay, honey?" Stupid question.

She is beyond words, just moaning, her face twisted in pain. Oh great, another midnight run to emergency. I hate that place. Wait and wait and wait. It is usually a four-hour round trip that always feels inconvenient to me. How many times do we have to go there in a child's life?

Vivi reads my mind: "I think we should take her to emergency."

"Lovely. All right, let's go. Shiloh, can you walk?" She doesn't answer, just reaches out to Vivi, slowly getting to a standing position but doubled over. We get in the van; the girls sit in the seat behind me.

"I don't understand why we always have to wait so late to deal with things. We'll be up half the night now. Good thing there's no school tomorrow. Oh shit. I probably don't have change for parking. It's ridiculous to charge people to park in the emergency lot, especially when there's no place to get change."

Against the silent backdrop of the girls, I can hear myself. Bitchy, whiny, unpleasant. Shiloh is suffering, and I'm making her feel worse by complaining about having to help her. I hate myself for it. Best say nothing. I park and walk beside Vivi, helping Shiloh.

I approach the desk. "Excuse me, my daughter has extreme abdominal pain."

The nurse points to a machine behind me. "Take a number," she says firmly.

Grrr. I hate this place. Take a number? What if she has a burst appendix and dies before you call it? I wrestle with the machine to get my piece of paper. We wait.

I have sat in emergency waiting rooms over the years for nut allergies, asthma attacks, a broken toe, a broken arm, and Keyz overdrinking. That was probably the last time. She was thirteen years old. It is a bad memory. Maybe that's why I'm so edgy. I look over at Shiloh. She looks defeated.

"Girls, I'm sorry for being so cranky in the van. I don't know what's wrong with me to make you feel worse when you already feel so awful. Please forgive me."

Vivi nods. Shi once told me that she has a crazy mom, too.

At last, Shiloh's name is called. We go to the desk, give her info, and outline the problem; then, we sit and wait some more. Finally, she is called again, and we go through the doors to an examining room. And wait. I'm not a good waiter. Thankfully, it isn't long before a handsome young doctor comes and introduces himself. He is soon gently prodding Shiloh's tender tummy.

"We'll do some blood work and give you something for the pain, but I'd like to get a CT scan in the morning."

The result of that is that Shiloh is admitted directly to hospital, which makes me feel even worse for being such a crank. The short version is that they think she has Crohn's disease, a condition in which the bowel becomes inflamed. It takes a week or so of treatment while they wait to see if surgery will be necessary. Things settle down satisfactorily with treatment, so surgery is averted for now, but the condition has a 70 per cent chance of recurring in the future. This is a distressing diagnosis for a sixteen-year-old girl, besides the embarrassment of having to explain gross personal details of digestion and elimination to friends who don't know what Crohn's is.

The following year, her grad year, Shiloh has another flareup and is in the hospital; she is tube fed for a whole month. Surgery is again narrowly averted. I go visit almost every day, but it is a good half hour drive each way, and we can't do much when I get there.

One night, I arrive later than usual, and Shiloh is in her bed smiling, surrounded by friends who've come for a visit. It is so nice to see her happy. She hates being there but tries not to grumble. I can see she is depressed, though.

*

Nineteen-year-old Shiloh looks hesitant as she sits on someone's castaway couch that now graces our living room in the white ghetto. "Mom, I'm going to move out."

"Really? Where are you going to live?" A strange mixture of happiness and sadness mingles in my chest.

"With Kali."

Kali is Shiloh's dear friend and mentor. She'd been her youth leader at the Baptist Church when Shi was in high school. She is several years older than Shiloh, the only daughter of her dad's second marriage and, therefore, a little privileged. Her parents helped her buy a one-bedroom condo in Coquitlam, a suburb of Vancouver, ten minutes from where we live. They live nearby.

Shiloh has been working for an arts studio for about six months. Part of me feels rejected, but I am happy that she is making decisions for her life. I can understand her wanting to go. Even medicated, I'm not the easiest person to live with.

"Kali's apartment is only a one bedroom. Where will you sleep?"

"Maybe the couch."

"Well, Keyz and I will miss you, honey. When are you planning on leaving?"

"In two weeks."

"Oh, that soon. What about Kali's dog? Won't you be allergic?"

"No, I'm okay with her. She doesn't bother me too much."

"Okay, good. Well, that's that, then."

I know that I get on Shiloh's nerves the way everyone's mother gets on their children's nerves sometimes. The bond between mother and child is like a thick tug-of-war rope, with lots of prickly bits sticking out but strong, very strong, not easily broken.

(After about a year or so of living with Kali, who got another dog that Shiloh is allergic to, Kali's parents, Bonnie and Samuel, offered to let her stay with them. Shiloh and Kali were planning a trip to India—

Kali's family is Fijian Indian—and they were well off, owning a flooring business at which both girls worked for awhile. They offered Shiloh six months of free rent while she saved her salary to go to India for three weeks with Kali and another friend. It was partly a visit to a ministry that the girls support, started by Kali's family, called Sunshine Angel Mission, which provides food, clothing, and education to impoverished children. I was with Shiloh the night before she left, keeping her company after hours at the arts studio where she worked, until about 11:00 p.m, helping clean up while she painted individual little personalized wooden keepsake boxes for the four or five orphan girls whose names she knew. She had the book she wrote about the Biblical story of the gospel, Adam and Eve's fall from grace, and Jesus's sacrifice. She illustrated it with beautiful hand-drawn cartoon characters. I noticed Adam and Eve bore a resemblance to Disney's Aladdin and Princess Jasmine. With help from a contact in India, it was printed in Hindi to hand out to the children. She brought me back a beautiful purple sari and some jewellery.)

So, Shiloh claims her independence, which means Keyz and I have to move. In subsidized housing, it's one bedroom per person. With Shiloh gone, we are overhoused with our third bedroom.

"Hey Shiloh," I say, dropping by her new place in the evening a few months later, after we've both finished work. "Do you want to go on the Blues Cruise with me? It's on Sunday afternoon in two weeks. Brickhouse is playing."

"Really? Yeah, sure. I'd love to go."

"Okay, it's only a maybe right now because I got a ticket for Drago, but I think he's with his other girlfriend for good now, so he probably won't come. If he doesn't, you can."

"Sounds good, Mot." Mot is a nickname derived from the first three letters of mother. In my manic phase just before my breakdown, I had an idea of the girls and me opening a takeout cafe from our house. Our subsidized housing building was under leaky condo construction for eighteen months, so the place was crawling with guys who had to eat. We were going to call it Mot's and Dot's, Dots being a shorthand for daughters.

As it turns out, Shi does accompany me on the cruise, which is an annual event hosted by the local band Brickhouse. A three-hour tour of Burrard Inlet on a sunny day on a boat loaded with people, music, dancing, food, and drinks.

Shi and I have gone below deck to get something to eat. We get our food and sit talking as we eat.

"Oh, Shi, I just remembered something I was going to tell you. You know how I did that demo in Shopper's Drug Mart recently handing out samples of Depends Undergarments? Well, it was a hard give because nobody wanted to take them, but then this woman and her daughter and granddaughter came in. The daughter was really pretty and nice, and she said, 'I'll take one. I have Crohn's disease. They're good for travelling.' So I gave her a few. I just was thinking you might want to use them on the plane when you go to India on your trip."

Her face darkens. "Mom, shut up," she hisses.

"Why, what's wrong? I just thought—"

"STOP. No. Don't say another word."

*

For me, moving is one of life's greatest stressors. Thankfully, at this time, I have a guy hanging around, hoping to move in. That is a great gift in my hour of need. This is Drago, a small handsome, dark-haired Croatian man. His blood-alcohol ratio is 1:1, equal parts. He is never sober, existing in a state of hardcore alcoholism that means he sleeps very little, which is handy because we do a couple of all-nighters packing and cleaning, dropping off loads at Value Village in the dark, under the sign that says, "No Dumping."

He is a godsend. I've noticed a pattern in that regard. Although some of my loser guys leave a messy footprint, sometimes the right guy is there when I have a specific problem or need. For example, my mom helps me keep my fourteen-year-old van insured and running, but it gets to the point the only thing holding it together is the bullet-hole stickers I put on it. So, I start dating a mechanic. That is Drago.

As I mentioned, because he needs a place to live and he's narrowed his options to another woman and me, he is very helpful. I am really annoyed with Keyz, who is no help at all with moving. Leading up to the move, she sleeps on the couch, unwakeable for seventeen hours, even at crunch time. That is one of my first clues she is pregnant. She is sixteen and looks much the same as she has for the past few years, with black hair and a pretty face and long eyelashes. She goes through a phase of drawing on strange, long black eyebrows until she takes her nail technician course, and her instructor says no one has black eyebrows. After that she modifies them slightly. A few years later I see the movie *Amy* about singer Amy Winehouse, who died at twenty-seven from an alcohol overdose, and she reminds me of Keziah and vice versa. Amy also had a striking appearance and many creative interests. And like Keziah, she had insecurities, used heroin, and had an eating disorder.

I insist Keyz has an abortion because I don't want to raise her child and I don't trust her to do it. I explain the difficulty of being a single parent and that I believe it's better for children to have two parents, which she reluctantly agrees is ideal. Plus, I am concerned about the health of the baby from all the alcohol and drugs. She won't consider adoption. I ask her if she knows who the father is and she admits she doesn't, could be any one of the few guys she's been having sex with during weekend parties. Twenty-eight years after my abortion, she's having hers. I was just barely nineteen. She is sixteen.

She is very unhappy with me but very happy with the drugs they give her to do the procedure. I am afraid she'll get pregnant again, just for the high. In the recovery room, she gets a text on her cell phone telling her that her old friend from school, Tiger, has attempted suicide and is in Vancouver General Hospital. It's a strange coincidence that they're both dealing with medical issues at the same time.

Still groggy, she cries for him. "Mom, can we go?"

"Of course, but I thought you two weren't really friends anymore, that you didn't really like him. You haven't seen him in ages." Keyz has a busy social life, which often includes coke-fuelled orgies on the weekends with several guys and girls.

"Mom, he tried to kill himself. He'll be happy to see me. Let's go."

On her way out, she practically empties a bowl of condoms into her large purse.

"Keyz, you don't need that many. Put some back."

She keeps walking, saying, "They said we could take some."

We drive to the hospital and find a large room on the psych ward. Tiger is sitting on a small couch playing a game with some girl. When he realizes it is Keyz, his face lights up, and he says, "You came."

"Yo, dude, wassup?"

We hang around for about half an hour. Tiger often came by the house looking for Keyz when she was out with her other friends. I felt like I should invite him in because it was often cold rainy evenings when he showed up, but I was afraid to, lest he become too regular. Any other people in the house make me nervous, yet I felt guilty turning him away.

I ask Keyz about his situation. He is in foster care of some kind, with his grandma maybe, but he lives far from the school, so he hangs around the neighbourhood after school with no place to go. He is a polite, somewhat nerdy lad. He breaks my heart.

As I sit in that hospital, I want to cry for us all—my little daughter, who is inwardly devastated by the loss of a baby she was sure would be a welcome addition to her life ("All the teen moms at school say it's the best thing that ever happened to them"); Tiger, who is so lost and alone and unloved he feels life isn't worth living; and me, who is familiar with both their pain as well as my own, feeling like a total fuckup, a pain-creating machine.

Life is hard.

Keyz tells me the abortion is the reason she started using smack, a slang term for heroin. I counter with the fact that she's been doing alcohol and drugs to excess for years before she got pregnant, and I'm not going to accept the blame for that. Her repertoire includes alcohol, marijuana, ecstasy, MDMA, various kinds of pills, LSD, cocaine, heroin, meth, and crack. I don't think there's a drug she hasn't tried. I know of four emergency room visits related to her drug use.

There's no telling if I made a mistake with her abortion. I discussed it with several friends, and they all agreed it was the only right and responsible thing to do if she wouldn't give it up. I was concerned about how her drug use might have affected the child. I knew I was not up to taking on a special needs grandchild, and I was pretty sure with her track record I'd be left holding the diaper bag.

The following September, Keyz, Shi, and I are at Starbucks having a coffee, and Keyz's eyes well up with tears. "You don't even remember, do you? This is the month my baby would have been born." I never gave it another thought once the deed was done but to breathe a sigh of relief and thanks. But from the moment a woman, of any age, finds out she's pregnant and that her body contains another life, she becomes a mother in her heart.

I don't know what happens after we die, but I make up scenarios, which include unborn children on earth becoming the children they were meant to be in the other realm, and I've imagined a beautiful little girl with the longest eyelashes in heaven walking up to Keyz, lifting her arms and saying, "Mama."

*

On moving day, my brother Gary, my dear friend Art, and the friend I hire with the moving truck grunt and sweat as they wrestle furniture and appliances to our new abode, a two-level, two-bedroom townhouse in Pitt Meadows, ten minutes farther away from Shiloh and my job selling flowers in a kiosk at a mall in Port Coquitlam. This is still subsidized housing. Drago is working on moving day at his job as a mechanic.

I like this new place better. The walls are a pale bluish colour, which makes me feel peaceful. I have a huge bathroom compared to the last, with enough counter space to have a bouquet of flowers in the bathroom and enough room to house my second-hand washer and dryer.

I have a housewarming party and tell Keyz she can invite her friends, those who helped with the move. The day of the party, Keyz asks if Corey can come, as Geoff can't. I relent. They mostly stay up in her room except for passing through the crowded living room to the patio to smoke. I see the back of a kid in a brown jacket and instinctively think that I don't like him.

I ask Keyz about him later, and it turns out that it was Corey. He starts to come around a lot. One day as I am passing by Keziah's mess of a room, I notice my roll of tin foil on the floor among the debris. What the hell is she doing with my tin foil? I notice some small blackened pieces on the floor but don't pay much attention.

I can't remember how I find out that Keyz is doing heroin, but Corey introduced her to it. Now I understand my gut feeling about him. I get her a little job working with me at a trade show doing demos. She is supposed to be selling potato chips, but she looks miserable. She keeps complaining she is freezing. She won't smile. I am annoyed at her performance, but somewhat gratified later when she says, "That was awful. My feet are killing me. I don't know how you do it." Much later she tells me that was her first time being sick from heroin withdrawal. She claims she didn't know it was addictive.

But I still don't remember if she told me she was doing it before that or how I found out. Sadly, a lot of Keziah's life is like that for me. I can't remember the details of her birth, or many specifics about her life. She kind of existed on the periphery of my own. Shiloh knew her far better than I did. I don't think I read to her much. I was just too busy. She clung to me like a baby monkey and hung on for the ride. She wasn't articulate like Shiloh, making it hard for her dad and me to bond with her. She was hard to understand when she did speak. I bonded better with Shiloh because it was easier having one child than two, and she was my little buddy. By the time Keyz came along two and a half years later, it was just more overwhelming to do everything that was required, I guess. Shiloh understood her though. I do remember she was cute as a button; she had a pretty little face.

One day when they are still quite small, Keyz runs through the living room and grabs one of Shiloh's drawings off the coffee table and crumples it into a ball, laughing like the devil. Shiloh starts crying. "Mommy, Keziah wrecked my picture."

I go from the kitchen to the living room to survey the destruction. Keziah stands there, waiting for the consequence. I go over to her and pick her up.

"Shiloh, come over here, please," I say. "Keyz, look at Shiloh. She's crying because you hurt her. You need to say sorry."

Keyz sits mutely in my arms. "Keyz, look at Mommy. You have to say sorry to Shiloh for hurting her."

Keyz looks down. She isn't even two years old, but she knows what is happening. I am surprised at her reluctance to apologize.

"Keyz, we are going to sit here until you say sorry." I see her squirming with discomfort in her heart. She is a tiny little human being with an instinctive aversion to admitting and making amends for her bad behaviour.

We wait quietly. Finally, she drops her head and quietly says, "Sorry, Dilope." That was what she called Shiloh then. I can see her bottom lip quivering.

"Thank you, Keyz. That's a good girl. Now Shiloh, you say, 'I forgive you.'"

She does as directed, and we have a group hug.

Sometimes saying you're sorry is the hardest thing to do but the quickest and best way to mend a relationship. Forgiveness is usually easy to extend if someone offers a genuine apology but hard to if they don't, at least for me. Maybe that's why God expects us to repent. Is God like us? I don't know about all that.

Boris and my mom felt it was important for the girls to go to Christian school. Mom helped pay the tuition. They wore red Stewart tartan uniforms. Because Boris wanted me to work in the shop at least part-time when the girls were both in school, I used drive thru restaurants as a convenient substitute for healthier meals sometimes or for after-school snacks. My cooking was much like my mother's—meat for protein, potatoes, rice, or pasta for carbs, and two different coloured vegetables. Despite my attempts to feed my family healthy food, we all seemed to be heavier than ideal. I think Keziah's chubbiness really became a problem for her by grade three or four. She stuffed her feelings about our family breakup and ate to compensate. Of course, she got teased. Kids picking on each others' weaknesses and calling names even happens at Christian school, to my chagrin.

By about grade six or seven, Keyz was already becoming somewhat rebellious. She drew a moustache on a picture of the principal's face, who was a woman and a pastor's wife. She begged me to let her go to public school. By that time, my lifestyle was so hypocritical to Christianity I relented without too much pressure. The school had decreased the tuition to make it more affordable, but as a white-trash family, I didn't really feel we belonged there anymore. At one time, it had been like a family. Now, it was just another example of failure.

Keyz was drawn to provocative feminine fashions from an early age. When she was eight years old, she asked me to buy her thong underwear. I said no way. She asked if she could get her ears pierced. "I'm reluctant, Keyz. I'm afraid if I let you put holes in your ears, you'll want them other places next."

One day at the dinner table when she is about ten or eleven, I notice a bump under Keziah's white school uniform shirt.

"Keyz, lift up your shirt."

She blanches and says, voice quivering, "I don't want to."

"Do it anyway, please." I gasp when I see a dangly metal bejewelled ornament gracing her belly button. "Keziah, what did you do?!"

"I pierced my navel."

"You did it yourself?!" She nods.

"Take it out."

"Mom, please."

Shiloh pipes up. "Mom, I think you should let her keep it."

"Take it out."

Sadly, she removes the bling thing. I never really knew what she was up to and usually assumed it was no good. She bought push-up bras for her tiny breasts and got me to drive into Vancouver for warehouse sales of tiny low-rise jeans with one inch zippers.

Some time shortly before my psychotic breakdown, we drove to the downtown East Side of Vancouver to an Aritzia warehouse sale. They have armed security guards at the entrance. They take women's purses at the door. It is unnerving in my condition. Who does that? Apparently, it is a security precaution against shoplifting, but how do I know they won't steal from me?

Again, I feel like I am in hell, waiting while young girls are milling through racks and racks of extremely expensive cheaply made clothes. Security guards are everywhere. Keyz finds something she wants to try on. We are directed to a curtained-off area, one big space where everyone changes in front of each other, no privacy. Bizarre.

I buy her a pair of booty shorts that I tell her she is only allowed to wear at home. And maybe something else, I forget. As we are leaving, I look into the dark eyes of the security guard at the exit and say, "If I say I'm sorry I came here, will you promise I don't have to come back?" His expression doesn't change. He looks at me like the psycho I am.

On our way back to the car, a guy in a wheelchair eating McDonald's fries asks me for change. I say, "No, sorry, but I'll give you a cigarette," which I do. I smoked on and off through my forties. I finally quit about six months after my bipolar diagnosis; being asthmatic, the cough was killing me. He sticks the cigarette behind his ear and throws the rest of the fries, container and all, on the sidewalk. Asshole, I think to myself, and we quickly jump in the car and lock our doors.

On the drive home, I say, "I want to stop by Matt's on the way home." Usually, Keyz would resist, but she is happy with her new clothes. Matt is a drinking buddy of mine. He drinks a bottle of rum every night after work. I've seen him do a full face plant from a standing position. I've sat around his kitchen table and drunk with him for three days, a few times. I drank with him on Keziah's twelfth birthday.

That day, the girls go shopping at Value Village while I drink with Matt and then go pick them up. They are mad at me of course, rightly so. Matt tells me to bring them back to his house. He is a loner but never wants to surrender my company when he gets it.

"Hi girls, how's it going? Find anything?"

"Not really."

"Okay, well, I'm going to pick up some stuff, and we're going over to Matt's."

"Mom, NO," Shiloh says, resolute.

"Yes, we're going to give Keyz a little party. Come on." I walk out, hoping they'll follow. "Let's get a bucket of chicken at KFC and an ice cream cake at the DQ."

"Really, Mom?"

"Sure, what kind do you want?"

"Oreo, please."

"You got it."

Even though it is a sucky birthday, what matters to Keyz is that I am spending money on her. It's a self-esteem issue. I always feel good spending money on my kids because it is like a release valve for my guilt about everything I feel like I should do but don't and everything I feel like I shouldn't but do. We get our stuff and drive back to Matt's.

"Knock, knock. Hey, we're here. We got chicken and cake. Let the games begin. Matt, this is Shiloh and this is Keziah, the birthday girl."

"Hi. How old are you?"

"Twelve."

"Would you like some Coke?"

"Yes, please."

Soon, there is a knock on the door and some friends of Matt's stop in briefly. We invite them to have food and cake. Nothing like partying with strangers. I know Keyz feels weird. After they leave, we settle around Matt's high-top glass kitchen table on swivel stools. Matt says, "Since it's your birthday, you can have a beer, if you want one."

I see Shiloh's eyebrows raise in alarm. My level of drunkenness by this time is such that I allow it, but I can still feel misgivings in there somewhere. Keyz snuggles her beer, figuratively speaking. Here we are, a man, a woman, and two kids, almost like a family. We coast on the good feelings of our shared adventure for awhile. Keyz loves her beer. Matt offers her another one.

"Okay, but that's it," I say.

As Keyz gets into her second beer, she grows a perma-smile. Her head is resting on her arms crossed on the table. She is attentively listening to Matt rant.

"So, you can have fun, but you have to know your limits." Keyz is nodding. The more boundary talking he does, the happier she seems. *Nanny 911* is one of her favourite TV shows, which indicates to me she's craving the parenting she lacks.

And then something happens. I don't know what. I can't remember. Maybe she says something he misinterprets or spills her beer or...? And everything just slides sideways. Matt gets into a fucked-up mood, as some drunks are wont to do. The best thing to do is get up and say goodbye, which we do, but there is a certain amount of hashing out that has to be endured first.

Shiloh was the only sober person in the room, so supposedly her version should be the most reliable. And her version is that Matt is a jerk. Probably. I gave up on our friendship after that, which I maintained for several years, sober. But then he called and invited me over one night, so I drove half an hour or so, and shortly after I got there, he got a call from his cousin inviting him to a party an hour from his place. He wanted me to drive him there. He was already so plastered he was weaving his way to my car.

In the car, I said, "You know, I gotta tell you I kind of feel used. You invite me over, and then you want me to drive you an hour out of my way, so you can drink when you're already so drunk you can hardly walk. I don't think so. I'm done."

It's hard to maintain relationships that get too imbalanced by someone's substance use and abuse. I've lost friends when I was drinking. I understand. Sometimes a friendship is held together by the substance use and abuse, but often it's what pulls it apart in the end.

One last thing I want to say about Matt is my heart aches for him in his suffering. The thing I feel worst about in my awful dark days of parenting is leaving my kids home alone for a weekend while I drank with Matt. Before I left, I was screaming like a psycho. I yanked the phone jack out of the wall so they couldn't bug me. I can picture them standing there together in the living room looking scared. They were probably about eleven and thirteen. It was only once but that was more than enough.

I am so ashamed of myself for this. Those poor little girls. Sometimes I thought they'd be better off in foster homes. Or would they be? I was terrified they'd be molested. Or maybe they'd be better off with my mom, but it wasn't fair to put that responsibility on her. I know there are thousands of kids growing up in dysfunctional homes like ours, where there's not enough time, money, parents, community, or love. I know because a lot of my kids' friends came from those homes. I came from one, as did my dad and Boris.

I sometimes can get really depressed and overwhelmed thinking about it. What is the solution? Where do we begin? I took parenting skills classes occasionally. The first one was when Shiloh was eighteen months old and I was already struggling, and I took one when Keyz was about eleven or twelve. I don't think that's enough. They say it takes a village (and a vineyard) to raise a child, and I think there's something to that. But sometimes I think human beings are here for a reason—to become who we are and to experience self-actualization. The conditions we grow up in can be compared to different types of soil, to borrow a Biblical analogy. A plant that grows among rocks becomes stronger, in sand, more resilient, and in weeds, more competitive, or whatever. Okay, that analogy was disappointing.

One time when I was distraught about all the things my poor kids suffered at the hands of their mood-disordered, alcoholic mother, I said to them, "Girls, I just feel so bad about all those awful times when I was drinking. It breaks my heart. Will you please forgive me?"

Shi said, "Oh, Mama Bear, we kind of forgot all that now. Don't worry, we love you."

Sweet, undeserved forgiveness from a child. Or rather, so much grace and so much compassion and acceptance from a child. Perhaps our children teach us as much about love, or more, than we can ever hope to teach them. Certainly, I have found the challenge of mothering the biggest educational experience, as well as the most demanding school curriculum, of my entire life. And the biggest lessons waiting for me from the school of mothering were just around the corner, although I didn't know it yet.

16

The Good, The Bad, and The (Un)lucky

A few months after Boris and I separated, I saw an ad in *The Georgia Straight* for auditions for a play. This was in 2003. The girls were nine and eleven. I was forty-two. I tried out and was cast in the lead female role in a play called *Pilate*, written by a Seattle playwright. This was going to be its Canadian debut.

I am playing Pilate's wife, Claudia. My husband Pilate, is being played by a tall, handsome guy, younger than me—a Christian with a difficult history, named Terrance. The rehearsals and show are at First Baptist Church on Burrard Street in Vancouver. One of the other guys in the cast who plays several bit parts is called Ace. He reminds me of that famous dancer, Fred Astaire. He is closer to my age, late forties. His hair is thinning on top, but he has a lamb's tail. After rehearsal one night, we sit outside on the steps of the old church and chat. He holds no religious beliefs, and this is his first attempt at acting. He has no phone.

"What makes you believe in Christianity? You strike me as an intelligent woman. Do you know Christianity's reputation for killing anyone who disagrees with it, like the Spanish Inquisition for example?" Ace baits.

"I don't really know a lot about that. All I have to go on is my personal experience, and I've had experiences that I don't know how to account for other than God."

"Interesting. I wish I could believe. But all scientific evidence leads me to believe that we are matter, and when we die, we are absorbed into the earth, and that's it."

"That's kind of a dismal forecast. It seems to me that we are spirit and matter. When we leave our material bodies behind, our spirit continues to live in some other realm."

We continue bantering back and forth until I suddenly realize the time. "Oh my, I've gotta run. The Skytrain closes at 1:00 a.m. It's been nice talking with you Ace."

"I'll walk you to the station."

"But you have your bike."

"That's okay. I can walk beside it."

"Okay, if you like. You don't have to."

"I want to."

"All right then. Let's burn."

I sense that Ace likes me, but he is tentative. However, during the run of the show, he gets bolder. I have eight costume changes, so sometimes I just have to do a quick change just offstage, as I don't have time to go back to the dressing room. One time, I leave the stage and start undressing before I see Ace and his friend Garth sitting there, watching. "Get out of here," I hiss.

After the show one night, I go into the change room, and Ace is bare except for his underwear. He has an athletic physique, with beautiful legs that would make a drag queen jealous. "Oh, nice body, Ace. Thanks for showing it to me." I know it is deliberate.

I am excited and nervous to be playing this role, as it's the largest dramatic role I've had and I'm taking the opportunity seriously. There is a lot of dialogue and a kissing scene—well, a one kiss scene—that I can't seem to get through in rehearsal without messing up every time by laughing or something. These episodes make me aware of how uncomfortable I really am with intimacy while being very attracted to my fellow actor. I feel like a young girl being kissed by a boy she likes for the first time, which is what I'm supposed to be feeling because that's what the scene is about, but it's real and I'm shy and awkward.

It is Laila, the director's, first attempt at directing a play, and I'm extremely impressed with her talents. She's an intelligent and artistic middle-aged woman that should have been exercising her skills much sooner, I think. My character ages from a young girl to an older woman, and Laila helps me show that transition through voice, attitude, and body language.

On opening night, I suddenly feel inspired and divert from her suggestions in a seductive scene by rubbing my stockinged foot across my husband's crotch while sitting on his desk. I thought it worked great, as it infused some fresh energy and got a rise out of him, but at intermission, Laila comes storming into the dressing room yelling, "Who told you to do that? Why would you do that? I'm the director! You don't just suddenly add things in during a performance!" I've never seen a director lose their shit like that, ever. She was absolutely correct though. It was a rookie mistake, even though I wasn't a rookie and knew better. But I also knew I could trust Terrance to work with it, which he did. She was particularly upset because she was sitting with friends in a church and didn't want them to think she'd directed that lewd move. I'm sure she told them she didn't. She certainly told me. I felt a bit rattled after that for awhile. It would have been better if she'd waited until after the show to give me her notes, but maybe she was afraid I'd gone rogue and wanted to nip it in the bud.

Terrance, my husband, is also the main set designer and does an outstanding job creating an amazing design complete with columns to replicate Pilate's palace, fashioned after a scale model he made from toothpicks and cardboard, which was a feat in itself. Some of us actors helped to construct the set at warehouse space loaned by a local theatre company, which then had to be transported to the church for the two night run of a show we rehearsed for months. I remember holding my breath watching Terrance dangle precariously from a tall ladder painting pillars and hanging lights.

Just before we are about to go onstage the first night, I am standing in the dark wing just offstage. I have the opening line, and I'm deep breathing, preparing myself for the moment when I step into the light, my mouth opens, and the magic begins. Seconds before my entrance, I feel a tall, warm presence in the darkness behind me. Terrance wraps his arms around me, in a moment that melds him and his character into me and mine. It is divine, an unforgettable touch that awakens Claudia in me.

Because the play is being performed in the sanctuary of the First Baptist Church, we run it Friday and Saturday night, and then have to tear the set down before the service Sunday morning. I am there helping with tear down until about 3:00 a.m., and this is after an unfortunate occurrence toward the end of the play. My co-star makes a sudden change to the slap scene near the end of the play, in which he swings his arm to hit me in the face, which we had rehearsed a million times to make it look realistic, but instead he swings the other way. (It just occurred to me this may have been a little payback for the foot in the crotch.)

Fortunately, I was completely in the moment and responded appropriately, but it threw me off, and as I fell to the stage limp, I felt my head hit the floor and heard a loud collective gasp from the audience. In the few ensuing lines of monologue when my husband Pilate doesn't know whether he's just injured or killed me, I feel his tears fall onto my face, which is thankfully pretty numb, along with my head. I didn't black out, but as I am helping with the teardown, I develop a headache and wonder if I may have a concussion. St. Paul's Hospital is just down the street, and I consider getting checked out but decide the show must come down, so I keep working.

Originally, we were expecting the playwright to come and see the show, but plans were changed, and, honestly, I was relieved. I know I'd have been more nervous knowing he was there. It was a good play, though, based on historical events but modernized with a cool dream scene as well as the romantic, violent, and emotionally moving scenes. It was the kind of play actors dream of, containing many opportunities to learn and grow. I felt that I'd done a pretty good job. I count it a huge privilege to have worked with so many talented people. It helped restore my confidence during a time when the rest of my life was falling apart.

My mom comes from Creston to see the show on the Saturday night, accompanied by my friend Russ. After the show, I change quickly and go out into the dispersing audience to see them. Mom's eyes are shining, and her voice wobbly as she says, for the first time I recall, "I'm so proud of you." Russ says, "You're very talented." Nice, thanks.

At the cast party, Ace sidles over and sits next to me. "This is kind of depressing, don't you think? I'm really sad the show is show is over. I'm going to miss everyone. It was a great experience for me."

"Yeah, there's always that bitter sweetness to finishing a show," I say. "I like the sense of accomplishment and that we came together as a team that sort of evolved into a family and we did our thing and now it's on to the next."

"No, I'm really feeling emotional about it. I'm not ready for it to be over. It reminds me of when my mom died. We were seven kids, and then my dad left. I was really angry. I was mad at my mom because while my dad was still there, she found my pot plant in the garden. I begged her not to tell my dad, but she did. I felt like she'd betrayed me. Our relationship changed after that, got distant. After my dad left, she'd go out to the garage every night for awhile, and we weren't allowed to bug her. We didn't know it, but she was studying to take her real estate exam. She got her license and worked hard and made millions. Then she got sick. I was the only one who could take care of her. Everyone else was too busy or involved with their own families. So, I lived with Mom and took care of her. It was hard at first, but then it was really good. I considered it a privilege. We reconciled, you know. And it really hurt me when she died. I wasn't ready."

Ace's eyes glisten.

"That's too bad. I'm sorry to hear it."

He draws a shaky breath. "Yeah, me too. Anyways, what are you doing tomorrow? Maybe you, Terrance, and I can have coffee?"

"Yeah, probably. You'll have to talk to him, but I'm in."

The next day when we go to meet Terrance at his apartment building, two older gentlemen are just coming out at the same time. They recognize us, and one says, "You were in the play last night, no? Such a good job you did, all of you. It was amazing. Are you professional actors?"

No, but thank you. That was a high compliment I've always valued. It's out of sequence here, but I wanted to sneak it in. And while I'm at it, I want to give myself credit for what Terrance said was a "brilliant instinct" in rehearsal to throw the last few drops in my wine glass at his back during a contentious scene, even though we didn't use it onstage. It was akin to the brilliant instinct to put my foot in his crotch, in my opinion, but I'm flogging a dead horse.

As it turns out, Ace comes home with me that night. He walks into our beautiful home with a sneer on his face, nodding his head as if to say, "Okay, I see." He says, "This is so gauche."

How rude, I think. Who walks into someone's house and says something like that? I'd never even heard anyone actually use the word "gauche."

A couple of months later, when I walk into his apartment, which is on the corner of Main and Hastings, noted for being the poorest postal code in Canada, I say, "Oh, this is nice," even though it stinks of stale cigarette and pot smoke and is a pigsty with clothes all over the bed and couch, which is all the furniture there is in the tiny bachelor suite. Oh sorry, there is a small table and mismatched chairs. It is a hovel, decorated with dirty dishes and empty cupboards. It has the grossest shower I've ever been in.

I still can't for the life of me figure out why he called my very nice house "gauche" when he first stepped inside, given his own shabby digs. But some of the time at least, he seems to think I'm glamorous.

I call myself Wacky Jacquie.

"Why? Why not Classy Jacquie?" he asks.

"Well, for one thing, it doesn't rhyme, and for another, it's not true."

Ace is always trying to change his friends and me into something we aren't. I find it annoying.

I forgot to say he didn't sleep with me the night he came over after the cast party. Before I could have the privilege of having sex with him, I had to understand that his last girlfriend hurt him, and he hadn't had a relationship for nine years. I had to promise not to hurt him. As far as I'm concerned, promises are for kids. I don't make promises, as I can't handle the responsibility. However, I said I'd try, and I guess that was close enough. So now, this first time we have sex, he is pumping away, and I sense liftoff is imminent, so I say, "Don't come inside me. I don't have any birth control."

Pump, pump, squirt, inside. Fuck, I think to myself. What an asshole. I specifically said don't, and he does. A month later at the walk-in clinic, a doctor confirms that I am pregnant. I cover my face with my hands.

"Oh, my god, no."

He looks at me apologetically for delivering the bad news. "I take it you wish to terminate?"

"Oh, shit, yeah. I'm forty-two years old, and I've already got two kids I can barely support. Dammit."

When I tell Ace, he says, "I'm not opposed to the idea of keeping it. My children keep getting aborted."

"Well, I am. There's no way. I'm making an appointment at Everywoman's."

I don't want the girls or Ace's friend Garth, who has become my boarder and taken over residence in Boris's Lazyboy in front of the big screen TV, to know about the abortion. We make up some excuse for being away for the day. Ace doesn't have a driver's licence, so I drive my van, with him as the passenger. As we are approaching the left lane where I have to turn, Ace says, "Pull up a bit. No, back up."

"Why?"

"Why can't you just do what I tell you? There are sensors under the pavement that will cause the light to change faster if you activate them with your tires."

"Who cares? We're here. We've got plenty of time. God, Ace, why can't you support me instead of putting me down and telling me how to drive."

I start crying. "On this of all days. This is your fault because you didn't listen to me, so fuck off."

He becomes contrite then, transforming from his usually arrogant, bossy self into the quintessential feminist partner, impressing all the women at the abortion clinic with his calm supportive demeanour. I swear half of them are wondering why they can't find a man like that. I feel like telling them this prick is why we are here.

Anyway, the dirty deed is done, bringing the death toll to children of my womb to three. I drive us home. I lie on the leather couch. We watch a movie, and Ace brings me snacks, drinks, and a blanket. I am sure it must be obvious to my boarder what we've been up to. Ace's uncharacteristic behaviour is a dead giveaway. I feel like a fool but say nothing. I am trying to get used to a metallic taste in my mouth from the IUD I had inserted into my uterus after the abortion to prevent further problems.

Ace does another play. I go to the cast party. He is busy talking to the girls in the lobby, and I go down to the stage and start dancing to the canned music playing. Nobody else is there except a guy who comes to me and says, "Do you jive?"

I say, "I'll try." It is a blast. He is a good strong lead that does most of the work. I love jiving with someone like that.

Ace comes in and says, "What are you doing?" Stupid question.

"Dancing," I say, as I let go of the guy's hands, and he drifts off.

"We need to talk about this."

"Why, what's up?"

"Why are you dancing with another man?"

"Because you were talking. Also, you don't dance, right? He asked me. What's the problem?"

"Don't act like you don't know. This is my cast party, and you're dancing with someone else."

"Again—" He cuts me off.

"We'll talk about this later."

From then on, he ignores me. My bullshit tolerance is pretty low by now. The girls and I leave. He is mad about the dancing and the leaving, and the fact that his hemorrhoids hurt. He insists that I spend the weekend figuring out why I dance. I do not have a clue what he is talking about. I dance because I enjoy it. That's it. That's all.

But to him that is not it, nor is that all. I am beginning to feel oppressed. I can see I'll never make him happy. He tells me he thinks I have bipolar disorder because he and his brother have it, and he recognizes the symptoms. I disagree, although I talk to my doctor about it. She also disagrees. Several years later I am diagnosed with this condition after all, but that was after major new symptoms developed.

Anyway, I knew he would break up with me and that I'd keep my half promise not to break up with him. And that's exactly what happened. He was upset that I didn't try to get him back.

There's something about other people that irks me. I do not know if this is because I now do have bipolar disorder or if there is some other reason. When I was first diagnosed, I picked up a pamphlet at the hospital for my mother that described the condition, but since I gave it to her, I'll have to Google it. Typically, and generally speaking, bipolar disorder is a mental health condition defined by periods/episodes of extreme mood disturbances. Bipolar affects a person's moods, thoughts, and behaviour. It's divided into two categories, bipolar 1 and bipolar 2. In order to be diagnosed as bipolar 1 as I am, you need to experience at least one manic episode and one depressive episode. My first manic episode was when I quit my job and went to Montréal on the train. My second was when I wanted to go be with my children in heaven and ended up in the hospital.

But for me personally, I feel like it refers to heightened emotions at all times, so that a move or a trip can generate extreme anxiety for me when it's just a normal thing for other people. I joke that I overreact and then overapologize. For example, I live in an over-fifty-five, low-income building, and the elevator ranges in smell from fumy to reeking sometimes. If I get stuck in the smelevator with someone and they either talk about the weather or some other such boring thing or they don't talk at all, I can become irked beyond all reason. Sometimes when people are talking, I can find the subject so dull that it's as though I leave my body and hover in observation of the phenomenon of conversation, feeling completely disconnected from the situation. People's need to talk all the time can irritate me this same extreme way. Car alarms, leaf blowers, garbage trucks, emergency sirens, and shouting voices are other sounds that are quite ordinary, but they can quickly disturb my calm and put me in a state of extreme anxiety or irritability.

What else irks me in this way? When people don't tip their server, when women pee all over the public toilet seats trying to avoid germs, when people don't push their paper down in the garbage can and it falls all over the floor, when they talk during movies or TV, when they mooch my food but don't share theirs, or when they buy me gifts I don't like, want, or need but feel compelled to keep. I suppose everyone has their list. What sets the bipolar person apart from the rest is the inability to tone down the reaction to an appropriate level in the moment. Everything flares up to its highest possible volume in an instant. This is where the medication can be quite beneficial, as it helps to control the response and to tone it down to a manageable level.

I had a hard time being a wife and mom sometimes. I felt selfish. I said I wish I wasn't this way. It doesn't seem like a nice way to be. It seems like a flaw. But now that I'm divorced and bereaved of all my children, it makes it easier to be alone. So, to me, this is a bit of unexpected grace in my life—a recognition that even though I've disliked myself for it, maybe I'm the way I am for a reason and I could try to accept myself more.

17

Desperate Digressions

When Boris and I separate, our rent is still 1,100 dollars a month. I don't want to move because it rocks my world. I still love this beautiful house, our "happy house," as we had called it, but I know I can't afford to stay. I take in a couple of boarders who end up not working out. My mom helps me pay the rent. I have no income, so I apply for welfare, which I am denied despite my genuine tears. I can't remember why. Was it because I didn't look needy enough or because some politician changed the rules and made everyone do a job search before receiving assistance? I'm not sure anyone explained it to me. In frustration, I scream, "It's no wonder people come into places like this with guns and start shooting people."

I am told to leave the premises, even through I am already going, and in a follow-up letter, I'm told my threats render me unwelcome at the office, pending an apology. This is post 9-11, when uttering threats in public places is taken much more seriously than it was before. I don't go back. I have already received the paperwork directing me to a job club where I'm offered assistance in getting employment. Through this contact, I get a job through a telephone interview, demonstrating the benefits of a new household insulation product in Home Depot stores on weekends.

The day of my first shift in Abbotsford, nearly an hour's drive from home, I am so nervous and hungry I lock my keys in my van twice in an hour. I don't eat breakfast, and I stand behind a table with no breaks for five hours, trying to entice people to talk about a subject I personally find mind numbingly dull. I pester people to fill in market research questionnaires. At the end of my shift, I pack up my gear, load it in my van, and drive home, 125 dollars a shift. The money is good. In 2008, the recession supposedly necessitated a drop in pay to one hundred dollars a shift, but it's still worth doing. By then I'm servicing local stores in Coquitlam and Port Coquitlam. The company has made a serious dent in the market, which I like to think I'm partially responsible for, and we've added Rona and Lowe's to my schedule, which are a longer drive out, to Burnaby and New Westminster but not as often, only once a month.

One day I'm at my demo table at Home Depot in Vancouver when two young guys come in. Their energy is up. We start bantering good naturedly, joking around. One laughs at my facial expression and says, "You should do comedy."

I say, "I do." He's cute, early to mid-twenties, smaller guy, but I like small guys because they're more like women. We start flirting. He invites me to his place. I tell him, "I'm off at two. Where do you live?"

He says, "Are you serious? Oh my god. I'll tell you what, we'll hang around here while you pack up, and you can follow us to my place."

"Sounds good."

We carry out the plan. His friend drives off, shaking his head.

My new friend says, "Come on in. Would you like a glass of wine?"

"Sure, thanks."

We sit on his couch sipping our wine in a basement suite, obviously male decorated. His display of treasures includes a tarantula spider in an empty fish tank with a screen on top; he also has a couple of lizards and a snake in other tanks.

"Uh, that kind of freaks me out. Has it ever escaped?" I ask.

His name is Alfonso: the guy, not the spider.

He laughs. "No, no, don't worry. You're safe here."

To this day I can not explain why I left work with a total stranger to drink wine and inevitably fuck. But there is energy between us, something we both feel. I imagine my mother reading this and saying out loud, "It's undoubtedly lust." I'm almost twice his age. It's flattering to have a young man want you. I'm a cougar. It's my job to hunt. Still, I am nervous. I explain I have two daughters at home. I've never done this before, left work in the middle of the day to have afternoon delight with a stranger, and sober at that. I can't help telling him a bit of my sad story, which makes me cry a little.

"You want to smoke a joint?" I ask.

"Oh man, I used to be chronic so I'm trying not to smoke."

"No problem. I don't want to be a bad influence on you. Do you mind if I have a puff?"

"No, go ahead, but do you mind going outside? I'll come with you." We go outside and up the back steps to the backyard.

I pull my pot pipe from the pouch in my purse. Being broke, I can't afford to waste pot smoking joints. I sprinkle a few grains into my pipe, light it, inhale, hold, and exhale. Two or three puffs is enough.

Alfonso decides to have one.

"Well, what do you want to do now?" he says.

"I don't know. I feel really weird. I can't believe I came here. But I think we both know why we're here so... I guess I'd like to take a shower if you don't mind."

He laughs. "A shower? Okay, go ahead."

"I won't be long. Just want to freshen up, you know."

I go to the bathroom and close the door. It seems grimy. Will I get clean or dirty in here? I hate using other people's showers, especially men's. I note the mouldy grout, the smelly shower curtain, as well as the taps, which my dyslexic brain burns or freezes me with. Even the soap looks dirty. I do a quick rinse, soaping the important body parts. I get out, dry off (oh god, what's been wiped on this towel? I can't believe I'm doing this), and try to turn some toothpaste into mouthwash with a swift swish. I open the bathroom door. Alfonso is lying on the bed in his underwear.

"Come here," he says.

I scurry over to the bed, drop my towel, and jump under the covers.

"I'm so freaked out," I say. "I can't believe I'm doing this." Even though I've slept with many guys, I've never deliberately gone after someone in broad daylight like this and with someone so much younger than me.

"It's okay, just relax and enjoy it."

We start to kiss. Soon my hands are running down his body. My hand passes over the front of his underwear.

"Oh my god, what is that? Did you put a baseball bat in there?"

He laughs. "No, that's just me."

"Seriously? Let me see it."

He slips the elastic waistband of his boxers over and down, and I gasp.

"It's huge! Oh my god, that's the biggest cock I've ever seen, and I've seen a few. It's massive. You're not a big guy. Where'd you get it?"

"Touch it," he says, and I do, slowly stroking the soft skin. My fingers don't close around it; it's that big. I'm thinking to myself, perfect, just my size. I climb on top of him and guide him gently with my hips and hand to enter me. What a sensation. I squirt and he comes at the same time. Afterward, he says he's all amazed at my squirting, as he has never seen it before.

(If you're not familiar with the phenomenon of female ejaculation, I can explain it a bit here. It's the gush associated in erotic lore with the arousal of the fabled G-spot. Other professionals say there's no such thing, and that it's a paraurethral duct secretion that occurs regularly for some women but by no means all. I don't think there's a consensus about it. I've found some guys are turned on by it; others don't notice or don't comment. My woman lover Nella was a little freaked out by it, not having encountered it before. I find it pleasurable, if a bit messy; it's a relaxing kind of diffuse orgasm that's less intense than clit orgasm but more pervasive and easier to achieve in my case. I haven't had a lot of clit orgasms with men.)

"Well, we both surprised each other today, didn't we? That was amazing," I say.

"No kidding. I can't believe how you could take me. Girls I've been with complain it's too big, and it hurts."

"Well, you can hurt me with that bad boy any time." I smile. "I've gotta go. Don't want my kids asking questions about why I'm late. Thank you, young man. Are you going to give me your number in case I'm ever in your neighbourhood again?"

"Yeah, I guess so."

"Great, thanks again. I had fun. See ya."

In fact, I don't really know exactly where his neighbourhood is in relation to anything else. I call him another time but get lost on my way over there and give up. I don't see him again until about five years later, when he walks into Rona while I'm there. He comes up to my table in the back of the store.

"Hi, you don't remember me, do you?"

"Of course I do, Alfonso. You're hard to forget. How are you?"

"I've been hoping I'd see you again. Um, can I talk to you?"

"Sure, spill it."

He lowers his voice, needlessly. It's Rona, there's no one around. "I'd like to see you. I can't forget how you squirt. Will you give me your number?"

"Sure, here. Call me. It's nice to see you again." Somehow in the space of these years, I got confident, and he got shy. He calls me with a meeting place. He's smoking a cigarette in his truck when I pull up. He looks around furtively. We run to the door which he unlocks. The place is devoid of furniture, with Gyprock on the walls and various tools lying around on the floor.

"What are we doing here? What is this place?" I ask.

"I'm renovating it for work. Um, well, sorry, but we can't go to my place because I have a girlfriend now."

"What?! Why didn't you tell me that?"

"I was afraid you wouldn't come."

"Classic. I wouldn't have. Oh well, we're here now. Come over here and let me feel Woody again."

"I love my girlfriend, and I don't want her to ever find out about this, but I had to see you one more time just to experience it again. I don't know if it's memory or fantasy anymore. I just want one last time."

"Well, your secret's safe with me. I've got to admit that I've thought about you, too. Okay, so let's do this thing."

We kiss and then he breaks away to make an impromptu place for our joining, dragging a paint tarp over to where we're standing. We begin again, but we feel guilty, rushed. I'm on top of him like an olive on top of a toothpick. "Just let go, relax," he says, and whoosh, there it is. I'm filled with the seed of his mighty member, and he's covered in the generous sea of my coconut milk. He's trying to wipe it before it hits the tarp. I'm laughing. It's been fun again.

I do insulation demos on weekends for ten long years before I finally decide my mental health is at risk if I continue. Boredom is a killer for me. I hate getting up early. I hate driving, and I hate being bored. The last couple years I spend writing rhymes about how much I hate my job while I'm at work. I reframe the situation to make it seem I'm being paid to write rhymes, but I'm just writing too many, and it has to stop. So, I retire from demos, with no regret whatsoever. I like talking to people, and I don't mind selling products, but if there're no people, I just squirm in my skin and feel like blowing my brains out. Alfonso never comes by again to relieve me.

I say I'm a cougar. I don't actually hunt young men, but I am separated. I drink heavily, and I am also sexually active and good looking. I always feel weird saying that. But compared to a lot of women my age who have lost the definition of their bodies under a comfy layer of soft padding, my drinking and smoking maintain my curvy figure under 130 pounds, and my double D's haven't lost their power to attract, even if they need a little cheat to stay up in the cup.

Through my boyfriend Curt of the time, around 2005, the cook with the missing front tooth, I meet Carrie, a woman in her early sixties, who lives in our neighbourhood. Carrie and Curt worked together many years ago at his first job and reconnect coincidentally at the Hook and Handle. Curt introduces me and she stumbles over to me, plants a big, soft, wet, warm kiss on my lips, says, "Hello, Darling," then turns to Curt and says, "She looks like Holly." Holly was his ex-wife who has since passed from lung cancer. Carrie is hammered but invites us over to her house to party some more. We buy cold beer from the store next door and make our way the few blocks to her house, which she enters saying, "Just sit there in the yard. I'll be right back." She doesn't return. In a while we go in to say thanks and goodbye and find her passed out on the couch still holding a can of beer upright.

We sit in the backyard with our beer. One of her sons, Jordan, a handsome young man in his early twenties, and her daughter-in-law Addison, who is married to her other son Jared, come out and make small talk.

"You wouldn't have an extra beer there, would you?" one of them asks.

"Oh yeah, sure, sorry, I should have offered. Here," I say, passing them each a can.

*

As my friendship with Carrie progresses, I learn that beer is like compost to fruit flies in this house. Everyone drinks, all the time, and there's never enough money or beer. Carrie has an outrageous, wicked sense of humour. Her speech is coloured with jokes and sayings, such as "I don't drink water. Fish fuck in it." She acknowledges she is an alcoholic and always will be; her attempt at recovery some time ago was unsuccessful. She suffers from depression, and beer is her medication. People drop by the house where the door is always open as long as they bring something to share. Upstairs, at Jared and Addi's place, Carrie's husband, Sam, avoids her bad moods and verbal abuse. Coke and beer are welcomed equally. Sam's not much of a drinker. It's a nonstop party 24/7.

It becomes my home away from home. I want to make it into a reality TV show, called *Carrie's Kitchen and Sam's Backyard*. Carrie is my new best friend, surrogate mother, and drinking buddy. When her blood alcohol level is optimum, she's one of the most entertaining, funniest people I've ever met, with a good and generous heart. When it drops, we sit at her kitchen table and cry together. For my part, I'm crying about the mess I've made of my life—my marriage, the children, finances, Christian school, everything. The kids are now teenagers and I feel overwhelmed, unable to perform as a good mother. I feel sorry for them having to live where we live and not have the stuff their friends have. At Carrie's, I find people who are more dysfunctional than me and my kids. It's like a group home, except it's all one big sad family. Everyone is filled with shame, regret, disappointment, hurt, anger, rage, failure, greyness, monotony, despair, hatred, bitterness, resentment, blame, hopelessness, frustration, and fear. We keep each other company as best we can, trying to keep our heads above water, trying to stay alive.

One of the people who hangs around Carrie's is T-Jay, a young guy in his twenties. He used to date Addison and be a heroin addict. He reminds me of Pee Wee Herman. He often has earphones in his ears. One early afternoon, he shows up at my house with a six pack and lets me listen to his music. It's rap, and it's extreme and offensive, talking about fucking and killing. He smiles when he sees the look of shock on my face.

"Why do you listen to that?" I ask.

"It makes everything else seem saner," or "It silences the other voices in my head," or something. Years later, I listened to Keziah's iPod, when she was no longer with us. It was the same kind of music. She started listening to rap music in elementary school with my disapproval. Finally, I was listening to it with her, when it was too late to help either of us understand the other better.

T-Jay and I crack into the beers. "We should find you someone," he says. He has a narrow face and wears a baseball cap backwards. He's cute in his way.

"What do you mean?"

"We'll put a profile on Plenty of Fish."

"What's that?"

"It's an online dating website."

"I don't want to do that."

"Come on. It'll be fun."

We grab the beer and go upstairs to Shiloh's room where the computer is. I feel guilty for smoking in there. T-Jay makes me a profile for an amusement. For occupation, he types "hand model."

"I don't get it," I say.

"It's from Seinfeld. George became a hand model."

"Oh, I never watched it." That's because I didn't get the remote for the twelve years I was married to Boris.

The website asks, "What's your idea of a first date?" T-Jay puts, "Beer and K-D." We laugh. By then we've each had three beers, which is enough for me to pull him into my bedroom, where we start to have sex.

"Wow! Your Chinese name would be Long Schlong Dong," I exclaim. His cock is enormous, thick and long, even though he's a small guy. And believe it or not, it's two tone. I don't know if it's a birthmark or what, but if he is ever charged with a sex crime he'll be easily identified with those markings. There's nothing like a good fit, whether it's cock or shoes. Very satisfying.

We are getting dressed when I hear the girls coming home from Christian school in their tartan uniforms. T-Jay and I go downstairs.

"Hi girls, this is my friend T-Jay."

Shiloh looks at me with a discerning eye, then at T-Jay. Her eyes say, "I can't believe you." Her mouth says, "That's disgusting."

T-Jay looks uncomfortable and says, "Well, I'm gonna bounce. See ya."

"See ya. Thanks for the beer and everything."

I try to lighten the mood by chattering about the Plenty of Fish thing, but Shiloh isn't having it. "Mom, you make me sick. He's way too young for you. Don't you ever think about the example you're setting for us?"

Clearly that isn't something I need to worry about as my children are parenting me. Do I feel bad? Yes, of course I do. I just don't know what to do about it. I feel bad all the time. I'm living in a piss-soaked white ghetto with no hope of getting out. I don't have enough money or time or energy. I'm trying to escape myself and my sordid life. Internally, it's dark all the time. I hate myself. I hate my life, I hate my ex-husband,

and I hate my boyfriends. Everything I do to try and change these feelings is guilt inducing. Please, please, can't somebody help me? I'm naked and ashamed. I feel sick about the damage I'm doing to my innocent children, but I can't stop. I don't know how. I don't know what to do.

One day when we're drinking at Carrie's, I give T-Jay my bank card and PIN number to go to the bank machine to get cash for beer. I'd rather stay and drink than walk to the store and carry another case over. And another. He's young. He can do it for us. Long story short, after I'd spent about one hundred dollars on beer to keep the party going, I found out T-Jay bought himself a t-shirt and ball cap with my bank card at the nearby skater shop. I lost my shit. I told him he had to pay me back and he did, remotely. I never had any interest in him after that. And he stayed away from Carrie's for quite awhile too.

I meet the third big cock I have known years later at a Plenty of Fish live event, a buffet lunch in Surrey. I am hesitant, arriving a little late, finding a table by myself at the perimeter. A guy soon comes over and starts chatting. He does a little psychological game with me that's supposed to indicate what kind of a person I am. It's a personality test called the Cube that you can find online. He tells me to imagine a number of things, including a field, cube, ladder, and horse, and write their sizes, colours, shapes, and so on. Each object represents an aspect of your life, such as your mind, ego, goals, and ideal partner. I am intrigued. After the brunch, we exchange numbers, and he walks me to my car, pausing to say, "I'm going to kiss you." And he does so before I can object. He leans in with his body so I can feel his third leg. Again, I am intrigued. I learn that he doesn't wear underwear, just lets it hang. We date a few times and fuck a few times, but there's no chemistry. The last couple of times he doesn't even remove my clothes, just lifts up my dress. The sex is as cold as a bag of party ice.

One day, I'm at his house, and he's showing me his favourite porn sites. Then he says, "Hey Jacquie, my birthday is coming up. I belong to this sex club in Surrey. You can pretty much do anything you want there. I was wondering if, for my birthday, you'd be into doing a gang bang? Here, I'll show you the website."

"You mean I'm the only woman getting fucked by a bunch of strange men? Well, I have to think about it. Nope, not interested, sorry." I'm pretty open minded and willing to play along as long as it's safe, but there is nothing about this situation that appeals to me. I don't even like guys that much. One at a time is plenty for me. When he mentions that it gets expensive to pay for dates when you're going on a lot of them, I email him my notice. Bye-bye, big guy.

The good thing about having sucked so many big cocks is that now that I'm a senior I can take a whole handful of pills in one swallow.

Interesting side note: This guy has crossed my path multiple times over the years, at the mall where I sold flowers for awhile and at live music venues where he was playing bass and drums or attending jams. In fact, I ran into him recently and got to ask him what the personality test he did on me the day we met was about, as I'd forgotten some details. In his recollection, the sex was excellent. We're casual friends now.

I can joke about these things in retrospect, but these were, in fact, my dark years, my darkest years, where shame stained my soul like red wine stains white carpet. My children, eleven and thirteen, stayed home alone while I drank in the dysfunction of Carrie's family.

"Mom," Shiloh says. "Please don't go over there again."

"Come with me. You can play with Adam." He's Jared and Addi's three-year-old son.

"No, we don't want to come. We want you to stay here with us. We don't like it there. We don't like the dogs."

"I won't be long."

"You always say that, and then you don't come home until after dark, and we're scared. And you always come home drunk. You're mean when you get drunk."

"I am not."

"Yes, you are. You get mad too easily."

"Well, come with me then."

"We don't want to. Stay here."

"No, I can't stand it here. This place is a mess. Maybe if you guys helped clean up once in awhile, I'd feel like being here. Look, I can count eight dirty glasses just in this area alone. Why can't you just use one glass? And half of them aren't even finished. Start doing the dishes right now, and I'll stay."

Shiloh looks at me with accusing eyes. "Come on, Keyz," she says sadly as they go upstairs together, away from the kitchen, away from work, and away from me. I am free. I can justify my drinking today.

But always, deep inside of me, in my centre, are the accusing eyes, the sad voices, the guilt, and the shame. There is never a day that I forget my childhood hatred for my dad, who ruined my life with his drinking, who scared me and alienated me, and now, I am turning into him. I am giving my daughters the life he gave me, only worse, because there's no sober mother here to rely on—to steady the ever rocking boat and maintain balance. My children are alone, on their own. They cling to each other, Shiloh imitating the parent and becoming Keziah's caretaker.

Looking back, I can't help wondering sometimes if that isn't why they left the earth so soon, nearly at the same time. There was one particular ten-day bond that connected them to each other in a final way, during one of the darkest periods of our life together.

One sad winter night when they were still both so young, still in their early twenties, just finding their way as young adults in the world, Keyz flew to heaven, and the bond stretched like a bungee cord, pulling Shiloh from the earth when it reached its maximum stretch, ten days later. I know that doesn't make sense in the natural order of things. No one could have planned the accident that took Shiloh's life so soon after Keziah's ended. It was just a very freak occurrence, but maybe there's a whole other set of dynamics going on in an unseen world. A woman I was talking to at a music jam recently reminded me of the story *When Bad Things Happen to Good People*. Life is like a tapestry, with a beautifully detailed picture on one side and a knotty mess on the back side. We usually see the back side.

I'm afraid to thaw. It's been seven months. I haven't worked but for a few days. I still tell people the story in conversation unemotionally. I meet a woman who lost her twenty-year-old daughter in a medical malpractice who tells me she was numb for two years. "Then my feelings woke up," she said, "and I wished I could go back to being numb. You'll know when it happens." This scares me. I tell myself everyone is different; this may not be my experience. Maybe it will be more gradual for me. Maybe writing this book can mediate the grief lying in wait for me in some way. I can hope.

18

Keziah

One thing of many about Keziah that I always admired was her willingness to make restitution for her wrongs. I don't know if that's because of when I asked her to apologize to her sister at two or another time. After the party she had while I was at Grandma Morton's funeral, there were two holes punched in the walls. I later found out she made at least one of them, maybe both. I told her she was responsible for fixing them.

I had left her and Shiloh alone for the weekend while I travelled to Calgary with my sister April for the funeral, leaving my brother Gary as the watch dog. He was living with his girlfriend across the street at the time. Keyz and her friends apparently ran him out of the house in his sock feet. Shiloh was out with her boyfriend. By the time they got home around 11:00 p.m., neighbours had already called the police. I think Keyz was about fifteen. She had a party, which was quickly overrun by kids looking for trouble, who trashed our home. I came home to beer cans in my garden, my favourite plant smashed flat. There was dirt, blood, and broken glass, even holes in the walls, as well as damaged furniture. In reality, nothing I owned was worth much money, but I also didn't have much money to repair or replace it. The feeling of disrespect was more damaging than anything I actually lost. Oh yeah, both girls had their laptops stolen. Shi's was a gift from a relative, and she grieved the loss of its contents.

So Keyz and one of her guy friends acquired a can of spackling and did the repairs, which I found remarkable. She never squawked beyond one yelp of protest when I threw out her extensive bong collection and all her other drug paraphernalia. It came to a big black garbage bagful.

But maybe that's because she'd already moved on to harder drugs than weed.

She resigned herself to leaving her first purchase with Quizno's pay, a six-hundred-dollar large-screen TV, with me to compensate for the money she'd stolen from me and for other debts. She never squabbled about restitution. She made it and carried on. She didn't seem to hold grudges. She was a brave and hopeful soul who got sideswiped by the breakup of her family, which sent her spinning into dark places alone.

In 2008, when Keyz started high school in grade nine at Terry Fox Secondary School, she quickly found her niche in the SWED group at school, a cluster of likeminded kids whose motto was "smoke weed every day." At school, they'd hang out on a corner of the sidewalk like a little gang of misfits. They'd hang out at our house when I was at work and write SWED with permanent marker on Keziah's bedroom walls, her mattress, and anything and everything they owned and on any available surface. Back in my day, a joint was easily concealed almost anywhere. In her generation, people carried around heavily padded bags to hold hundred-dollar bongs and bottles of water. Since she was low on the totem pole financially, until she learned to steal that is, she offered our home as a hangout. She travelled to downtown Vancouver to the 4/20 celebrations on April 20, which promote pot smoking, and she proudly uploaded a picture of herself with Marc Emery on her Facebook page.

Keyz was like me, an isolationist. For a while after leaving a recovery house to live with me, she rented a little bachelor suite, which was beautifully furnished and decorated by the owner. There, she would gleefully purchase an array of cleaning products and would dangerously do drugs alone. "I love my cleaning products," she'd say.

She wanted to get a job, but the lure of easy money from escorting was too strong. She'd started working at Quizno's subs at fourteen and then worked at A&W in Creston, when she lived with my mom after the party debacle. But I learned that even before she left Vancouver for Creston, she had a date or dates that gave her enough money to get her tongue pierced before she left. She was fifteen years old then, before she'd started using heroin at sixteen. She'd post ads on Craigslist Personals and have plenty of options. Jesus. She made two hundred to three hundred dollars an hour. I couldn't compete. I didn't even make twenty dollars an hour working at the seniors' residence. I've wanted to be a sex worker as much as I've wanted to be a lesbian. They're both afforded so many advantages, so much more freedom than the average working girl like me. But I knew I didn't truly belong in either camp. I was stuck in the middle, though sadly not even the middle class.

She inevitably fell back into escorting. Sometimes she'd call me when she was bored while waiting for dates from an apartment downtown, which was managed by an agency. That was safer. Sometimes she'd put an ad in the personal casual encounter section of Craigslist and minutes later she'd say, "I have a date."

Keyz always had a high pain tolerance. She pierced her own navel twice, but she told me later that tongue piercing was the most painful thing she ever experienced. And interestingly, the piercer told her that her tongue was shorter than normal, possibly accounting for her distinctive accent. All the earnings from her job at Quizno's at that time were going to pay to replace Shiloh's laptop, which was stolen at the party when I was at Grandma Morton's funeral. It never occurred to me to make a house insurance claim. I mean, even so, it wasn't a break-in. I wasn't there; the thieves walked through an open door.

Of course, I was concerned, as every mother is, about teenage pregnancy and safe sex. I told my teenage daughters to please use birth control if they were planning to have sex. I offered to help them procure it. I told them about my experience and regret. I was worried about the dangers of the internet. I'd heard about some kid getting a blow job at a high school dance and was alarmed, so I asked Keyz when she was fifteen if she was sexually active. "Have you ever given a guy a blow job?"

"Eeew, gross, Mom. You think I'd put some guy's piss stick in my mouth?!"

I was relieved. For her sixteenth birthday, I wrote in her birthday card, "Sweet sixteen and never kissed a piss stick!" I believed her when she said it, but then I later learned that she fucked some guy off the internet at fifteen. Keyz was a rapper. She got my love of rhyme and wrote three awesome raps, which she performed at Narcotics Anonymous meetings to commemorate periods of clean time: thirty, sixty, and ninety days. I have one on my wall called "A Dopeless Hope Fiend." Her anxiety before performing would be mental and physical, which made her wonder if she could perform her rap. Shi and I would comfort and encourage her.

When her time came, she stood behind the podium, and she looked small in the crowded rooms. Then she opened her mouth and expressed her truth in words that shot forth in a line, and wrapped themselves around each other, her rhythms binding her heart to ours.

She gave a tight, pleased smile as the applause followed her back to her seat, and we whispered kudos in her ear to affirm her greatness. Her friends shouted "Yay, Keyz!" Afterwards, we went somewhere to eat and celebrate. I was so proud of her at times like those; other times, I felt so much pain for her, as if she were a child I had already lost, even when she was still here with us. She fought her battles privately in her room. She set impossibly high standards for herself from the time she was a child. She had inherited my perfectionism.

Keyz loved to cook. I often imagined her going to chef's school and owning her own restaurant. She would arrange her meals attractively with garnishes. I'm remembering a night when I was at work at the seniors' residence and my girls were home alone. Eleven-year-old Keyz was baking, and her long hair got caught in the electric mixer, leaving her with a bald patch and a concussion. I didn't leave work to go home when Shiloh called my workplace because she said there wasn't much blood and my shift was over soon. It was another one of my regretful parenting decisions.

Food was a frenemy for her. She developed bulimia in about grade seven, eating bags of apples and slimming herself down, from chubby to a slim ninety-eight pounds over a short period of time.

I was working. I didn't really see it happening until suddenly the change was obvious. From then on, she would use any means to maintain her weight. Drugs helped her with that. She lived with a voice in her head that always told her she was fat no matter how she looked. She was beautiful with a petite curvy body, along with lots of class and style. She had blue-green eyes like butterflies lashed to the max, smooth soft skin, and long hair, which was often thickened with the extensions that she dyed black—a stunning contrast to her ivory skin. She dressed seductively, but she was often too high to care, as she often put together outfits that maximized her curve appeal.

She took advantage of Grandma Myra's RESPs to take a course to become a nail technician. Unfortunately, her heroin addiction flared before she completed her last exam. But she managed to get a job at a salon briefly before customers were unsatisfied and complained that she seemed tired.

She made it a goal to complete her course, though, and later, during a period when she was clean, she studied, wrote, and aced her test, receiving a certificate of completion, which she proudly framed and hung on her wall.

"Mom, I'm so proud of myself."

"I'm so proud of you too, honey. That's a real accomplishment."

Keyz always struggled with anxiety and feared any kind of performance, although one year she wanted the lead role in the school play. So, she auditioned for it, and got it. Her acting talent was evident. Shiloh and I have that ability, but Keyz had always shied away from it before. I was impressed with how well she did, but it was a one-time effort.

Keyz had a bit of a speech issue. She had ear infections as an infant. Was that an indicator that her ear tubes were too narrow or that they had been scarred? I was always trying to diagnose things. She said nothing for a long time as a toddler, unlike Shiloh, who was articulate. Then, when she did speak, it was garbled and difficult for anyone to understand, except Shiloh. My friend suggested I take her to a speech therapist because at three years old, she should have been talking better. So, I did. They tested her and said she was normal (what?!) and that different letters come later for some kids. She should have all her sounds by eight. If not, come back.

Well, by then we were all covered in dung from the family breakup, so it fell off the list. She was mostly okay, but there were always some sounds she couldn't pronounce as well as some she could say only with some effort. Her voice was also soft, making it difficult for me to hear her the older my ears got.

She had a dental anomaly she was self-conscious about, where her eye tooth came in right beside her front tooth on one side, much like my brother Gary, only his are that way on both sides. She also had flat, pronated feet like mine, a gene passed down from at least the time of my mom's dad, who avoided the war with this trait.

I sometimes feel sorry for people who don't have children or don't know their biological parents because being a part of a gene chain is so interesting. I have the paternal Morton bags under my eyes. "These bags have luggage tags," I often say. I also have the Morton nose. You can look at your own features and see where you got them by looking at your parents and relatives. It's fun, and sometimes sad, to see what parts of you your kids get.

Eventually, Keyz was diagnosed with borderline personality disorder and post-traumatic stress disorder. She also struggled with bulimia, perfectionism, obsessive compulsive disorder, and various addictions. Yikes! We might as well have handed her a bag full of loaded handguns to play with when she was growing up.

What happened to Keyz—accidentally overdosing alone on drugs—was not her fault. The real Keyz I remember from her childhood was a happy little girl who bounced out of bed in the morning, loved her sister, and her desk full of craft supplies, where she played creatively. I took those supplies from her when she was five because my neatness overdrive had no tolerance for mess, so I had to get rid of her fun. That was surely a mistake. Most of her issues surfaced after our family broke up when she was eight, but her journals indicate she never really felt a part of the family and that Shiloh was a better artist. In fact, she said that she always felt like an outcast and as if she were rejected by us, her parents, because we were busy with the business. She always felt like her dad favoured Shiloh and that she never really knew her dad. She felt like a burden and had trouble speaking up because she felt what she had to say wasn't worth hearing. She and Shiloh didn't get along growing up, and she never felt a sense of belonging and acceptance.

In her writing, she uses the words "always" and "never" a lot. I think I learned in counselling that's called black and white thinking. I still do it myself, much too often, although I try to catch myself at it now.

Keyz wanted a daddy who loved her completely and who wanted to spend time with her and buy her things and be affectionate with her. That's not what she got. She got a distant daddy who preferred Shiloh, whom he could understand and who took up all the room he had in his heart for kids. He'd thank her if she made him eggs and toast when her mom stopped doing it, and that made her happy.

And she wanted a mom who could set clear limits and create a safe home space for her and her sister to grow up in. It's not what she got. She got a volatile, unpredictable mom who tried her best to look after the family but just wasn't always good at it.

One time when Keyz was a teen and I was a single mom, I lost it with her. I had to put a lock on my bedroom door after my prescription sleeping pills went missing and she and her friends damaged the door jamb trying to break it. I had to establish some boundaries. She and I were hurling words at each other and got engaged physically.

I yelled: "You think you're stronger than me, that you can just do whatever you want to in my house? Think again, little girl. You'll never win over me. I'll always be older and stronger and smarter than you."

She was kicking and flailing. I knew I had to take her down, teach her some respect. So, I put her on the ground. I've always liked wrestling. My brother and I used to do it every night after supper until he started to win. I sat on her and pinned her wrists down. At this point, if I were with my brother, I'd start to dangle a ball of saliva over his face, hopefully retracting it before the thread got too thin and it fell of its own weight. But this was Keyz. She wriggled and squirmed until she was absolutely certain there was no escape and then started to cry.

"What's the matter?" I asked.

"I miss my dad. I want a dad."

This was totally not what I was expecting. I wasn't a hundred per cent sure she was telling me the truth. It could have been a manipulative ploy just to get me off. I'd used it myself with a guy once. But it worked. I got off and sat beside her while she cried. "It's not fair. Why don't I have a dad?"

My heart went out to her then. Poor kid. Of course, she needed a dad. Every little girl needs to feel there's someone big and strong and on their side in this world, someone who loves them, tells them they're beautiful, keeps them safe with boundaries, and protects them against ravaging intruders. I hadn't had that either, so I really felt her pain.

"I don't know, Keyz. I'm sorry. It isn't fair."

Over the next few years, when Keyz would complain about her dad—who never remembered birthdays, except his own, or gave Christmas gifts—I would encourage her to talk to him, hash out their relationship. One time, I heard her on the phone with him. She had spent ten months at Westminster House in one of her several attempts at addiction reduction and recovery and was learning to express her feelings. All the girls in the program had group counselling and Narcotics Anonymous meetings every day. Her dad had never done any recovery work, so he was defensive, saying, "It was hard for me too, you know."

But when Keyz was in her addiction, she sought out her dad as someone to use with. It was something they had in common now.

"I felt sick about it, Jacquie," Boris said later. "I didn't want to do it, but she wore me down. I know it wasn't right."

I understood. I thought of giving her beer on her twelfth birthday.

I understood how using a substance together could forge a bond between a parent and child and how it could create a sort of rite of passage for the child into the adult world. Of course, that didn't stop him from borrowing forty dollars from her, which he took a year to repay, and then only because she got really mad and tired of his delays.

At some point, Keyz got an injection infection. She'd break off needles in her body. Soon her foot was double its size, red and unusable. She spent three or four days in emergency on methadone battling the flesh-eating disease. Every time I'd go to visit, Boris would be there. It was awkward and aroused feelings in each of us of being a family again. I would have preferred not to see him, although I was glad that he was making an effort to show some care. She seemed delighted with all the parental attention. She was on IV antibiotics because I remember her holding her IV pole while Boris pushed the wheelchair down to the basement cafeteria for Tim Horton's. She was lucky because she'd had a few previous similar infections, but I think this incident was the worst. She received good care.

At some point, the astute building manager at the subsidized townhouse Keyz and I had moved to when Shiloh moved out realized Keyz was no longer living with me full-time, and I therefore had to move out of the two-bedroom townhouse we'd been in. But Keyz had lived in all sorts of different places. Between sixteen and twenty, she had lived with me, lived with Corey and his mom, gone to detox and recovery places, lived with me, gone to detox and recovery again, lived on her own, gone back to detox and recovery, rented a place with Shiloh, and gone to detox and lived in a recovery house in Richmond. Her best clean time was the ten months she spent at Westie House in New Westminster.

On the phone one day she said, "I have thirty days clean." This would have been in December 2014, or so.

"That went fast."

"For you," she said.

She was allowed home to the ground level suite that she shared with Shiloh on weekends, which was usually when I saw her.

I'm remembering a particular rainy Saturday evening in February 2015. Shiloh and her boyfriend Ryan have gone to Vancouver Island for the weekend. My phone jangles around dinner time with the loud distinctive ring that indicates Keyz is on the other end of the line.

"Hi Mom. What are you doing?"

"Nothing, really, email. Lazy day. What are you doing?"

"Nothing. I'm just at my house. Can we still do the driving lesson tomorrow?"

"Well, you beat me to it. I was going to call you today because I'm not sure my car is still insured for you. But besides that, I have to talk to you about the elephant in the room. You can't drive my car when you're using drugs."

I hear the tears in her voice when she asks how I know.

"Shiloh and I noticed last week when I was over for dinner."

"But how could you tell?"

"Well, we know you pretty well. The behaviour is pretty obvious. When you go outside and come back in a good mood it's usually a sign. You move differently, like you've got al dente noodles instead of bones. Plus, I saw marks on your arms."

She sobs as she explains. "No, Mom, I haven't been using needles. Those are scars from before."

"So, you've just been smoking heroin?"

"Yeah, for a week. I feel so stupid. Why can't I get on top of this?"

"It's not easy, Keyz. It can only be done one day, hour, or minute at a time. I'm proud of you for trying. You just keep trying until you get it. Recovery is a lifelong process, and relapse is a part of it. I wasn't going to tell you this, but I had a drinking relapse after six years of sobriety, at Christmas time. I'm only telling you to hopefully encourage you, so you realize you're not the only one. Don't be too hard on yourself."

"I can't believe it, Mom. Six years?"

"Your dad was clean for about twice that long. Don't give up."

"Are you still coming for dinner tomorrow?"

"Sure, thanks. What are we having?"

"Chicken and stuff."

"Sounds good."

"Do you want to go dancing tonight?"

This is an odd request. Keyz and I never go dancing together. In retrospect, a possible indication, along with the tears, that she is already high.

"I dunno. Maybe. I don't know the places to go in New West, do you?"

"Not really."

"I'll do some Googling and call you back. Talk soon."

I research veues with live music and find a few. Just as I am about to call her back, a wave of exhaustion comes over me. I just feel like crawling into bed. I am still in my pajamas. When I think about showering, doing my hair and makeup, and driving thirty minutes from Maple Ridge to Burnaby, where the girls live, through the dark rainy night, I completely lose my energy at the thought of it. I phone Keyz back.

"Hi honey. You know what, I found a few possible places, but I just got really tired. Do you mind if we don't go?"

"I guess not."

"What will you do instead?"

"Well, I guess I could call my friend and go to the SNL meeting." This is the Saturday Night Live Narcotics Anonymous meeting held weekly in New Westminster.

"That's a great idea, Keyz. Do that. I'll see you tomorrow. Love you, bye."

I get up late Sunday morning and putter about, surprised Keyz hasn't called me to tell me what time to come for dinner. I call her. No answer.

I do whatever and then decide to go over there, as I haven't heard from her and my calls aren't being returned. Cue ominous music for the drive. I arrive at their house about 5:00 p.m. Her bedroom light is on behind the blinds. I am a little concerned. It is beginning to get dark, but I have a strange feeling that light has been on all night.

I knock. No answer. I yell. No response. I try to peek through the window but can't see anything. I go and knock on the kitchen door. Nothing. Maybe she went out to get some food for dinner. I try calling again. I am starving so I decide to go eat and come back. In the deep place where I knew Emmanuel wouldn't need his soother, I know Keyz is dead on the other side of that door.

When I come back after eating, nothing has changed. The light is still on. I sit in my car. What to do? I see her landlords, a young couple, come out of the house from upstairs and chase each other playfully. How do they afford this nice house? Should I ask them to let me in? I should, but I don't want to. I'm not ready.

I look at my watch. The Sunday music jam I enjoy regularly at the Billy Miner Pub is set to begin by the time I drive back to Maple Ridge from Burnaby, where Keyz and Shi live. I'll just go to the jam and decide what to do later.

I say nothing to anyone, but I have to keep forcing waves of nausea away whenever I think of Keyz. I've chosen pleasure over pain. No, I've chosen a distraction to give me a bit of time, instead of dealing with what's in front of me head-on. I have to gather myself together for what's to come. When I get home after the jam, I call the recovery house to see if by some miracle Keyz has shown up for her curfew of 11:45 p.m.

"No, she's not here, and she's only ever been a couple of minutes late. The girls here haven't been able to get a hold of her all day. Can you go over there again?"

"Yes, I think we have a problem. I have to. I will. I'll call you when I know anything."

But in my heart, I already know. I hate to disturb the landlords so late, but thankfully and ironically the following day is the Family Day holiday, and they are up. Wojtek, the young Polish guy answers the door while his Chinese wife, Ling, stands at the top of the stairs.

"Hello, I'm Jacquie Johnston, Keziah's mom. I'm really sorry to bother you so late, but I'm wondering if you can let me into Keziah's suite, please. Shiloh is in Victoria for the weekend. I haven't been able to contact Keyz, and I'm worried."

"Yes, sure, okay, just a sec while I get the keys."

We walk around to the back of the house, and he tries the key, and another and another, which don't work. "Sorry, wrong keys. I'll be right back."

The light is still on. I am trying to prepare myself for what I am about to see. He comes back and tries again with no success. Oh, for heaven's sake. Label your keys. He tries the kitchen door, which opens, but the handle to Keziah's space doesn't have a key lock, so we can't get in that way.

"Sorry, I'll go look again."

"I have to make a phone call." This is taking a lot longer than I expected, so I go to my car where I left my cell phone to call the recovery house and explain. Wojtek comes out again holding a key over his head and mouthing, "I found it." I am talking to the recovery house staff person when he comes running back around the house motioning me to come. "We're in. I'll call you back."

As I run behind him, I hear Wojtek say, "She's on the floor," just before I see her. I stop at the threshold. He keeps going to kneel beside Keziah's body, which is lying on the floor parallel to her bed. "She's cold," he says, after checking for pulse and breathing, of which there are none. I look at Keziah's young body, dressed, thank god, in a black bra and grey sweatpants, stretched out with her arms over her head, crossed at the wrists. Her skin is a pale grey, and her lips are a dark blue. She is perfectly still, forever asleep on her "down" pillow. (In drug slang, heroin is also known as down.) She looks like she is resting after doing a dose.

"Come away. She's gone," I say. Wojtek looks up at me. "Come on. She's— Leave her." I begin to cry.

Wojtek comes and stands beside me, putting his arm around me and also begins to cry. He calls Ling who comes down the back stairs and joins the teary huddle. "What happened?" Wojtek asks.

"She had a drug problem. She was in a recovery house. She must have overdosed."

Ling said, "What? She did drugs? I didn't know."

"You wouldn't necessarily. Did you notice she was only here on weekends lately?"

"No."

They both share recent family losses they've suffered. Everyone has trials to bear.

"I have to call the recovery house and the ambulance, I guess."

I just keep standing in the doorway, looking at my dear little dead girl. No matter how obvious, the feeling of disbelief settles over me like a shroud. I call the recovery house. "She's gone," I say, loath to saying the D word.

"What do you mean?"

"She's dead." I hear a yelp at the other end of the line.

"I'm so sorry. Is it okay if I tell the girls here tomorrow at our noon meeting?"

"Yeah, sure, whatever." What does that have to do with me?

I call the ambulance. When they arrive, I explain that Keyz probably overdosed. They go in, look at Keyz, and get a blanket to cover her. The guy stops before he puts it over her face. I am grateful. They call the police, as her bedroom is now technically a crime scene until the cause of death is determined. I am asked if I want a VSW. "Yes, please," I say. I could use a victim services worker right about now. Soon the police and coroner arrive, and the VSW and I are asked to wait in the kitchen. She is a lovely woman named Beth, who keeps me company until about 4:00 a.m., when the business is done.

As we are talking, I suddenly realize I am supposed to be leaving the following Sunday for Mexico to attend a writing retreat hosted by my friends Annette and Rodney. Being low income, Mexican vacations only come to me with a windfall of some sort. I don't gamble, so my best bet is gift money. My one previous gift of money was when my stepmom Bunny passed away a few years earlier, after several years of dementia and a bad fall. She and my dad had been together for twenty-five years, off and on, and my dad gave us each a few thousand dollars from her life insurance payout. In this case, Boris's mom had passed away recently, and he paid me five years worth of delinquent child and spousal support. It was not a lot, after I gave the girls half. But still, it was enough for this trip, and I had been so looking forward to it.

"I guess I have to cancel my trip," I say to Beth, the VSW, who is waiting in the kitchen with me to hear back from the cops who are investigating Keyz's room. "But I didn't buy cancellation insurance. It'll just be a waste. It's a shame but, oh well."

"Why can't you go?" she asks.

"Well, I have to plan a funeral, obviously."

"Maybe it would be good for you to go to get away by yourself and grieve privately. Writing is healing."

"Well, I'd love to go, but it seems so selfish." I've learned since then that VSWs are big on self-care. So, her response was not as surprising as it might seem.

"Why couldn't you have the funeral when you get back? What's the difference?"

"Yeah, maybe. I'll have to think about it and talk to my family. It's Shiloh I'm most concerned about. I wouldn't want to leave her here alone."

Just then a policeman enters the kitchen, doing a poor job of trying to hide a baggie of needles behind his leg. "Well, I think we're about done here, after the coroner comes in to speak with you. Do you want to say goodbye?"

I shake my head no. The coroner, a lovely young woman, comes in. Odd job choice, I think. "First of all, I'm so sorry for your loss," she says. "Based on my findings, you are probably right that your daughter overdosed, although I'll do an autopsy and let you know if the drugs were contaminated with fentanyl. The evidence suggests that it was accidental. We found no suicide note or anything to indicate otherwise." A small sigh of relief escapes me.

The coroner calls me later to say they found no fentanyl. Keyz died from an overdose of heroin and cocaine.

"Do you know when she died?"

"Based on the condition of the body, I'd say last night some time, close to midnight, with some certainty."

"So, the official date of death will be yesterday, not today."

"That's right, February 7."

"Thank you so much. Goodnight."

They leave, taking Keziah's body with them. Beth and I turn off the lights in the kitchen and lock the door, returning to the threshold of Keziah's room. "I guess I should take her purse and phone."

Beth gets them for me, and we turn off the light and lock the door.

I go home feeling sick. I cry all night, can't sleep. I am scheduled to work that afternoon, a Monday. I might as well, I think. I can't sleep or cry anymore.

I call Boris on Monday before I go to work.

"Hello?"

"Hi, it's me. Can you talk right now?"

"Yeah, yeah, I'm okay. What is it?"

"It's Keyz. She suffered a fatal overdose on Saturday night."

"Yeah. Where is she?"

"She's in the Vancouver General Hospital morgue."

"Yeah, so we should go visit or what?"

Obviously, he's missed the words fatal and morgue. "Boris, she's dead."

At that point I hear a sound reminiscent of a wolf howl which becomes continuous howling sob noises. I hold the phone and wait, blinking tears. Finally, I say, "I'm sorry."

He stops howling enough to blurt out. "That's terrible. I can't work now."

"You're at work?"

"Yeah, at the woodworking shop. I have to go. I'll talk to you later."

"Yes, later. Bye."

I think, I hope, Keyz could hear that wherever she is. I hope she knows how her daddy wailed for her. She'd be gratified to know how much he loved her.

The whole time I am smiling with puffy eyes at customers as I wrap flowers I am picturing Keyz lying in that position. It is almost as though her image is superimposed on everything I see, tattooed on the back of my eyelids. The position in which Keyz died in hockey terms is known as penalty—arms crossed above head giving signal of stoppage in play. Game over. In sign language, hands crossed at the wrists means work. Her work is done.

My journal entry for February 10, 2015, reads: Since my last writing, my beautiful, funny, wise child Keziah was eaten, beaten by a dragon, wagging its wicked tail. A scaly beast with jagged teeth devoured my darling frail. Her body cold now, lips of black. Tell me for certain she's not coming back.

I call Shiloh's cell in the morning. "Hi honey, how are you? When are you planning to get back today?"

"We were going to catch the 5:00 ferry. Why?"

"No reason, really. Can I see you tonight after you get home?"

"Why, is something wrong?"

"No, I just miss you. Call me later."

"Okay, love you. Bye."

Boris and I agreed it would be best to tell Shiloh in person together that night. Unfortunately, just after this call, her cousin Jennifer, Boris's niece, sends her a text saying, "Is it true about Keyz?"

When the recovery house girls found out they posted in memoriam notes on Keyz's Facebook wall, which Jennifer sees. So, Shiloh calls her dad, and he tells her. She and Ryan, her boyfriend, then race to catch the next ferry, which results in a speeding ticket, fine, and impounding of Ryan's car at the ferry on Vancouver Island. It will cost him about one thousand dollars to get it back.

Shiloh comes to my apartment, distraught. We hug and cry. I tell her the story. She sits on my couch all day crying, reading, and responding to texts. Shi has a lot of friends. After hours of texting she says, "I'm going to write something on Keyz's wall." I don't know how Facebook works, but it seems like a good way to let people know.

When she is finished, she reads it to me:

I don't know if there was a person I loved more on this planet than my beautiful sister Keziah Johnston. She was a shining star. If you don't know, she's no longer here to make you laugh (... everyone, always!), or sit with you while you cry (...me, when I needed it), to encourage us, to persevere with us, to fight for us and for herself.

But hey, we have that hope and assurance that she is at beautiful peace now, right? Just gotta keep coming back to that through the burning heartache (heartache like I've never known) of losing her. She was so loved. And she (so) loved so many of you. Thanks for your love and prayers. Thanks for being the kind of loving, laughing, crying, journeying souls to uplift her (and me, and our fam). We want to celebrate the beauty that Keyz was and will continue to be in all of our thoughts of her for the rest of our lives.

So please join. If you knew Keyz, if you loved her, we'll have a celebration of her life in the beginning of March (more details to follow). In the meantime, remember her. Relive the good times and the struggles. Smile at the way she was, think on the way she impacted your life, be comforted in the way you may have affected hers, laugh at her hilarity, meditate on her tokens of wisdom (she was such a wise little one).

I will miss her sooo deeply, and I know many, many of you will as well. I am so thankful for the time we had with her, and I am sooo thankful to be her sister. Now what God? She's in your hands.

It is a beautiful loving tribute to her sister, her best friend. She doesn't mention how Keyz died, which of course people naturally want to know. I guess to Shiloh, it isn't as important how Keyz died as it is that she died.

I beg her to put the phone down, but she won't, can't, doesn't. I am worried about her. She sleeps with me for two nights. I sense I am getting on her nerves. We go to the funeral home together. "I want to see her," Shi says.

"Honestly honey, she didn't look good. I don't want you to remember her that way." She acquiesces. We clean out Keyz's apartment at the request of the landlord. Shi wants to sleep in her own bed that night. "Are you sure, honey?" There is only the kitchen separating her from Keyz's room. She nods. "Ryan will come over."

"Okay then."

I work a day then take a day off. My family, every single one, tells me to go on my trip. Shiloh says, "Go Mom. I'll be okay. Grandma Myra said she'd come, or I can go there. Bonnie and Samuel said I can stay with them. And I've got Ryan." Bonnie and Samuel are Kali's parents, the family Shi lived with for awhile.

Shiloh, Boris, and I meet at Old Spaghetti Factory one evening to talk about the memorial service. Boris lives in Surrey. The restaurant is a short twenty-minute drive from his place. Shiloh comes equipped with a notebook and is writing things down as we speak. She is going to work on it while I am away, and then we'll have a week together when I get back. "Is a week enough time? Maybe we should bump it up another week," I say.

Shiloh bristles. "No, Mom. You're making people wait long enough as it is. People need to grieve and get on with their lives." She is right, of course. She wants Boris to build a simple wooden urn that she will decorate.

Travelling—like moving, performing, and many other things—stresses me out. Besides the stuff I am packing for the trip, I have several bouquets that have been delivered to my place, which I am going to leave with Shiloh, plus a few things she left here. She is staying with Ryan at his dad and stepmom's. I call her the day I am leaving. "Hi, Shi. I'll bring the stuff over tonight around eight-ish, okay?"

"Okay, Mom. See you later. I love you."

In fact, it is almost 10:00 p.m. by the time I arrive at Ryan's dad's house. Drew answers the door.

"Hi, how are you?"

"Oh Jacquie, I'm so sorry about Keyz."

"Yeah, me too. It's still hard to believe. She and Shi were so close."

"My mother lost a child, my brother, when I was a kid, and she was never the same."

"I'm sorry to hear that. It's hard. But listen, I've got more flowers in the car. I better go get them."

I make a couple more trips and stand in the kitchen again with Drew, expecting Shi to come out any minute. "Are Shiloh and Ryan asleep already?"

"No, they're watching a movie. Do you want me to get Shiloh for you?"

"Oh no, I don't want to interrupt their movie. Just say goodbye for me. Thanks, Drew, see you later."

I go back to my car thinking how funny it is that Shi didn't come out and say goodbye. I should have maybe asked to see her. They could've paused the movie, and I could have said goodbye. Instead, I get in my car and drive away to meet my friend Ed, a friend I sometimes go to movies and live music with, who is letting me park at his house and is giving me a ride to the airport in the wee hours.

By the next evening, I am landing in Manzanillo, Mexico, and taking a cab ride to my destination, Libé, a small Pacific coastal town. Annette and Rodney, the workshop leaders, have been going there for a few years, so they're familiar with some of the locals and assure us it's safe. The first time I went to one of their retreats there, I stayed with them in a rental house with a pool. This time I've made arrangements to stay at a casa that rents out rooms. For the last few days, I move to a hotel with a pool—to treat myself a bit before going home to face the dark time waiting for me there.

The workshop classes are held for a couple of hours Monday to Friday mornings from nine to eleven. Each day we learn about certain subjects, such as show don't tell, story structure, characters, outlining, point of view, and raising the stakes; there are also wordplay warm up exercises as well as free writing time, and individual coaching. The group usually meets for dinner, and there are several touristy options such as the lagoon tour and exploring the town. There is also a farewell dinner and a literary reading night.

Shiloh didn't appreciate the silver pillbox souvenir I bought her last time, so I told her before I left that I'd bring her a Frida Kahlo souvenir. Shi worked at an arts studio for three years after high school and taught her students about Kahlo's work, which they all felt inspired by. I look through all the little shops for Frida Kahlo stuff. There are earrings, fridge magnets, bags, t-shirts, journals, pictures, et cetera. I email Shi asking what she wants me to bring her. I don't hear back, so I continue to look.

I am staying at a guest house called Casa de Veronica. The houses in Mexico often have high walls that serve as security and privacy. I go out to the backyard, lie in the hammock under a shady palapa, a grass roof, and think about Keyz. Someone I don't know sent a spam email the day she died, reading "The gods conceal from men the happiness of death, that they may endure life." I find that comforting. Honestly for me, the meaning of her death isn't so important. I focus on her escape, relief, and peace. As she was an addict, there is a logical susceptibility to her outcome, a known, accepted risk. However, neither she nor I believed it would ever actually happen, I don't think.

But behind the façade of addiction lies another possibility: She died of loneliness. I wonder if that evening might have gone differently if I'd made the effort to go over and go dancing with her. I don't know if she went to SNL. My guess is probably not. That might have saved her. I can't wallow in guilt, my natural reaction. I regret my decision because of what happened, but would I regret it if she went to SNL and everything was okay?

Shiloh and I looked through her phone a bit to try and piece together the events of her last evening on earth. A recovery friend she was texting told her to "Get rid of that shit," referring to the drugs. Another recovery friend, a young man named Brody we spoke to later had told her not to do any more that night. He was with her for a little while just before her fatal dose, when he had to leave. She reached out for support to three people that night. She also called her dad, but he missed the call. No one was there for her in the moment she desperately needed help. But even if they had been, if we had been, it might have happened anyway, if not in that moment, then later. One can't spend all one's time second-guessing tragic events or taking all the blame for others' desperation. That would just take us all down.

I still sometimes feel the aftershock her of her permanent absence, a wave of nausea rising from my stomach up through my head. It's when I think about never getting to see her, touch her, laugh with her... Oh my god, I can't remember her laughing. She had a wry sense of humour, and her voice implied amusement, but I can't remember what her laugh sounded like.

In Mexico, I let myself cry. The beauty of my surroundings is soothing. Brightly coloured blossoms abound, little geckos scuttle, hummingbirds dart, and I rock, alone with my grief. For some reason as I am rocking in the hammock, I keep thinking of Keyz pushing her foot on that glass kitchen table we had. I warned her repeatedly that it would break if she kept pushing it. And suddenly one day, we heard a loud crack. But was her constant pushing deliberate or subconscious? Could she have stopped herself from doing it if she'd tried?

I was in Mexico when my sister called Boris to tell him about Shiloh being killed in a fatal car accident ten days after Keyz's death. I asked him later what his reaction was when he heard. He said, "Yeah, I don't know. I don't remember really. I was still in so much shock about Keyz that I didn't react much. But boy, that hit me hard when you told me about Keyz."

I gave Boris Keziah's phone after she died because he needed one. I hadn't even looked through it. He dropped it, and it broke a few days later. It was like she was gone again, all records erased. I kept Shiloh's phone after she was gone. I looked at it a lot in the days that followed. In the few months she'd had it, she had taken 1,184 photos. It gave me great comfort to scroll through them and to see the world through her eyes. But then I got accidentally locked out, and Apple couldn't recover access for me. It was another significant loss.

One thing I really have to say is how bad I feel about Keziah's stuff. Her landlord called and wanted her belongings removed immediately so her room could be rented. I had just moved into my tiny bachelor suite with no storage. My sister April, her daughter Jocelyn, Shiloh, and I went through Keziah's stuff, boxing and bagging it up. I was overwhelmed. I mostly just cleaned out the bathroom. I saw the plastic packet her deadly dose had come in. The police had taken all the needles and other paraphernalia. I had to hang on to the bathroom counter. It was surreal. I had to keep reminding myself that I am in the room where I found my daughter's dead body and going through her things. We chose memory items, but I no longer have any of them now, and I don't remember what they were.

There was the little pink quartz Buddha I'd put in her Christmas stocking one year that she had loved. I learned that rose quartz is a symbol of unconditional love and therefore a message of the forgiveness I had sought from her. I gave it to her, and now she was giving it back to me. And a vibrator that my sister found in one of her drawers. My sister April said, "Man, I've never seen anyone grab something so fast." This is one of the sick, crazy, true things that actually happened. "Make sure you wash that thing well."

One of the moms from the Christian school the girls attended offered to help with arranging meals; she also bought me a CD of Christian music or anything else I needed. Her daughter, who was a classmate of Shiloh's, painted portraits of both girls that were on the stage at the memorial service. The principal of the Christian school came to the service, and they erected a memory bench for the girls at the school. One of the girls' teachers also reached out with memories and gifts at a lunch my friend arranged. Both the Christians and the lesbians from BOLDfest were supportive. I really didn't have any close personal friends at that time except for Ed, my movie companion, but people come out of the woodwork at a time like that. Only one of either of the girls' teachers from grade nine to twelve came to the service that I know of, whereas the Christian elementary school community was remarkably supportive after such a long time.

I took Kezi's framed certificate from nail technician school and included it with the memory table at the service. Mostly, her stuff went to the front yard for pick up by a charity. A woman came along and asked if she could have the coffee table. I told her she could have anything she wanted. I saw her coming back in her small car, making trip after trip. As I was coming around the corner of the house, I noticed her opening Kezi's nail supply kit, a silver case with wheels. She looked at some nail polishes and decided to take the kit. I felt sick. It was such a personal thing, but what would I do with it? Where would I put it? It was a practical but painful decision to let it go, but one that I would cry over repeatedly after. I didn't even go out to Richmond to the recovery house where she'd been living to get her clothes and personal items. I just asked them to donate them or throw them away.

Keyz was my give away, go away, throw away girl. I didn't nurse her as long as Shiloh. I didn't bond with her the same way. I let other mothers—Mom and Rita, Corey's mom—raise her sometimes, and then when she died, I didn't kiss her goodbye. I also didn't have her prepared for viewing.

She came innocently into our family and was treated poorly by us, by others, and by herself. We loved her. We tried to look after her, but our care wasn't enough. We didn't know how to do it well enough. Shiloh was pretty good. She stood by her sister in dire times. Their love for each other was strong; they belong together, whether here or there. Keyz has her best friend with her, and that is as it should be. No more lonely. The place she occupied in my heart aches, breaks, and makes me regret so much. If only I could truly believe she's happy now, free, and in good company. I'm going to insist on believing it until I know for sure.

I am saying goodbye to you now, sweet girl. Goodbye, goodbye.

19

Shiloh

In Mexico I let myself sleep in, and I don't bother with the writing retreat unless I feel like going and the timing suits me. I send off another email to Shiloh, again with no response. So, I send one to her friend, Kali, her former roommate and now her supervisor at the office of Centura Tile Vancouver, where they both work: "Get that girl to answer me."

I hear a knock on the door at Casa de Veronica, the guest house where I am staying for the first week of my time in Mexico. "Hello," Annette's voice rings out through the screen. She is the writing retreat leader and my friend from Vancouver. She self-publishes self-help books and personal memoirs. I met her and her husband Rodney dancing at the Yale Hotel, a well known blues bar.

"Are you decent?" Annette asks as I come padding out of my room in a nightie I've hastily thrown on to greet her.

"Somewhat. You just woke me up but at least I'm dressed, sort of."

"Okay, so you're moving to the Cabo Blanco Hotel today, right? Rodney checked, and the check-in time is 4:00 p.m., so we'll come over and help you with your bags."

"I think I can manage, thanks. I have a rolling suitcase and a backpack, and it's a block away. Should be alright."

"No, no, that's what Rodney is for. Let him carry your suitcase. We'll be back at quarter to, okay?"

"I guess so, but it's really not necessary."

Annette leaves, and I head back to my room to shower and pack. I've spent the week in this place I've dubbed "the dirty dive." I don't want to step in the shower because the tiles are repulsive. I can't walk around barefoot. Supposedly the housekeeper lives upstairs. This place belongs to Rodney and Annette's friend, Phillip, who lives in Oklahoma part of the year. My theory is that the housekeeper is Phillip's girlfriend, and he puts her up here in exchange for some cleaning she doesn't bother with. I could teach her to clean grout with some bleach and a toothbrush. The floor isn't swept, and I find someone's old dental floss stuck to the floor, but it may have been mine. There's no face cloth along with the cheapest smelling block of unnatural pink soap, Mexican-dollar-store style. The sink is tiny and doesn't allow enough room on the edge to set my contact lenses and solution on, so I have to use the top of the toilet tank.

My strategy was to stay in the lower rent place for the first week while the retreat was going on, then move up to a nice hotel for a final five days to relax and grieve. This is a little grittier than I expected, but that's what I get for 175 American dollars per week.

I'm happy to be moving today. I'm pretty sure the check-in time was earlier when I made my reservation. I decide to take a chance and go over earlier. Sure enough, I'm all checked in by 3:00 p.m., so I go to Annette and Rodney's to tell them. Annette says she'll come over to the hotel with me, and we can go for a swim. She gets her swimsuit and cover-up on, and we walk the few blocks on the dusty, bumpy streets, and occasionally cracked sidewalks, trying to keep our flipflops on our feet. She comes up to my room with me and waits while I change into my bathing suit.

The hotel has a beautiful large pool tiled in royal blue surrounded by a cement apron, where other guests sit at tables under umbrellas or relax on white plastic loungers. Beyond them, the property has trimmed green grass, shrubs and flowering plants, as well as tall palm trees from which yellow and other birds flit. Friendly Mexican waiters that must be sweltering in their black pants and white jackets stroll at a relaxed pace around the grounds taking orders for food and drinks, which are served in plastic cups. There's a swim up bar in the pool, but it's not always staffed. I usually order a piñada, which is a virgin piña colada, a sweet mix of pineapple and coconut juices.

We get into the water, which is warm enough to be comfortable and cool enough to be refreshing. We swim, float, tread water, and chat until we're ready to get out.

I'm lying on a white plastic lounger, trying to avoid the periodic shade caused by the breeze pushing the fronds from a tall palm overhead.

Dots of pool water decorate my legs. The odd one tickles as it dries. The sky is a perfect baby blue as far as my eye can see. The palm fronds, like a fringed dancer's arms, lift and fall gracefully. I close my eyes and consciously enjoy the moment, the feeling of the sun warming my eyelids. Beside me, Annette texts furiously, head bowed to see over the top of her glasses. I'm thankful I don't have any technology interfering with my peace right now.

"I have to go to the bathroom," she murmurs.

"Mm hmm," I reply sleepily, though registering that she mentioned earlier she doesn't like the bathroom in the lobby. My mind wanders freely, blurring the edges between awake and dreaming. I am suspended in this state of bliss for an unknown amount of time. But then Annette's absence begins to make an impression on me. What's taking her so long? I open my eyes and look in the direction of the hotel lobby. What I see coming toward me blasts me out of my reverie.

Everything becomes surreal. I see my sister April and our old friend, Karen, the woman we lived with when Emmanuel died, walking toward me along the edge of the pool. What are they doing here? Coming to join my vacation? Why Karen? I've hardly seen her since the Maranatha days twenty-five years ago, although she and April have kept in regular touch all these years. As they approach, my mind reels, and I feel as though I am a character in a movie, and I don't know my part.

What is happening? I stand up. April and Karen are hanging on to each other, and their expressions are grim. Something about that posture seems strange. Are they here to surprise me with a visit? By the expression on their faces, I don't think so, but I can't imagine why they are here, if indeed they actually are. Maybe I'm dreaming, hallucinating, sun struck. It feels surreal. I greet April with a hug. "Hi, Seest. What are you doing here? Did you come to join me on my vay-kay?" Seest is our nickname for each other, short for Seestor, or "sister" with a Mexican accent.

April says, "I wish we were. Jac, sit down." She is two years younger than I am, but right now she feels considerably older. I return to my seat on the lounger and she straddles the foot end facing me. Karen has remained standing on my right side. April puts her hands firmly on my knees as if to ground herself, takes a deep breath, and says slowly and carefully, "Jac, I've gone to considerable trouble and expense to find you and come here in person to give you some terrible news."

"Is it Shiloh?" shoots out of my mouth, thinking of my unanswered emails.

"Yes, it's Shiloh. She took a week off after Keziah died and went back to work on Monday." It was now Sunday. "On Tuesday on her lunch break, she was walking on the sidewalk outside her workplace on Canada Way when there was a two car collision and one of the cars came up on the sidewalk and hit and killed her."

These words have the impact of a glacier flung from heaven landing on my chest, stealing my breath and forcing a loud wail to escape. "This can't be happening. I can't believe it. Are you fucking kidding me?" Tears stream of their own volition from all four of our faces. Annette is now standing on my left. "You mean I have no more children? How can this happen?"

Karen leans into me. "It shouldn't have happened, Jac. It should never have happened."

"She suffered contusions to her left hip and leg," April continues the story. "The force of the impact threw her backwards about thirty feet, and she landed on the back of her head. Witnesses at the scene did CPR and the paramedics continued it for an hour and a half, trying to save her.

"I had to identify her body as next of kin. She was in Royal Columbian Hospital by then. I was shaking. I walked this slowly." April uses her hands to demonstrate the reluctant pace of her feet. "She was on the other side of a window. The social worker warned me she still had a breathing tube in her mouth. She handed me Shi's glasses, and I just started bawling.

"It's always the glasses that get people, the social worker said. She lifted the curtain, and there she was. Yes, that's her, that's my little Shi-Shi, I whispered." April had lived with us when Shiloh was a toddler and she loved her to pieces, always buying her gifts. They'd lie on April's bed and cuddle when April came home from work.

April and I reach for each other. After some time of sobbing, I have to hear more. I'm aware the other people around us didn't come for this, but it's too late to move. I try to be quiet.

"I don't understand. Where was Shiloh again?"

"She was on the sidewalk outside Centura on Canada Way."

"But how could she get all the way over there on her lunch break?"

"What do you mean, Jac? She was right outside the building."

I suddenly realize I have been picturing the scene of the accident on Columbia Street in New Westminster, where she went for an interview eight months earlier for a different job that she didn't take, and they cautioned her about the busy street. In my shock, I forget where she works, although I was there a couple of weeks before.

"Oh, okay, now I get it. Sorry, I was confused."

"I'm just so relieved we finally found you, and I told you. I've been carrying this burden for five days, dreading the moment I had to tell you. I called Karen to see if she could come with me. I couldn't do it alone. I'm so glad you cried. When Emmanuel died you didn't cry, and it scared me. Did you cry when you found Keziah?"

"Yeah, I did. The young couple, her landlords who let me in to her suite, cried with me. I cried about Emmanuel, just not immediately because I was in shock. I don't like to grieve in public. I cry at home alone. But wait a minute, why would they try to save her if she was dead? That doesn't make sense."

"I'm not sure. There's a lot I don't understand either. I'd like to get some more information when we get back. They attempted to revive her for so long, I guess, because she's so young." (Later medical reports from the hospital indicated she still had a weak pulse at that time but no eye movement.) I picture my only daughter lying on the grass, at least I hope she landed on grass instead of the street. Her eyes are open and unmoving; her neck is crushed to bone gravel. April uses the medical terminology because she's an occupational therapist. But that's what it means. All by herself, surrounded by strangers, while her mother frolics three thousand miles away. Well, not frolics, exactly. I am wandering around Mexico in a state of shock, mourning the death of my other daughter.

"Uh, Jac, there's something else. The media have gotten involved, and they're waiting for notification of next of kin to release the story."

"What? Why?"

"I guess somebody at the scene mentioned that Keziah had just died, so they want to tell the story, but they're waiting for us to tell you and get your permission."

I don't know what to think of that. It is all too much to process. I am still reeling from the feeling that everybody in heaven and on earth knew about this tragedy before I did. I have the sense that I'm being watched, and that all eyes are on me, waiting for my reaction to an event they've already seen.

April says something about Shi's friend and former roommate Kali hearing the crash and noting that Shiloh was late returning from lunch. She was scared to go look. When she finally ventured out, she saw Shiloh's boots and knew then that Shi had been in the accident.

"Her boots? Weren't they on her feet?"

"No, that's the thing. The impact caused her to fly out of her boots." I think of the country song "Angel Flying Too Close to the Ground."

"Someone suggested Shi might have been suicidal after losing Keyz, but apparently she saw the car coming toward her and tried to get out of the way. She just didn't have time."

Thunk. A boulder drops in my gut. Jesus, she had the moment of knowing. Oh god, that's the worst part. I wish I hadn't heard that. Did she feel herself fly through the air, land on her head? Or did she black out on impact and feel no pain? Please let it be that. I want, no, I need to believe it was so fast she didn't have time to fear or feel.

April says, "When do you want to go back? We can stay or go at your command."

"Well, if it's all the same to you, I'd just as soon stay until I planned, which is another five days. I just started the best part of my vacation. I have no desire to encounter any media, and I'm in no hurry to deal with burying two children. I could use some time to process this. We have a week to plan the service when we get back, which will be a double ceremony now, dear god. I can't believe it."

"You can just relax. We're planning the service for you. Ryan, Shi's boyfriend, Kali, and Jocelyn, my daughter, are helping with the arrangements. We're all meeting up at the church as soon as Karen and I get back. We had to move to a bigger location, now that it's a double ceremony, and thankfully Willingdon Church in Burnaby donated the use of the church."

"I can't believe I have no children left. It's so bizarre. I feel like I'm in a movie, and everyone knows what's going on except me."

"I'm sure you do. But it was complicated finding you. My co-worker Mika found out where you were by Googling writing retreats in Mexico, and I recognized a picture of you online from the last time you went on the retreat. From that, we were able to contact Annette. She's been keeping an eye on you since yesterday. I was so afraid you'd hear about it somehow before I got to you."

"Yeah, I noticed a few things about her behaviour, how she was keeping too close an eye on me, for example. But I thought that was because she was worrying about how well I was doing in my grief state over Keyz. Well, you guys must be getting hungry. We should go drop your stuff off in my room.

"You can stay with me if you want. I have a king-sized bed and a single. It's perfect. I didn't order it that way, but we can share the king, April, and Karen can have the other bed. Let's go. I'll show you. Annette, thanks so much for everything. We'll be in touch."

We go to the room to get ready for dinner. I suddenly remember something. "Oh my gosh, you guys, I have to show you the last email Shiloh sent me. I wrote her a note when I got here.

Hi Shi, I made it. Sorry I didn't say goodbye. Drew asked if he should get you, but I said not to disturb your movie even though I really wanted to give you a huge hug goodbye. But since you didn't come to the door, I thought it wasn't that important to you. Maybe you didn't hear me at the door.

Blah, blah, blah...

Thankfully the other guy staying here is an IT guy, who helped me connect to the Wi-Fi so I could email you. Write back if you want but no obligations. Love you, darling, hope you're ok. Mom.

And listen to what she wrote me back:

MOM! I was so mad you didn't say goodbye! :P Of course it was important to me! I hadn't seen you in days and you were going away! If there's one thing we've learned... it's you never know when your time is going to come, ya gotta make the most of the little moments. What if Keyz didn't come say goodbye to me when I was going to the island? :(

I just couldn't hear you from the back room where we were watching. Drew interrupts us thirty times when we're watching a movie. Take a lesson from him ;) :P Don't tell him I said that though. And it's not actually thirty times. But he def interrupted our movie AT LEAST four times. Four times for sure. Actually five cuz he interrupted it to bring me that stupid bag of stuff after you told him not to interrupt us! :P

And you know, it used to kind of frustrate me, and it frustrates Ryan too, but then I started to appreciate that he talks to us. And he pops in just to say things. If he just left us alone, we wouldn't have the same relationship. It's kinda nice. But it's okay either way. I'll be content either way, interrupted or not. But know you can ALWAYS interrupt me for a hug, Mom. Or whatever. Any time. Love you so much. And I'm soooo sorry we didn't get a chance to say goodbye.

I'll message you more later. Hope you have a beautiful time! <3 <3 Love you!!!!! ShiCat

"Did you hear that?" I repeat. "You never know when your time is going to come. Weird. It's almost like she knew. But she couldn't know, could she? It's just ironic."

We walk to town and have dinner, then walk back to the hotel, and April and Karen collapse in their beds, exhausted. They were at the airport at 4:00 a.m. It's been a long wretched day.

I can't sleep, however. I go out to the lighted balcony in my nightgown with my journal while the bearers of the news sleep inside. There are palm trees framing my view of the two glittering stars I can see in the dark sky. Two stars, the only two in my view. Maybe we become stars when we die. Is that you, girls? I see you. I can imagine them saying, "Let's go see Mom and see if she notices us." Twinkling for a star is what waving is for a human.

Both my daughters died by accident. Ten days apart? Is that an accident? What on earth am I supposed to make of that? Every time someone dies, it stirs up so many questions for which there are no answers. I can't wait to hear the things people are going to tell me about the possible reasons for this. They have to; we all have to find some way for it to have redemptive meaning. Otherwise, it just seems like a waste, a loss. An unbearable cross, a dice toss, south-growing moss.

So far, we've come up with freedom from suffering and desire to be together. Fair enough. That's fine for them. What is the meaning of their deaths in the lives of those who remain, who loved them? That's a little trickier. It may be different for each survivor, and it may not be revealed immediately, if at all. The best and funniest explanation I hear is from my ex-girlfriend, Nella, who says Shiloh's accident was God saying, "Shiloh, get up here and help me with this kid, Keyz." Hahaha. It's good to laugh in the face of death.

It's easy for me to say Boris and I were shitty parents and Shiloh and Keziah didn't deserve us, or we them, and it's fitting that they are close in death as they were in life. They took care of each other. Shiloh wanted to be an orphan since she was three years old. Now she is, dream fulfilled.

It's Shiloh's twenty-third birthday on Tuesday February 24. The coroner is trying to keep her body in the best condition possible so I can see it. How many mothers have to see the dead bodies of their three children? I do. Why do I? What is it I'm supposed to learn or understand?

*

A month later, an RCMP Constable and my VSW, Beth, whom I'm still meeting regularly with since Keyz's overdose, meet with April and me at my apartment to answer questions about the accident. The female officer sits upright while we grill her for two hours. We want details. I'd heard Shiloh was listening to a podcast from her church on her iPhone, ironically about death, as she walked along Canada Way. A new driver and his friends were speeding as they collided with a vehicle that was making a wide right turn, out of the British Columbia Institute of Technology's parking lot. The wide-turning car, containing a mother and her small children, crashed into a bus stop. The speeding, out-of-control car then slid onto the median, back across two lanes of traffic, and up onto the sidewalk, hitting Shiloh and then being stopped by a telephone pole.

"But if she tried to get out of the way, she'd be hit on the right hip," April posits.

The officer says, "Not if the car was behind her."

I suddenly feel like a puzzle piece has been placed. "Oh, so she was walking along, the accident happened, she turned around to look, and wham, she got hit."

She nods. In my mind it's a slow motion movie that I construct and scrutinize for details, but I only have hearsay to go on.

"It happened so fast; she wouldn't have felt anything."

I nod, emotion clogging my throat. "Thank you." I can feel the officer's steel-rod back and steely determination not to cry, but I can also feel she is close.

Back in Mexico, April and Karen want to celebrate Shiloh's twenty-third birthday somehow, a week to the day after she was killed, so Karen and I plan to have an hour-long massage. As I am walking over to Annette's rental house for directions to the massage therapy place, I notice two butterflies dancing in a tree, one yellow and one orange. Yellow was Shi's favourite colour. They flutter about and both pause on branches so I can get a good look. Two stars, two butterflies.

Annette and I start walking, and she says, "Oh, look at those pretty flowers." There in an empty lot blooms a little patch of purple and yellow flowers. Shi and Ryan's wedding colours. They had dated on and off since high school, and I found out after she died that he'd been planning to propose the following month on their anniversary, but it was already understood they'd be together for the long term.

After our massages, Karen and I return to our hotel room, shower, and get ready for dinner. Later, as April, Karen, and I walk to Annette's before dinner, a huge flock of birds swoops low over Karen's head, and before I can comment on it, out of the blue, another one appears. I take these natural occurrences or sightings as signs. From speaking with other bereaved parents, I am not alone. I don't know if I'm imposing my beliefs or my desire to connect with them from beyond. But I know I feel better if I do, so I try not to let my logic knock it.

After dinner, we walk through town, get an ice cream cone, and end up at the Mexican Elvis impersonator's show, where we dance on the sidewalk for awhile then go in and have fun dancing for a bit. A real character—a middle-aged guy, with a big smile, wire-framed glasses, and who is fairly tall and very outgoing—comes up to us and starts dancing with us. I had gone antipanty, and he accidentally pulls my skirt up to reveal to the adoring crowd my bare butt cheek. I can't dip. "No dip, no dip," I hiss at him at the slightest hint in that direction.

After awhile, he and his wife invite us over to their table. Turns out they're Christians from Calgary. We're still in Libé, Mexico, for the last five days of my trip. On the walk home to our hotel, which they are also staying at, Karen and I are walking ahead, and April tells them the story. When they catch up, he gives me a big hug, says God loves me, and asks if he and his church can pray for me. I say yes, even though I am in my red dress, hardly dressed the part of a grieving mess.

A few moments earlier, as people were leaving the bar when the music had stopped playing, a woman came over and said, "Thanks, ladies. You were a delight." Shiloh Delight Johnston, Happy Birthday.

I feel guilty for enjoying the evening so much, but Shiloh would have loved it. She was an amazing dancer. At the housewarming party we had at our house after Shi had moved out, my guy Drago said to me, "Look at Shiloh." She was bopping away, pure enjoyment on her smiling face.

Being in Mexico when Shiloh was killed and believing in a telepathic connection, I wondered what I was doing when she died and why I didn't feel something. As far as I can determine, taking the time change into account while she was dying, I was in ecstasy at an unexpected discovery I made on a walk into town during Carnival week. In my journal I wrote:

February 17, 2015

Omg, today in town, I saw a young Mexican guy with four flats of live rainbow coloured chicks. He was selling them for less than a peso each. They were so gorgeous. All the gringos were negative about it, but I've never seen such a sight. Maybe I can get Annette to take a pic and email it to me. I want to buy three chicks to have as yard pets while I'm here, pink for Keyz, yellow for Shi, blue for me.

I asked a little boy with good English, "What happens to them? Do they get big or do they die?"

"Depends how you take care of them" was his sensible reply.

20

Postmortem Posts

The morning of Keziah and Shiloh's funeral I was nervous. A funeral is akin to a wedding if you're the bride or the bereaved mother. It's a big production with a large audience, all focusing on you. My long-time friend and hairstylist Amber, who had generously beautified me for Emmanuel's funeral and my wedding years ago, offered to come and do my hair before the service.

"Oh, would you, Amber? That would be great. Thanks so much. It starts in Burnaby at 10:00 a.m., so could you come around 8:30 a.m.?"

"Yeah, it won't take me long; your hair's so short. I'll just blow it for you."

I was cursing the early hour, but since Willingdon Church had generously offered the use of their sanctuary, we had to work within their time frame. I was still second guessing the food decision. April and I met at the church with Pastor Angela and her team. The church was offering to provide tea, coffee, and sweets, and based on their experience with a previous young person's funeral, they didn't think anyone would even eat them.

Since the service would be close to lunch time, I thought we needed to provide sandwiches at least, plus meat and cheese and fruit and veggie trays. That's what Shi and I were going to do for Keziah's service, which was going to be held at mid-afternoon. ICBC, our provincial vehicle insurer, was paying for Shiloh's funeral, so we could afford to get some extra food. I'd never been to a memorial service that didn't have food. It didn't seem right to me, yet I knew it would be a further imposition on the church in terms of acquisition, storage, volunteers, et cetera. Plus, we had no idea how many people to expect.

I didn't know what to do. I called Mom to get her opinion, and she said to leave it, as the Calgary cousins wanted to go for lunch before one of them had to fly back that same day. The church was providing sandwich trays for the family room. So, I left it but not without misgivings. So many people had contributed to this event, giving their time, energy, and money, yet I couldn't wait for it to be over. One day at a time, sweet Jesus.

I didn't need Amber to do my hair. I really just didn't feel like being alone with my feelings. I needed a distraction. Somehow, I ended up being late. Mom, Aunt Lorna, my brother, Gary, and his girlfriend, Teresa, who had driven up from Creston together in Mom's car, were waiting for me at a nearby motel. I was to lead them to the church in my car. We sped through the city, with me revving with inner anxiety. We'd requested no press, but it was nerve-wracking anyway.

We were ushered from the parking spots saved for us to the family room, which was jammed with people standing, waiting. I couldn't even discern all the faces. I went straight to Drew, Ryan's dad, and told him about Shiloh's email to me about saying goodbye. And then it was time to go.

I pictured sitting with Mom and April. But as it turned out, Karen and her husband, Andrew, who were not family, took one side of me. And when we got to the reserved area, relatives, who should have been in the family room, were already there, somehow confusing everything and creating a schmozzle in front of the packed sanctuary of over nine hundred people, as we were told later.

The one good thing was that as we were walking in, I suddenly heard the song "Ain't No Sunshine When She's Gone" by Bill Withers, and its sad familiarity soothed me. I'd made music suggestions to my niece Jocelyn for the photo montage, which were politely rejected, and since she'd offered to do it, I let her do it her way. This one song was a surprise concession. I wish I'd had the presence of mind to also ask for Norman Greenbaum's one hit wonder, "Spirit in the Sky." Maybe somebody could note that I'd like that played at my funeral, please.

I felt like a zombie, unable to register much. I remember there was a worship band, led by Ryan, with guitarists, a drummer, and two female vocalists, one being Kali, Shi's friend. There was a small display beside the pulpit, which consisted of two portrait paintings of the girls by Shiloh's school friend, Sasha. The two simple wooden urns holding my daughters' ashes were stacked on top of each other, were surrounded by colourful bouquets left on the stage by sympathizers, and were topped by a vase containing a selection of white flowers—roses, lilies, gerberas daisies. As well, a larger bouquet of yellow roses, white lilies and peonies purchased from the flower shop where I'd been working the last few years, sat on a pedestal to the left of the pulpit. The stage itself was massive, with a large black absence around these small presences, appropriate for the occasion. There were also beautiful bouquets from other friends and acquaintances gracing the steps leading up to the stage. We had arranged two small memory tables in the lobby, with mementoes of the girls, including artwork, baby books, journals, photos, eyeglasses, a beautiful lamp, perfume, jewellery, an empty handbag, and more flowers in my daughters' favourite colours, white for Keziah and yellow for Shiloh.

Pastor Mark, one of the pastors from Willingdon Church, led the service. He asked Ryan and the band to open with a song. Then he invited Kali's father, Samuel, up, and he introduced him and his wife as the "brown parents" of their adopted "white daughter," which got a laugh. Then he prayed for us all and, mostly, that God would be glorified. To start the sharing, Pastor Mark read a prayer poem Keziah had written a few weeks before she died, thanking God for helping her stay clean that day. For the next forty minutes or so, people got up to share their memories of the two girls. Kali read a two-page letter from one of Shiloh's best friends who was on a mission trip on the other side of the world when she died. Her other best friend, Nandini, spoke about what a rare and precious and great example of a friend Shiloh was. Three girls got up together, Kezi's recovery friends from Westie House, and shared Keyz-isms that made us laugh, thank goodness. "If you said, 'Hey Keyz, you look great today,' she'd say, 'Go on.'" They mentioned that she had trouble loving herself, but they sometimes thought that she loved chicken and almost any meat product more than she loved them.

A fellow bipolar poet friend of mine named Phillipa who'd come from Kamloops got up and performed a poem about the ugly side of death, in contrast to the sombre but hopeful notion of Christian death leading to union with God. She was also a Christian. In fact, I'd met her in a church mom's group when our kids were small. Years later, we did a poetry slam together. She'd often feel the urge to get up and perform her poetry in church. It wasn't for everyone, but once after I shared my testimony at the mom's group, she spontaneously improvised a poem for me that

260

was amazing, and I admired her talent.

My mother got up to speak at the mic. We watched her face contorting as she struggled to control her emotion, half-smiling apologetically, as she waited to be able to speak. Finally, she began, and suddenly my brother Gary was standing beside her with one arm around her shoulder. He looked away from her. His eyes filled, and I saw a tear literally shoot from his right eye. From his left one, a tear rolled down his cheek and dropped. My mom talked about the "fun, fun times" she'd had with the girls in the summers stargazing and other "fun, fun things." She mentioned they'd both had their struggles but faced them bravely and with perseverance, and she had the utmost respect for both of them. "And their mother" were the last few words she managed to whisper before sitting down.

Sylvain went up holding Raziel, his three-and-half-year-old son, with his fourth wife, Rachelle, who wore dark glasses throughout the service to hide her emotion. He also teared up as he expressed the loss of his son Emmanuel's sisters. He made us laugh telling us Keziah called him "brah," the way people say "bro" in Ebonics. Shiloh taught me about Ebonics, as Keyz and a lot of her friends spoke Black rapper lingo. It's a portmanteau of ebony and phonics. Our subsidized white ghetto home was in the suburb of Vancouver called Port Coquitlam, which we shortened to PoCo and which Keyz and her friends called PoCompton— after the city in Los Angeles, which was home of the Bloods, the notorious gang, and the home of West Coast gangsta rap. Sylvain said usually he wouldn't like it if someone called him brah, but he liked it when she did. Another laugh. The laughs are what I remember.

I'll just mention here in passing that Sylvain and I met after a twenty year hiatus around the time I was living in the white ghetto with the girls, shortly after my separation from Boris, my breakdown, and my bipolar diagnosis. He had tried to contact me through my mom, who had refused to pass on his calls in an effort to protect me, but she gave in the third time he called. When we finally spoke, I discovered that he and Rachelle were living in Port Coquitlam, only blocks away. He invited me over, and we caught up. Since then, they've had us over for holiday family dinners and parties, and we keep in touch. Sylvain works as a DJ and musician for private house parties; he also performs at legions and seniors' homes, and he often invites me to his gigs. I used to be the gig nanny when Raziel was little, when Rachelle would join him on stage with her gorgeous voice. They harmonize beautifully in song and in life.

Boris got up during the open mic at the funeral eventually. Later, April and I discussed how he talked about himself more than the girls, as did his best friend, who included mentioning a Christian song he'd written, that went to twenty-six countries. Boris did say that I'd done a good job with the girls, which to me is ironic as fuck because while I did the job, I don't think I did it well. But in comparison to him, yes, I guess so.

Many people shared, including friends of both girls, the principal of their Christian elementary school, and Ryan. A girl that Shiloh and Keziah and I knew got up and sang a song about God's love, a capella. She had struggled with addiction as a seventeen-year-old when Shi and I were in a community theatre play with her many years before, and we had just happened to cross paths again recently. Afterwards, my sister April, who was in the front row, grabbed and hugged her, bawling. It was a moving performance for many, but for me, not so much. I was so frozen from the weight of that glacier that landed on my chest when I heard Shiloh died. I could hardly absorb or respond to anything.

The church offered us DVD copies of the funeral service, so I rewatched it recently for the first time, more than five years later. I also reread my journal from that time. I noted that Boris's niece, who was part of the group that mixed up the seating arrangements, sat in front of me. She had a couple of friends with her. She has had her own struggles with addiction, which Boris later attributed to her behaviour that day. She would cry and say things like "I can't handle this." She then left the service with her entire entourage. They went in and out this way about three times. It was overly dramatic, rude, distracting, and disrespectful. I wanted to slap the back of her head and tell her to sit down and shut up. Honestly.

After the service she snagged me in the lobby while I was talking to friends who had approached me on my way there from the sanctuary. She wanted me to listen to her sing a song. A video camera was set up for people who hadn't had an opportunity to share during the service. I sat and listened, thanked her, and went to speak to some other people. But I was inwardly resentful of giving her even a few minutes of my time after she'd irritated me so much already and when I knew people were waiting to talk to me. When she wanted to meet up the next day, I said no.

I spoke to more people, can't remember who, and then someone came and told me to go to the family room for some lunch. I was starving, having foregone breakfast. I ate two delicious ham-and-Swiss croissants before Boris dragged me off to go through the basket of cards people had brought. His uncle told him there was money in theirs for him for funeral expenses and other things, so he made me sit there and go through every card to see what cash or cheques could be extracted. When we were done, he left, leaving Mom and eighty-six-year-old Aunt Lorna and me to carry the flowers, urns, and other items down to my and my sister's cars.

I wish I could have a redo of that day. Or not. I don't remember any brief conversations I had with anyone. I was in a daze, overwhelmed. My sister's daughter had made blank scrapbooks for people to write condolences and comments. But many of Shiloh and Keziah's friends wrote directly to them instead, in Facebook fashion, I guess, speaking to them as if they could hear them.

All I can say is I'm so sorry there wasn't lunch served at the funeral for you. Call me, and I'll buy you a meal. Someone pointed out, hoping to soothe my anguish, that even if we had enough food for five hundred people, it would only have been half enough, since almost one thousand people attended the service, many of them known to the girls or me and many of them acquaintances from our various communities. Still, I'd rather have run out than not put out.

*

When we got home from Mexico, I learned that someone had started a GoFundMe campaign to raise donations for memorial park benches for the girls. A memory park bench was an idea Shi had had for Keyz. These were thoughtful gestures. But the ask was fifty thousand dollars, which seemed excessive to me. I didn't know the cost of benches, although I heard that in Vancouver, they were twenty-five thousand dollars. I wouldn't place the girls' benches in Vancouver. It just sounded kind of ostentatious to me, and not just me, as I read in the comments after the news article about the benches.

Oh yeah, the media. Backtrack to before the funeral. I received an email from Kali the day after April and Karen arrived in Mexico, saying the media was impatiently waiting for permission to print the story, now that I'd been notified.

"Yeah, okay, I guess," I replied back, not considering the implications or even that I had a choice. I was in shock.

One of the implications was that suddenly unknown numbers of people now knew my business, only not all of it. Jocelyn and Kali did a dozen or so interviews. Somehow, in every version, there were errors—the big one being that the girls and I were from Coquitlam. The girls lived in Burnaby at the time they died. Shi had lived in Coquitlam but Keyz never had, nor had I since they were very young.

At the end of online news articles, readers can sometimes post comments. I didn't see any of the articles until after the comments sections were closed. I would like to address a few in particular. One woman wondered why I would go to Mexico after my daughter had just died instead of holding my other daughter close. Ouch. Good point, especially in retrospect. I did have some guilt about going and still do. It sounds and looks bad. But would my being here have made any difference to what happened to Shiloh? No. Maybe being away was a grace in my life so I didn't have to be handed her glasses and see her in the morgue with a breathing tube in her mouth. Who knows. Maybe I would never have recovered from seeing that. If I'd been here, the press would have been interviewing me, and my privacy would have been invaded far more even than it was.

My privacy is valuable to me, which may sound strange in a memoir like this one that discloses a lot of personal information to the world. But it's different when you choose to disclose something in your own time and in your own way. It's different from when a stranger, like a reporter, wants personal information from you on the spot when you're in a state of shock—information that will be shared with strangers. I don't have a cell phone. I'm not on any social media. I am thankful my image and comments were not associated with those articles. I say really weird things sometimes, things I regret later. Rather than judge myself harshly for my decision to go to Mexico after Keziah died, I prefer to think perhaps it was better that way. Most of the comments other people wrote in response to the media coverage were compassionate; a few were disturbing. I did feel afterward that there are mostly good people out there.

The cause of Keziah's death was questioned by some. Due to the stigma attached to drug addiction, Jocelyn and Kali were trying to be respectful by being vague to the reporters. Articles mentioned "unknown causes," "suspected drug overdose," "unexpected and not intentional," "yet-to-be-confirmed causes," "tragedy family has chosen to keep quiet," "drug overdose," and "believed succumbed to an overdose." On one site, someone remarked regarding the phrase "undisclosed causes" that it obviously meant Keziah had committed suicide and that I should speak up to break the stigma around mental illness.

I would like to break the stigma here associated with the death of young people in general. I agree that telling the truth is the way to go. I wasn't the one being interviewed, and in the situation, I understand and appreciate the discretion Jocelyn and Kali showed, even though it left us open to the even bigger stigma associated with teen suicide. I personally breathed a sigh of relief when the coroner found no evidence for it because for me, it's just so hard to think Keyz was in too much pain to want to continue living. It's easier to take knowing the overdose was almost certainly accidental, although it doesn't make the loss of her at such a young age any less painful.

I have a few general thoughts regarding intentional suicide. I know of or have heard of over a dozen successful or unsuccessful attempts at suicide that I can recall in my lifetime, and in every case, I've felt a deep sadness. Yet I respect the decision. It is a sacred one, a courageous one, a transcendental one. For loved ones who grieve, it's as deep as any loss with the added pain of wishing it could have been avoided. My eighty-one-year-old uncle, who was a farmer in Saskatchewan, shot himself. To me it seemed a natural and compassionate act to himself, similar to what he'd show a suffering animal in his care—a brave, dignified choice. I have never considered my fellow humans any less for having taken that course. I'm sure we've all considered it at one time or another. I know I have. As a young teenager, I imagined hanging myself in the broom closet of the Baptist Church. I always admired Dorothy Parker's poem "Resumé," copied here.

Resumé
Razors pain you;
Rivers are damp;
Acids stain you;
And drugs cause cramp.
Guns aren't lawful;
Nooses give;
Gas smells awful;
You might as well live.

I'm remembering my last conversation with Keyz. I felt a warmth between us as we talked. I sensed disappointment but not despair. She was with a friend right before she died. She'd been clean for around thirty days up until a week or so before she died and was only smoking, not shooting heroin—if she was telling the truth. Therefore, her tolerance was reduced. If she'd bought needles that day and already done enough heroin and coke for her friend to warn her she'd had enough, her last dose of the day could have been her last dose. As it was. Her depression often made her want to eat. Her overeating made her want to do drugs to be thin. When she'd go to treatment, she'd eat instead of using, then relapse so she could use instead of eating. That may be somewhat simplified, but I think it's true. Also, at this time, she was living in a recovery house and was out for the weekend, with no structure and nobody to hang out with, so she fell back into old patterns of behaviour.

The only thing that raised a question for me was that she wrote the date on her to-do list for that day, which was unusual. She was the queen of to-do lists, making little squares for her checkmarks beside each item, but she didn't often date them. Another thing that might or might not have been coincidental was that she finally cleaned up her extra room that she used as a wardrobe. She reported it happily to me in our last conversation. And sure enough, when we went to get her stuff, it was spotless. Since the drugs put her into cleaning fits, it might not mean anything other than she'd been using during the day and not that she had cleaned up in preparation for leaving.

Without a doubt, depression is a silent killer, and we need to acknowledge and destigmatize it. It's possible Keziah killed herself recklessly, ignorantly, accidentally. We know she died of a drug overdose. Whether it was intentional or not, we don't know for absolute certainty, nor can we. In my heart, I don't think it was suicide, except in the sense that drug addiction itself is a slow suicide. She often talked about wanting to get her driver's license, get a car, buy a house, find a boyfriend, and get a puppy or a hedgehog—most of the things a lot of young girls want, I guess. She finished her nail technician course and wanted to get a job, although the lure of escorting for "easy" money was hard for her to resist. Apparently, she looked forward to seeing one of her escort clients with whom she got along well and enjoyed seeing. She wanted to get clean and live a normal life.

Another comment I'd like to address came from a guy who thought people should bypass the plan in the GoFundMe campaign for memory benches and donate directly to charity. I agree with that also. As it turned out, the benches turned out to be much less expensive than believed. I put Keziah's bench in Moody Park in New Westminster because it was where she lived her best life, drug free for ten months, in Westminster House. There is a huge recovery community in New Westminster, and I wanted her friends to have easy access to the bench. It cost about 2,700 dollars. I placed Shi's at Lafarge Lake in Coquitlam, where she and I used to walk near her other homes. It cost about the same.

Keziah's bench plate reads:

In Memory of Keziah Johnston
May your beauty "go on" forever
Your love, friendship, humour and style
Are gifts that will always bring us a smile.

Shiloh's plate reads:

In Memory of Shiloh Johnston
Watch in the sky
For signs of Shi.

Shi loved the sky, often saying, "Mom, look, isn't it beautiful?" And I just saw the everyday sky, nothing special, even though I like the sky too, but I mean at the times she mentioned it, I didn't feel like I saw what she saw. Also, Shiloh's plate is a reference to the two stars I saw in Mexico and several times since, at significant times, as well as to birds and cloud formations, and to the idea that she's ascended, I guess. She had taken some spectacular sky photos on her phone that I got locked out of and lost. So sad.

There were several thousand dollars left in the fund after purchasing the memory benches, so I made donations in my daughters' names to Westie House, a couple of other recovery places Keyz had been in, the Mood Disorders Association, Crohn's and Colitis, and a ministry in India related to Shi's trip there. I don't think I ever saw the GoFundMe page, but when the money was distributed, I wrote a note of thanks and detailed the donations for Kali to post. I have no idea who gave, friends as well as strangers, I imagine. The kindness from all is deeply appreciated.

One of the upsides in a tragedy like ours is that it's really amazing to experience the outpouring of kindness, sympathy, and generosity that it generates. The worst situations seem to bring out the best in people.

21

The Sentencing of Kenneth Narayan

It's June 13, 2017, almost two and a half years after Shiloh was killed. The alarm rings at 6:00 a.m., jarring me out of a deep sleep, like a knife cutting into a birthday cake. I carefully feel for the snooze button with my eyes closed and push it just before I am submerged by sleep again. The next time it rings, I mumble to myself, "Gotta get up" but push the snooze once more. A few minutes later, the alarm rings again, and this time wakes me up. "Okay, okay, I'm awake." But I can't resist the urge to rest my eyelids just for a second before I get up.

The next time my eyes open my first thought is "Oh no, please don't tell me I've slept in." The clock confirms that indeed I am behind schedule but by minutes, not hours, thankfully. I get up, put the coffee on, step into the shower, and in an hour, I am ready to go out the door, straight into early morning rush hour traffic. I take my coffee, a bottle of water, and a snack bag of prunes, as a substitute for breakfast, for the trip.

My destination is the Burnaby RCMP detachment, where I will meet with my new VSW Carol, and Constable Erica Cooke, the RCMP officer in charge of the investigation of the accidental death of my daughter Shiloh. Carol told me I can ride with them downtown to the courthouse, and I accept their generous offer and screech into the parking lot a few minutes after 8:00 a.m., our planned leaving time for downtown.

A youngish woman wearing a nice trench coat is waiting on the sidewalk.

"Jacquie?" she asks, as I approach.

"Yes, sorry I'm late. Are they gone already?"

"No, not yet. I'm Parm, like Pam with an r. Unfortunately, Carol is

270

ill, in the hospital actually, so I'll be replacing her today."

"Oh, that's too bad about Carol. I hope she's okay."

"If you want to come with me, we'll go get the car."

From a nearby parking lot full of cars, Parm approaches a beige Ford Taurus that begins honking its alarm and doesn't stop—no matter what buttons she pushes on the fob—until we get in and she starts the car.

Parm drives back to the main doors, from which emerge Constable Erica Cooke, a tall woman in full uniform with a faux hawk earned when she shaved her head for Cops for Cancer. She adjusts the seat to accommodate her long legs and begins piloting us through the heavy traffic while noting drivers looking down at their unseen cell phones and telling terrible driving stories from her job as a traffic cop.

I'm not sure if this trip to court is an official part of Constable Cooke's duty as the head of the accident investigation or her personal interest in the case. Today, we are going to juvenile court for the sentencing of Kenneth Narayan, the seventeen-year-old driver of the car that hit and killed my daughter Shiloh in the accident. Kenneth, his mother, father, and lawyer are waiting outside the appointed courtroom.

My sister April, her daughter, Jocelyn, and Jocelyn's boyfriend, Boyd, join us in the lobby of the law courts building. We turn a corner and see the Narayan family, and awkwardly make no eye contact as we pass. We find seats some distance away.

Kenneth is a handsome young man. His family came to Canada from Fiji. He and his dad are smartly dressed in suits and fancy shoes. His mother appears to be dabbing her eyes with a Kleenex.

We are told the court session begins at 9:00 a.m. In fact, due to another case and location change, it doesn't start until 10:00 a.m. By that time, Boris has arrived, getting lost in the building.

The Crown counsel representative, another tall slim woman in a dark brown pantsuit, starts the proceedings by describing the accident, complete with a booklet of photographs for the judge to refer to. Then she reads the victim impact statements that April, Boris and I have submitted earlier, which tell in our own words how losing Shiloh has impacted us physically, emotionally, and financially. She gives examples of other similar cases and the sentences they received. And finally, she recommends the following maximum allowable sentence: two years' probation with curfew, 250 hours of community service, and five years of driving suspension.

The defence lawyer has letters from teachers, employers, and others to say Kenneth is a good person, student, and employee. He talks about what a hardworking family he is part of—whatever that has to do with anything. He argues that most of the cases cited by the Crown counsel were after lengthy trials, and Kenneth has shown responsibility by pleading guilty, which he did at the last minute, so no trial was required. Again, I'm not sure what his point is. He tries to assign part of the blame to another driver whom Kenneth hit during the accident, even though Kenneth was speeding excessively at the time.

The lawyer does mention that Kenneth, who only had his driver's license for seven months when he hit Shiloh, had a previous incident resulting in a twenty-four-hour suspension, after being pulled over for an alcohol infraction. So, whatever the letters and his lawyer say, Kenneth disregarded the law at least twice that we know of in the previous seven months, one of which caused a death. He was injured in the accident himself, along with his passengers and the occupants of the other car he hit. The judge kindly gives her sentence at the end of the day, so we don't have to return to court. Thankfully. We probably wouldn't have. After much repetition of previously stated facts, her sentence is guilty of dangerous driving causing death, with a penalty of two years' probation, with a curfew at home with his parents from 11:00 p.m. to 6:00 a.m. for six months, two hundred hours of community service, and a four years' driving suspension. I feel satisfied that it's fair.

At one point, the judge asks if Kenneth has anything to say to the court. He stands up and says to the judge, "I just want to say I'm sorry." He doesn't look at us. I have to say I am really disappointed. I was really hoping he'd tell me directly that he was sorry he killed my daughter. It would have allowed me to forgive him more easily than this impersonal apology made to the judge. Nevertheless, I do my best to offer him forgiveness in my heart.

I am happy, or maybe just relieved, to hear his lawyer say he is depressed. Perhaps that's an indication of caring. I'm sure he feels awful about everything. How could you not? I feel sorry for him, a life ruined over a moment of carelessness—speeding in a hot car to impress his friends after a trip to McDonald's for lunch. It could happen to anyone. I just wish he'd talk to me. But he's young, and it's hard. I haven't seen the last of Kenneth. Hopefully by the time of the civil suit, he'll man up and offer a proper apology.

Much later, I came to understand that his apology was offered in a collective way in being spoken to the judge, to everyone, to society in general, not just to me individually. Perhaps there was some attempt to protect my privacy and to soften the impact of his actions upon me by sharing them with the society in general and by not looking at my face. The way I am trying to soften the portrait I've had to draw of him here is by hiding his real name.

As for the civil suit, unbelievably to me, after five and a half years, at the date of this writing, we have not yet been to court and will likely settle outside of it. So, chances are I'll never see Kenneth again. He has served his sentence and is free in the eyes of the law and in mine. I wish him well. However, I could scream a hundred thousand times for the way the lack of closure keeps me bleeding, hanging on to an irreversible mistake made by a stranger that changed my life forever. It also, unfortunately, keeps me connected to Boris, who is now remarried to a Filipino woman, stuck in her home country because of immigration laws and then COVID-19. On my last attempt to assist Boris with the information requested by my lawyer for the civil suit, I decided I am no longer willing to give my time to help him receive money in compensation for the accident, after the innumerable times he owed it to me and withheld it, as I'm reminded reading old journals about the wretched days of court as well as endless visitations and payments. This despite the fact that Boris is now severely cognitively impaired. Once I tried to spell out a word for him, and he asked, "G, G, what's a G again?" As I told my lawyer in an email, this sort of thing is not conducive to my mental health or my ex-husband's life expectancy.

But to better explain why there is still no settlement, let me mention again that the province of British Columbia only has one main government vehicle insurer, the ICBC. In this particular accident, the young driver Kenneth was going between ninety and one hundred and twenty kilometres an hour in a fifty-kilometre zone. He hit a car which turned wide, whose occupants have made a civil suit for damages and injuries. He has countersued them for turning wide. Because there can only be one claim per family, I sued on behalf of both Boris and me, for Shiloh's death. Kenneth's passengers were injured and are also suing him. So, there are four lawsuits over this one accident, and ICBC has to appoint four individual lawyers to counter them. Unfuckingbelievable. And to add insult to injury, the death will probably be awarded the lowest payout because injuries can cost the victims a lifetime of suffering, but a dead person's life is basically resolved and worth relatively little from the point of the law. Between five and ten thousand dollars without a lawyer, according to my legal advice, split between the parents. That's why, I was told, if you ever hit someone, you should back up and drive over them again to make sure they're dead. Not joking.

ICBC is still in the process of assigning lawyers to the case. I was told I'd receive counselling and wage loss ompensation from ICBC. I guess that means some day. I could use it now.

*

December 17, 2020

Six years to the day minus two months since Shiloh was killed, there's breaking news: After speaking to Boris tonight about my annual spousal support payment, which is due this month, he informed me that he spoke to the lawyer's office this week, and the negotiations are complete. He thinks we should each be receiving a cheque very soon. He'd like to pay me out of his, which is fine. The lawyer did email an offer for our approval recently which must have been accepted by ICBC. The salt in the wound is that the lawyer's share is 25 per cent of the settlement, plus costs and disbursements, yet somehow the money he receives, including payment for helping me get permission to administer Shiloh's estate, is more than Boris receives and almost as much as I do. So, whether it's a lawyer or an escort, if somebody's making three hundred dollars an hour, somebody is getting screwed. Which is not to say I'm not grateful for the legal support received and not to say that my lawyer charges three hundred dollars an hour. It's more. Thank you Allan and staff for your patience with us these many years.

Rewind to 2015 again. I can't believe all my children have died, of accidental causes. Last night it hit me again. What are the chances? I can't find anything on Google about the probabilities, but I don't have to. I know it's rare, rare like sashimi. What if someone won the lottery three times, two of the picks ten days apart? It's just mindboggling.

I've already decided the *why* doesn't matter. People die. It's part of life. Apparently, 155,000 people die every two seconds on the earth. It's the circle of life, Simba. But holy shit, Batman, my two beautiful daughters, so nearly grown up, a mere ten days apart?

Is Boris correct? Did God take them from me as a judgment on me? The thing that doesn't make sense about that, though, is that He took them from him, too. No judgment on Boris? I never withheld the girls from their dad, even when I probably should have. He got lost in his addiction and wandered away from them. Oh, never mind. These thoughts lead me back down the road of resentment and blame and dislike. There's no point going there.

I talked to Gary on the phone a few days ago. He had a dream, apparently the same night and dream as Shiloh's former superstitious Korean boss Sheila, in which he saw Shi and Keyz together, happy. I want to see them, talk to them, hug them. I can't believe they're gone. I miss them so much every day.

As I have no scheduled activities, I decide to wash my floor. I hate cleaning. But I love the look and feel of clean. So, I get a bucket and start. When I get to the living room, which is also the bedroom, this being a bachelor suite, I pull the bag of sympathy cards and the guest books out from under the little table beside the couch. As I start to wipe the floor underneath the table, I hear a noise and see water running from a tipped over bouquet of flowers on the table. "FUCK!" I yell and grab the vase to upright it. Then I run with it to the kitchen sink to refill, which I do, leaving it there for now. I go back to wipe up the excess water under the table, which now holds only the framed photograph of Shi and Keyz that Kali gave me the day of the viewing.

After getting that area done, I move over to where the urns are. They are simple wood boxes made by Boris and filled with half the cremated remains of our lovely daughters. My mom has the matching set. On top of the stacked boxes, I had placed a gift from my mother. It's a Willow tree figurine called "My Sister, My Friend," consisting of two female figures standing close and holding hands.

One of the reasons I hate cleaning is because I'm lazy. I hate all the extra work of moving everything that is necessary to do a good job. So, even though my laziness has just caused a spill, I think I can just gently pull the two boxes out to clean behind them. But what happens? Somehow the figurine falls off and hits the floor. I shriek. Against all odds, it doesn't break but lands in a face up position on the cross bar at the bottom of the table, as though there were an invisible hand under there waiting to catch it. It was a similar crossbar that saved my big fat boarder's ass when she fell through my glass coffee table.

It is incredible. "You're okay," I exclaim to the figurine, still amazed at what I am seeing.

I start to cry. Is this the answer, the meaning I've been seeking? Is it an echo of the message of the No Shit Miracle when little Shiloh's poopy diaper was clean? If I hurt my children accidentally, God will make sure they're okay. There's grace to cover my mistakes, my foolishness, my laziness, and my lack of care.

But still, what are the chances they'd die ten days apart and both still so young? Maybe the same as the chances of a clay figurine falling from a height of fifteen inches onto a hard surface, not breaking, and bouncing into place balanced perfectly on a crossbar? Ooh, should I try and stretch or morph the metaphor to Jesus on the cross (bar)?

I look at the pictures I took. They're even more amazing than I thought. There's seemingly nothing supporting the figurine on either side. I was afraid it would fall while I was taking pictures, but I took a chance because it's so hard to believe if you just hear it and don't see it.

Oh, and I just had a double pickle with my brunch—two perfectly formed pickles attached to each other. Don't take a pic of them. I eat them, but they are so cute. I show them to the girls' picture. "See, this little pickle is just like you two, one a little bigger than the other, stuck together."

Later the same day... Okay, so get this. My friend Dee texted me to let me know I was invited to Chances, the casino, to see a Charlie Daniels tribute band. So, I go. With no communication about timing, Dee and I and her friend Chloe all arrive within a minute of each other. During the course of my conversation with Chloe, I learn we have the following things in common: We are both recovered alcoholics; we are both bipolar; we both love to dance; we each lost a daughter of the same age (twenty); we had children with chronic illness; we are both former Jesus freaks involved in the charismatic movement; and we both had cataracts. What are the chances we'd meet in a place called Chances?

And then what happens with all that coincidence and with Chloe? Nothing. I've never seen her again. She was Dee's friend. But this particular day is a defining one for me in terms of accepting and believing that the unseen influences my life.

22

Dear Diary, Dear Mom

Thursday, September 4, 2015

It's about seven months since the girls died. Today, I went to Thrifty's and bought some flowers. I was just admiring them on my table. I compared the reddish gerbera to the red lips on the picture Shiloh painted and hung for me, and I just missed her deeply, all over again. I still can't believe it. I just try to stay busy and not think about it. I try to watch TV until I'm falling asleep, so I don't have to think before I sleep. But I get a pang whenever I see something that belonged to them or hear somebody talk like them or see someone who looks like them.

I can't believe I'm going through this again, all this grief, walking through life without the children I bore at my side. Why did they have to die? I cannot help asking the question even though I know it does no good. I miss their missed calls. I feel numb. Numbness protects me from collapsing, hyperventilating, crying myself dry, throwing myself into traffic, smashing my head on a rock to stop the memories. I sometimes wish I could feel more and release it. I'm a bit zombified. Maybe my meds? Yet I'm afraid to feel the real sorrow. I fear being engulfed by it. TV time.

Friday, September 15, 2015

Sometimes, this world and the things we do in it feel so mundane that it makes me wonder what the purpose is. And it makes me wonder if there are other worlds and what they're like. Here on earth, there is an outer world and an inner world, which we simultaneously inhabit. The inner one interprets the outer one, which is somewhat illusory. The earth itself contains so much jaw-dropping beauty, designed to inspire and feed the souls of men. But the other humans, wow. Not so much, sometimes. I think the earth is a lovely playground where people come to learn to get along and often fail miserably. Return trips to get it right doesn't clash with my ideals.

There is a theory that we "pre-spirits" in the heavenly holding tank have some choice about our trips to earth. That interests me because I think if I had a choice, I would choose to live in Canada because I think it's the best country on earth. I'd choose to be bisexual because that's a good economy of gender, exploring two in one trip. And I'd choose to be female so I could experience the wonder of childbirth and motherhood. Though for the next trip, I'll probably request to be barren because I couldn't take the chance of losing another child. Mind you, for many women barrenness is a pain-inducing condition in which the woman experiences the grief of the loss of children without the benefit of having known them. Barrenness is a curse if you want children. If you don't, it's a blessing because you have natural birth control, although it robs you of the choice here on earth.

If life here is about learning lessons, children are a way for their parents to be stripped of selfishness. They come into the world completely dependent on their parents for everything they need to survive, with built-in defence mechanisms, like their high-pitched continuous screams that find the nerve centres in their parents' spines and brains. Even while completely nonverbal, they command the attention of all other humans in their proximity.

*

Having lost all three of my children, some people expect me to be suicidal or in the fetal position on the floor, awash in the amniotic fluid of my own tears. And well I might be, except I'm still numb and my knees are getting bad, so the floor's not a place I get to often. I sometimes wonder if I'm a hardcore badass bitch who deserves these terrible losses.

But then again, what if losing my children is something I requested on my previous trip to earth so I could learn some important lesson? Like learning about grief and sorrow as well as forgiveness and self-forgiveness for greater love. Intense pain sounds like a stupid thing to ask for though, to say nothing of the lives my children might have lived and the tragedy of their deaths. Some life lessons are terribly, terribly hard to learn, aren't they?

I've never really found life to be particularly pleasurable, but maybe that's because I am bipolar. I've always been on the depressed side of normal. My perfectionism was visible even to my grade-three teacher. In a spelling test, I was trying to make perfect letters, but I was too slow to keep up with the class, so I ended up trying write the words quickly at the bottom to make up for my slowness. But it felt like a conveyor belt of words coming faster and faster, and I got about three of the ten written out legibly.

My default setting is negatively realistic, so I don't see life here as much of a cake walk. I see more pain than joy, more loneliness than acceptance, more dysfunction than family, more difficulty than ease, et cetera, et cetera. I could go on with a list like that for a long time. Maybe that's why Christianity appealed to me at one time. It was supposed to fix everything.

I honestly think my children escaped a lot of bullshit. They got to have a lot of good times before they were taken away. Who knows, they might already be back in another incarnation. It's funny how when someone dies, you become obsessed with the idea of where they went and what they're doing. At the same time, I picture the girls in some heavenly place where they can fly, communicate with thoughts, have their same personalities but with perfected and healed bodies and minds, eat fruit off trees, swim underwater without holding their breath, visit others who have passed away, design with clouds, dance like divas, and follow me around my apartment. Until I turn on the TV. Keyz hated it. She just used hers as a huge nightlight. Every day they are beaming me their love, comforting me with their unseen presence. Thank you, beautiful girls. Blessings on you always.

I just took a break and sliced a pear into quarters. The first bite made me squeal with delight. It was perfect. The tangy sweet juice met my tongue as my teeth penetrated the tender flesh. Delicious! And it gave me an idea. I got the image of the girls eating fruit from a book a friend loaned me when Emmanuel died called *Intra Muros*, written by Rebecca Ruter Springer. You can find it online now. There's a passage in the book describing twelve fruit trees on a golden street in Heaven, an image from the Book of Revelation in the Bible. One thing I've learned about fruit on earth is it has to be ripe to taste good. How does fruit ripen? It happens magically, biologically, over time. A life lesson on earth is that timing is everything. It would be different in Heaven, though, wouldn't it, where time as we know it doesn't exist. Perhaps all the ripening has to happen here for perpetual enjoyment to be possible there.

Maybe Keyz had figured out that she would always be a slave to demons—body dysmorphia, OCD, PTSD, borderline personality disorder, depression, and finally heroin addiction—because she'd fought the good fight and hadn't overcome. Maybe she learned what she needed to know for this trip on earth. She became a person I respected as she worked on her recovery and worked hard to improve on the negative behaviours that supported her addictions, like lying, stealing, and putting herself in dangerous situations.

She spent four Christmases in recovery houses from the age of sixteen to twenty. When she was in, she wanted out, and when she was out, she wanted in. Usually, she'd last a month or so. I was really proud of her when I took her to her first house at sixteen. Keyz was a loner, and here she was suddenly in a situation where she had to live with a group of strangers. We were both anxious, but I left her there, amazed at her willingness to try. After ten weeks, there was a graduation celebration. I guess I thought she, and we, had beat it then—until Keyz started telling me all the ways those teens knew to manipulate and cheat. When she enrolled in Westminster House a couple of years later, she was in a house with several other girls. They had group every day, attended Narcotics Anonymous every day, worked on accepting responsibility for their behaviour and making amends, and shared household responsibilities for cooking and cleaning.

After a time, I was allowed weekly visits, to which for some reason I always seemed to be a bit late. This infuriated her and rightfully so. After six months, I think it was, she was supposed to move out because there's a time limit on services due to demand. However, there was a second-stage house up the street and she opted for that. I felt proud of her decision. It was there that she really seemed to be actively engaged in her own recovery. She wrote me a letter of apology for her unsavoury behaviour and accepted responsibility for it. We were sitting in my car when she handed me the envelope. I read it silently, appreciating the curve of her letters, her unique script. I thanked her. She was disappointed that I didn't cry. We often disappointed each other, it seems. Yet we were both trying so hard to get things right and to make things right between us.

Keyz *loved* Sriracha, a spicy chili sauce, which she put on everything.

I remember getting a huge bottle at Costco and taking it to Westie House. After she died, I swear, Sriracha was everywhere. Every major take-out chain had a sriracha dish on their menu. I knew I should have written them down, but I didn't. There are still lots. I always imagined that somehow Keyz had an influence on its popularity. And, it fact, it's become a staple in my house. I like it on scrambled eggs, anything with mayo, and I squirt it into any tomato-based sauce, like Bolognese, chili, or curry. I feel like she won me over from the other side.

Shiloh, in contrast, definitely had her worldview in order, and had learned how to thrive, despite less than ideal conditions. She ached to better this world and, perhaps, that's easier done without the limits of human constraints. Perhaps, she was ripe.

A couple of people have told me that Emmanuel was an old soul. Old soul? He was a baby. How can you tell? However, that bit of conjecture fits nicely into my theory that he, too, was a fast ripening fruit, and he came and left so that I might understand the concept of God's forgiveness in a fresh new way.

What does all this say about me? I'm a crusty fifty-four-year-old, hanging on the tree wishing someone would eat me.

Last night, I went out dancing at the Fairview and stopped in at Tim Horton's to get a mocha for the trip home. A young girl was working there. I said, "I'd like two things, please, a small mocha and can you please turn that off." Some machine that creates the ice part of smoothies or something was dinging. Then an alarm went off when the coffee was brewed. "There are a lot of noisy alarms here," I added. "I don't know how you do this job. It would drive me crazy."

She replied, "It's just life."

Just life. Annoying repetitive sounds. Maybe I have a low tolerance for life and babies crying. The server seemed nonchalant. The noise didn't seem to bother her a bit.

When I got home, I had a talk with Keziah's picture on the wall. I just want to take that soft, smooth-skinned face in my hands and kiss it. I know exactly what that forehead feels and tastes and smells like. I miss it so much. I hope she's happy, infused with love, a new seed in a new world filled with delight, self-love, purpose, belonging, or whatever good things we need there to thrive.

She got a bum rap here, really. A fresh start was a good thing. If she heard that, she'd say, "So, you're happy I died? You wanted me to?"

And I'd say, "No, never. Heartbroken, not happy. But I'm happy for you that your suffering here ended."

The feeling of being unloved coloured her perceptions. It was a hard cry tonight. My friend Arlene gave me a candle holder and a heart-shaped tea candle for Keyz's birthday, but I forgot to light it. I lit it tonight. It flickers while I write. Her picture's on the wall, but she's out of sight.

*

There's one final note I must make regarding some feedback I received from my dad after he read a draft of my manuscript this summer, when I was home for my fortieth high school reunion. (It's 2019 as I'm writing this.) He said he wanted to read it because he might not be around by the time it is published. He's eighty. I had mixed feelings about that. My relationship with my dad wasn't very good when I was younger, although I've grown to love and appreciate him. Becoming a parent yourself will do that to you. I didn't want him to be hurt by the things I'd written about him, but they were my truth at the time. However, I also didn't want him to sue me if I published things that offended him, so I let him read it. I also appreciated the fact that he was interested and willing to read it. He was embarrassed by my words and wanted credit for being a good provider, which he was. And I've come to admire him in other ways—getting and staying sober, and taking care of his partners, for example.

My mom can't, and won't, read my book because she says it's too painful. I emailed her recently and asked her why she thought that. Here is her response:

Hi Jacquie,

Because I think your book title is apropos and you have had a painful life with many disappointments and so many losses. I feel your pain, but I am not as courageous as you are, and I don't want to revisit those things. I chose your father when I was a child myself, not at all a good judge of character and not nearly mature enough to have a family of my own, so I feel responsible for the dysfunctional upbringing you had, all my children had. I never considered asking God to choose my husband, or even asking Him whether I should marry so young. I went forward blindly and willfully, and I've had so many years to regret that. I can see all the hurt and rejection you all felt, not because your father meant to reject any of us but because he was self-centred, so I took responsibilities that should have been his, and that allowed him to lead his own life without accountability. He definitely did support us financially but not emotionally or spiritually and not by example.

I love you all so much, as individuals and as part of my heart, and when I realized what a mistake I had made, I didn't know how to deal with it. I knew I should try to have you all honour your father, but that was almost impossible for me because of my own feelings of betrayal. I tried to live by the strength of my own will and ended up failing my husband and my children.

Vaguely, but not really perceiving, I knew there was alcohol addiction in his family and mental illness, mostly depression and suicide, but I never let myself think that would affect your father's life or mine because his own parents were such strong Christians, more evidently than my parents. Now I understand what the Bible says about the sins (or even characteristics) of the fathers being visited on the children to the fourth generation; then, I didn't understand. I feel guilty for perpetuating these weaknesses and having them projected on my children. You suffer with being bipolar, your brother is an alcoholic, and your sister followed my personality of compensating, in addition to the negative in-law characteristics. What is too painful is the fact that I so much wanted a family and was so inadequate as a parent that I am to blame for your pain.

You have an amazing talent. I have letters from you that show how you can express your feelings. I see in your life the courage and resiliency with which you have dealt with tragedy and I am so proud of you. You are so much more candid and honest than I can be. I hope my confessions help and give clarity.

Love you, Mom

This was some of my response:

Thanks, Mom.

It's interesting for me to see how much we've felt similar in our failings as mothers when we think quite highly of each other. I was reading Keziah's recovery journals, and I've said in the book what happened to her wasn't her fault. She came into the world a happy little soul that got sideswiped by the breakup of our family. Even before that I felt guilty for the way Boris monopolized my time and didn't give her the love and attention she deserved (and neither did I), which sent her spinning off into dark places alone. She felt unloved, which breaks my heart.

I feel guilt and shame about my parenting, yet she and I grew up in similar families, with emotionally distant fathers and an alcohol-addicted parent. In her case, both her parents were addicts. So, I say it wasn't her fault; it was my fault. I see now that we were repeating an inherited family pattern. Maybe you were doing the same.

In which case perhaps you can cut yourself some slack also. You and your sisters don't speak much of what it was like for you growing up, but I picture you, the "latecomer"—a quiet, shy, somewhat anxious little girl, who may have been a bit in the background, especially when your dad got sick. You're right. You were just a child when you got married, a young girl hoping to have a nice life and a family, but who didn't get a lot of attention or guidance when it would have been helpful and important. In light of your circumstances, you did a great job and an excellent one by the time you were a grandmother.

I don't want to bring up the past or unpleasant memories for you or to cause you any more pain. Please know that I love and respect you, and there's nothing wrong with not being a loudmouth schnook like me.

Thanks again for all the times you've taught, loved, cared, sacrificed for, and supported me and my family over the years in so many ways: setting a good example of fidelity and accepting responsibility, being so generous with your time, talents, and money, being a fantastic cook and housekeeper, allowing us to invade your space, and being willing to share ours at times, and always offering encouragement and reliability like a "This Way Out" sign in the darkest of nights.

As you've watched me grow and hopefully mature, I have seen the same of you. I have seen how your faith has led you into an exploration of becoming a better person, how a young girl met her challenges head-on and allowed the pressure to refine her into a positive woman filled with strength others can draw upon.

You da best, Mama. You da best.
Love, Jacquie

23

Epilogue, January 2021

Every day for years after the girls died, I lived with the thought that I too could die any day. The notion that anything is possible wasn't just a dollar-store plaque sentiment anymore. It was a reality I'd experienced. I'm still aware of my own mortality every day, but the feeling is less intense. As I write, the entire world is at war with an invisible enemy, a deadly-to-some virus. Many people I know have grappled with a severe fear of contracting it. To me, the fear is as detrimental to people's well-being as the virus may be. Now that I've lived through what I imagine is the worst thing that could happen to me, fear doesn't have much hold. Life is a calculated risk. We do our best to get through it by making life-affirming choices but that doesn't guarantee success.

We're all going to die one day. We don't have control over when that day arrives. Even attempted suicides fail sometimes. But the bright side is that as long as we are here, the possibility for something great to happen is equal to the likelihood of tragedy. While I have experienced unimaginable pain in the loss of my children, many people have suffered as much or more with their own losses. You can't compare pain. Pain is pain. Love is pain. Being alive is pain, but also sometimes joy, comfort, and laughter.

Over the six years since my daughters died, I've received many kind compliments from family members and friends about how well I've dealt with my losses. They've told me I'm strong, brave, and admirable. In this regard, I am humbled, unsure of what they know or see. From my perspective, it feels like I've cried, written, grieved, and talked a lot about my pain; being able to release and share has been healing. There seemed to be some grace for me to be able to accept my daughters' deaths, not when they were fresh, of course, but later, after I tunnelled through dark nights of sorrow, digging deep like a prisoner with a spoon escaping from a war camp, eventually surfacing above ground, free. One spoonful at a time, one day at a time. It's the only way to live. I accept death just as I accept life, which seems like the best choice.

One thing I find interesting is how imagining Shiloh, Keziah, and Emmanuel to be existing in another realm has opened my eyes to the world of nature. It's as though a curtain has been thrown back, and I can see through a window into the essence of life. I can't count how many times I see two things, sometimes three—two spiders on my window yesterday, ladybugs, maple tree spinners that land on my car, two leaves that blow in the window, two birds (although that seems less meaningful as they probably just like hanging out together, being flockers).

Every morning, I sit in my empty-nest apartment decorated in fifty shades of teal, six floors up, drinking my coffee, watching the maple tree outside my window transform through the seasons. In the spring, the ends of the bare branches erupt into triads of tiny, pointed leaves. Then bright lemon-lime green seed pods begin to form, hanging like colourful flowers or dangling earrings. These develop into the clusters of spinners that the wind will toss like confetti over the empty lot next door in late summer. Then the new leaves slowly emerge, filling in the spaces until the branches are hidden and a couple of crows build an unseen nest in them. An interesting thing I've observed about crows as I've sat near my window from one year to the next is that they're economical birds; they move a current nest twig by twig to another location rather than resourcing twigs.

In the aptly named fall season, the leaves drift to the ground day by day, slowly shedding and revealing the mossy branches once again, the strong wind sometimes giving the tree a brisk, final shake. I love watching windstorms hurl leaves and loose ends around the sky, seeing the birds struggling to fly against it or sometimes catching a backdraft that sends them careening.

I am grateful for many things in my life: an affordable home, an awesome car (I recently bought my first self-chosen brand new vehicle ever, a VW Beetle convertible that I drive "topless" year round as long as it's not raining too hard), generally good health, good friends, my family, a bit of money in the bank, and decent employment (virus-affected for now, allowing me some cherished writing time). Most satisfying is a healthy relationship I've enjoyed for the past few years with a lovely younger man, Daniel, who treats me well and doesn't seem to mind the fact that I look like I'm carrying twin grandchildren. Sometimes I think this fat belly of mine is a daily reminder that I was once blessed with children, a souvenir of my time as a mother. One gift that I received from my children is the joy of having them and the peace of not having to worry about them anymore.

Nothing can replace Shiloh and Keziah, and I still miss them. But one of the things that's filled some space in my life since I moved to Maple Ridge, just three months before they died, is finding a place in the live music community here which is where I met wonderful Daniel. He is an intelligent, kind, good-natured, and loving person as well as a hard-working tradesman. He has beautiful teeth to the point that sometimes I randomly say, "Show me your teeth." He's very affectionate, kisses me often and perfectly, and makes me laugh hard. I love him.

Attending performances and jams where I dance to my heart's content and hang out casually with regularly attending friends is one of my favourite pleasures. Well, it was until the virus almost killed it. There's been a small trickle of live music at times during the pandemic, but dancing is not allowed. The very notion is an affront to my deepest intrinsic human values but what can you do when you live in a zoo, as Daniel's mom, who often has Sunday dinner with us after a seven-year ongoing battle with cancer, likes to say. She's been extremely isolated during the pandemic, so her visits are the highlight of the week for all of us. He and I dance at home now. It's not the same as being surrounded by the pulse of the music and the energy of the people, but it's also fun, in its way.

Daniel lives a four-minute drive away in a rancher he renovated on Creston Street, the name of my hometown. Is that a sign? Yes, a street sign. We enjoy cooking meals together there several nights a week, now that COVID-19 has curbed our eating out habit, going for rides in the summer on his 2012 Harley Dyna Superglide Custom (it's as sexy as it sounds), singing while he plays guitar, and having extended chats and boinking sessions. People sometimes ask if we have plans to move in together or marry, both of which are hard on relationships in my experience. No such plans, just living the dream daily, four minutes apart, sleeping well. I think we have a perfect balance of independence and loving attachment.

My long-time desire to write a book—ever since my dear grade-three teacher, Miss Sheppard, inspired me by creating a cover out of pink construction paper for a story I'd written on the weekend and inviting me to read it to the class—will soon be realized. I am fulfilled, content, and grateful. I have accepted the outcomes of this lifetime with as much humour as I can muster and hopefully a little grace. Looking ahead, what do I see? Spring is coming to the cold, wet tree. Someday soon, we will be dancing mask free with our friends again, with joyful music playing across the room.

Acknowledgments

Songs referred to in this book include I've Got a Mansion by Ira F. Stanphill (New Spring 1949); Paradise by the Dashboard Light by Jim Steinman (Epic 1976); Sunday Morning Coming Down by Kris Kristofferson (Monument 1969); Ring of Fire by June Carter and Merle Kilgore (Columbia Nashville 1963); Spirit in the Sky by Norman Greenbaum (Reprise 1969); From This Moment On by Shania Twain (Mercury Nashville 1998); Constant Craving by k.d. lang and Ben Mink (Sire Records 1992); Come Now and Let Us Reason Together by Norman J. Clayton (c. Norman J. Clayton 1938); Kumbaya by Marvin V. Frey (c. Martin V. Frey 1939); Angel Flying Too Close to the Ground by Willie Nelson (Columbia 1981); Ain't No Sunshine When She's Gone by Bill Withers (Sussex 1971); Girls Just Wanna Have Fun by Cyndi Lauper (Portrait 1975); Oh the Blood of Jesus by Anonymous (Public Domain); and Da Giovanni (Yolanda Lisi Yvonne Laflamme 197?). Poems and books referred to in this book include Dorothy Parker's poem "Resumé," (originally published in 1925 and now in the public domain); and books *Intra Muros*, by Rebecca Ruter Springer (David C. Cook 1898); *Boundaries* by Dr. Henry Cloud and Dr. John Townsend (Zondervan 1992); When *Bad Things Happen to Good People* by Harold Kushner (Schocken Books 1981); and *Uncle Arthur's Bedtime Stories* by Arthur S. Maxwell (Review and Herald 1927). Movies referred in to this book include *A Thief in the Night* directed by Donald W. Thompson (1972) and *Amy* directed by Ashif Kapadia (2015).

It's impossible to thank everyone I want to because it took me so damn long to write this book that I can't remember anymore everybody on the journey who listened, cared, and contributed. You know who you are. Thanks and appreciation to you all.

I have managed to remember some, however. For unwavering

encouragement and support, I wish to thank Aunt Ione, Aunt Jean, my family, Kelly, Kathrin, Claire, April, Ann, Yvonne, Michelle, Cameron, Andra and the Soul Sisters, Sylvain le Musicien, and my darling Daniel: You're spoons for the tunnel.

Gratitude to gifted tattoo artist Trish and her client for the wonderful cover image. Trish's work and contact information can be found at www.raincitytattoos.com.

Thanks ever so much to Andrea O'Reilly and the editorial team at Demeter Press for championing a new writer like me, with a challenging story to tell. I couldn't have done it without your encouragement and excellent support!

And, finally, a million thanks to Emmanuel, Shiloh, and Keziah for making my life and the story I've made of it so much more interesting and precious and filled with extraordinary lessons by your presence in it. Unending love.